Other Books by
Shannon Hooper

Walking with God: Journal

Walking with God: Bible Study
(Coming Soon)

Abundance in His Promise:
A Prayer Devotional
(Coming Soon)

Walking with GOD

Walking with GOD

SHANNON HOOPER

M
Magdala

M

Magdala

Published by Magdala House Publishing
Nashville, Tennessee

ISBN: 978-0692304525

Subject Heading: GOD | CHRISTIAN LIFE | FAITH

Verses cited NIV, are from The Holy Bible, New International Version®, NIV® Copyright © 1973, 1978, 1984, 2011 by Biblica, Inc.® Used by permission. All rights reserved worldwide.

Verses cited ESV®, are from The Holy Bible, English Standard Version®, © 2001 by Corssway, a publishing ministry of Good News Publishers. All rights reserved.

Verses cited KJV, are from the New King James Version®. Copyright © 1982 by Thomas Nelson, Inc. Used by permission. All rights reserved.

Verses cited MSG or The Message Bible, are from The Message. Copyright © 1993, 1994, 1995, 1996, 2000, 2001, 2002. Used by permission of NavPress Publishing Group.

Scripture quotations marked HCSB are from the Holman Christian Standard Bible®, Copyright © 1999, 2000, 2002, 2003, 2009 by Holman Bible Publishers. Used by permission.

Verses cited NLT are Scripture quotations taken from the Holy Bible, New Living Translation, copyright ©1996, 2004, 2007 by Tyndale House Foundation. Used by permission of Tyndale House Publishers, Inc., Carol Stream, Illinois 60188. All rights reserved.

Verses cited GW are from GOD'S WORD®, © 1995 God's Word to the Nations. Used by permission of Baker Publishing Group

Cover Photograph: Pindyurin Vasily

Chapters

INTRODUCTION

*T*his was not a book I started out intending to write. It was something that God planted in my heart during the early morning hours, as I watched the first snowfall of winter. That seed developed into a neatly planned outline that ended up bearing little resemblance to the book that God would ultimately unfold before me. Perhaps, this is the most important lesson for us to learn in our walk with God. He is the great Author and Creator. His best is always superior to anything we could devise.

I had no idea where this journey would lead when I first sat down and began to pen the words that God was writing in my heart. With little more than the seed of an idea, God compelled me with the force of the Holy Spirit unequalled in my memory, to set out on what has been an exquisitely beautiful adventure with Him. As I write these last few lines, the emotions that I most profoundly feel are relief, peace, and joy.

I have fulfilled to the best of my ability, the requirement that God seemed to have set for me. Though, I certainly do not imply that anything within these humble pages was written under the kind of divine authority as the Holy Scripture He breathed into existence! His Word is the truth through which all else must be compared.

The whole earth is filled with awe at your wonders;
where morning dawns, where evening fades,
you call forth songs of joy. (Psalm 65:8, NIV)

To understand how life works, He gave us an instruction manual called the Bible. Just as He spoke and breathed life into the universe, 2 Timothy 3:16 tell us that Scripture is also *God-breathed* into existence.

God knows that we often learn best by example, and He gave us plenty of them in His Word. Through the pages of Scripture, He introduces us to a variety of complex, and sometimes deeply flawed, men and women who will usher us along an incredible and life-changing adventure. You and I will spend time with some of them along our journey together. Through their lives and their struggles we will come to more fully understand our own life, and hopefully, draw closer to God in the process.

Our walk with God is a journey to understand His heart more fully, to worship Him more authentically, to draw closer in relationship with Him, and to fulfill our divine anointing. With every step and every day along this path,

2

we will hopefully realize that the faith and trust we have in *El Eyon* (Most High God) is so much deeper than it was yesterday. As our faith and trust deepens and grows stronger, it produces the abundant fruit of obedience.

Have you ever seen the sign or bumper sticker that says, *'If at first you don't succeed, trying doing it the way your Momma told you'*? Let me change that just a little. We can do things our own way, but life is so much better, sweeter, smoother, richer, happier, and more successful when we simply do it the way our *Father* told us in the first place!

In the simplest of terms, this is the essence of *obedience*. It is cooperating with God's better plan, and doing things His way, so we may reap godly rewards.

When He breathed life into the universe, God gave us the gift of free-will. We don't have to follow His rules or do things His way. I've certainly done plenty of things in accordance with my own plans. I'm sure you have, too. I've also done plenty of things in accordance with God's plan. I don't know about you, but I'll take God's results every single time!

As I penned the words to each chapter, God revealed things that were profound, exhilarating, and transforming for me, in my walk with Him. He brought me closer to His heart with every step along the way. I know He will do the same for you!

I am simply awed at the beauty, simplicity, power, and love of God's ways. When I began this book, I didn't think it was possible to love Him, believe Him, or trust Him any more than I already did. Yet, I sit here now writing these words knowing that it was...because I do! Even if you do not believe that it is possible to follow harder after God, it is my prayer for you that every single night you lay your head down believing it simply isn't possible to love Him more, only to wake up realizing that your love, your faith, and your trust in Him are even deeper.

God is our eternal Father. His love for us is as boundless as it is stubborn. He will not let us go. He will not stop trying to lead us on the path of His anointing and make our crooked paths straight. It doesn't matter if we have spent every day with Him, if we have been away a long time, or if we have just come to Him. God has been with us since before we were knitted together in our mother's womb, and His love and passion for us, as His children, is limitless. We were created in the mind of God long before He created us in the womb. God has planned and prepared for us even before He created the world.

This is not a book of doctrine, denomination, or law. It doesn't matter if your background is Baptist, Pentecostal, Methodist, Catholic, Charismatic, Jewish, Buddhist, or even agnostic, or humanistic. This is a book about what it means to follow hard after God and to align our lives with the Creator of Heaven and Earth. This is a book about the boundless love of our Father and the sacrificial grace, hope, love, and Salvation we find through the death and Resurrection of His Son, Christ Jesus. This is a book about what it means to live our lives in the fullness of God's promise and purpose. Most importantly, this is a book about God's profound love and devotion to all of His children.

A church is not a building. It is a body of believers united in Christ. I do so love churches. I always have. I love everything about them. It doesn't have to be my church home or even my denomination. I am uplifted by the worship that happens inside their walls. Filled to the brim on Sunday morning or empty and quiet on a Tuesday afternoon, I am moved by the feeling of energy and sacredness that exudes from their pores. I relish hearing men and woman who have been called by the Lord to speak and teach on His behalf.

I sincerely hope that you have a church and a church family where you believe with all your heart that God has planted you in its fertile fields. If not, start exploring churches in your community and ask God to lead you where He wants you planted.

For centuries, great men and women of faith have written millions of words on the subtle differences and similarities of Christian worship throughout the world. I encourage you to read every single word the Holy Spirit directs you towards. As for our journey together, I will respectfully submit that our walk with God is built upon a foundation not of doctrine, but of *faith, trust,* and *obedience.*

For much of this journey that we are about to embark upon together, we will travel along with Moses and Joshua as they lead two generations of Israelites out of slavery in Egypt and into the Promised Land. We will examine how their journey of divine deliverance from bondage and into the land of the Lord's promise mirrors our own journey from Salvation's deliverance and into the land that God, by

5

His Word, has promised unto us as His children. Along the way, we'll meet a whole host of God's best, and some of His not so best, and see what God is revealing to us through the stories of their lives.

This is a book at is intended to be written in and used. Don't be afraid to write your own ideas, questions, verses, and anything that God brings to your mind. This is your walk with your Father. Let Him guide you along the way.

> *As we begin our journey together, this, I pray:*
> Dear Lord, Thank You for Your mercy, grace, blessings, and boundless love that You pour into our lives. Please open our hearts and our minds to receive Your truth and hear Your voice. Along this journey, please bring into the light of Your love all that has been shrouded and hidden from Your mercy and grace. Let us pour out all of ourselves at the foot of the Cross so that we may be filled fully and completely with Your Holy Spirit. Lead us on this journey together as You lead us in our walk with You. Reveal to us Your anointing for our lives, and lift us up to our highest Kingdom destiny. Lord, we are ready, willing, and hungry to be Your hands, Your feet, and Your champions. We are hungry for Your purpose and Your Holy anointing. Please lead us to the land of Your promise. God we praise You as the Lord of our lives. We thank You for the gift of Your Son, Jesus Christ, in whose Holy name we pray. Amen.

CHAPTER ONE

TO KNOW HIM IS TO TRUST HIM

"When I am afraid, I will put my trust in You. In God,
whose word I praise, In God I have put my trust; I
shall not be afraid. What can mere man do to me?"
Psalm 56:3-4 (NASB)

*J**esus** left no room for doubt when He said, "by this*
everyone will know that you are my disciples, if you love
one another"[1] (John 13:35). Before we are called to do
anything else in God's Kingdom, we are called to love. We
are called to love God and to love one another as an outward expression of our love for Him. It is my prayer that
through our journey together we will develop an even
deeper, unshakable, and passionate love of God. He certainly has a passionate love for us as His children! That
love is what will sustain us, even if our faith might be

shaken. It is also what will allow us to trust Him completely though we may be afraid. It is what will allow us to
be obedient even when worldly logic says we are foolish.
He is worthy of every ounce of love that we pour out!
There is no more beautifully transformative force in all the
universe than a close, personal relationship to the God who
created us.

Our worship, our good deeds in the community, the
way in which we treat other people, and live our lives is an
outward representation of an inward relationship with
God. It is the feet to our faith and the way we show the
world to whom we belong.

Without that passionate inward relationship and complete surrender of our lives, as demonstrated by our *faith*,
our *trust*, and our *obedience*, I submit that every other act of
religious adherence is merely window dressing on an
empty storefront. Doubt this is true? Have you ever been
called to love someone who was not very lovable? Has God
ever asked you to show someone godly love, who has
wronged you, betrayed you, wounded you, or was just
generally a horrible person? It wasn't easy was it? How
much did you have to believe God, trust Him, and surrender to Him, in order to obey Him?

When I search my mind for an example of true godly
love, I cannot think of a better example than Nashville's
Father Charles Strobel, his mother, Mary Catherine, their
family, and their charitable ministry, *Room at the Inn*.

Room at the Inn is both a Nashville based homeless
shelter and a cooperative of faith congregations in Middle

Tennessee that provide year round assistance to those in need. It is truly a godly place founded by Father Strobel. In Nashville, his is a name that brings to mind the very essence of Christian love and charity. Many people know of his life-long work to help those less fortunate. Not as many know how the *Room at the Inn* came to be founded.

Now if we are children, then we are heirs - heirs of God and co-heirs with Christ, if indeed we share in his sufferings in order that we may also share in his glory. (Romans 8:17, NIV)

On December 9th, 1986, Father Strobel's elderly mother, Mary Catherine Strobel, was found in the trunk of her car near the local Rescue Mission. She had been kidnapped while shopping at a local department store and brutally murdered. It was initially believed that the suspect may have been homeless. Mary Catherine was a beloved mother figure to many. She was called the *'Mother Theresa of Nashville'*, as she had spent her life working tirelessly for those less fortunate in the community. More than a thousand people attended her funeral.

Father Strobel did not wait for his mother's killer to be brought to justice, or for the homeless theory to be proven true or untrue. He saw a need, and in December 1986, the *Room at the Inn* was born. Four local churches agreed to assist by providing shelter and assistance to those in need.

After a tireless investigation by Nashville police, the suspect was later caught. As it turned out, he was an escapee from a mental ward who has since been linked to five other brutal murders. He confessed to the crimes, and by all accounts, took pleasure in reciting the horrific details of the homicide to detectives.

In keeping with his faith, Father Strobel, asked that his mother's killer not be put to death. Instead, the killer is serving three life terms in a Tennessee prison.

The *Room at the Inn* has since grown to 180 congregations in Middle Tennessee with more than 6,000 volunteers.

In our walk with God, our faith, trust, and obedience provide the foundation for everything else.

Godly love is not always about how we feel, but it is always about obedience to God's will. If you don't think that to *love one another* as Jesus commanded will, at times, require unimaginable levels of *faith, truth,* and *obedience,* let me ask you this: Could you show godly love to the man who brutally murdered your mother? Would you ask for his life to be spared? Would you accept the anointing to serve those who were once investigated for her murder?

God passionately cares about our eternal Salvation, but He has equal passion about our lives here on earth. Like the Israelite's deliverance from Egypt, our eternal Salvation is not the end of our walk with Him. It is actually only the beginning. God did not just rescue His Chosen People from slavery and then drop them off in the desert to live out their lives. He had something incredible planned for them even before their rescue. He wasn't just leading them away from something bad, He was leading them towards something greater than they could ever imagine.

God is called by many names: *Lord (Psalm 118:1)*, the *Alpha and the Omega, and the Almighty (Revelation 1:8)*, *King of Kings and Lord of Lords (1 Timothy 6:15 and Revelation 19:16)*. In Hebrew He is called El Shaddai (God Almighty), El Elyon (The Most High God), Ehyeh Asher Ehyeh (I Am Who I Am), Adonai (Master/Lord), El Gibbor (God of Strength), and El Roi (The God Who Sees) just to name a few. My favorite name for God is the one by which His Son calls Him – *"Abba, Father"*[2] *(Mark 14:36)*.

Romans 8:17[3] says that we are *"heirs of God"* and *"co-heirs with Christ."* By His sacrifice, Jesus prepared the way not only for our Salvation, but also for our adoption. We are children of God. The Father of Jesus is also our Father, and boy does He love His kids!

As Christians who have accepted Christ as our Savior and set our lives to follow after God, our eternal Salvation is secured. Still, our loving Father wants so much for us here on earth. He wants to fulfill His Kingdom plan in our lives. He wants to deliver us into the land flowing with milk and honey. He wants to crumble the walls of Jericho at our feet. He wants us to reach our highest destiny.

While Heaven is the ultimate land of God's promise, He has made very specific and personalized promises over our lives here on earth, as well. Our Promised Land is a place where these promises become our reality and where we can dwell more closely with God than anywhere else this side of Heaven.

For Him to pour out His favor into our lives, we must first cooperate with Him in our blessing. Does a good and loving parent pour out their treasures into the life of their rebellious and uncooperative teenager? Of course not. How about a child who does their work, has a great relationship with their parents, and is honest, responsible and trustworthy? Our Father longs to give His children the best, but because He is a good parent, He wants to ensure that His blessings will not detour our walk with Him.

Our walk with God is a journey to grow in our *faith*, our *trust*, and our *obedience* to our Father. Every time we choose to cooperate with Him by trusting Him, believing Him, and obeying Him, we are actually cooperating in our blessing.

Faith

As we begin this journey together, let us define what we mean by *faith*. For many years I listened to people toss around the word faith as though it were a mythical state of being. It always sounded like an undefinable and theoretical accomplishment. If it was discussed in any detail, folks much holier than me, would always provide some variation of *'you know it when you have it.'* How could you possibly know if you have faith if it's an undefinable condition that you first have to possess in order to know? Let's look to the New Testament for answers.

In the New Testament, the Greek words most often used for *faith,* are the noun *pistis* and the verb *pisteuo.*

> Pistis[4]: conviction of the truth of anything, belief, believe, faith, assurance, fidelity

> Pisteuó[5]: entrust, believe, to be persuaded of, place confidence in, to entrust a thing to one

To have faith in God is to believe Him, trust Him, have confidence in Him, and have fidelity to Him. We believe, trust, and have confidence in that which we have a personal and tangible connection. We trust what we know. By His divine love for us, God has chosen to reveal Himself to us so that He may be tangibly known to His children. He reveals Himself to us every day in words and in actions. Ephesians 2:8 makes clear the source of our faith is God: *"For by grace you have been saved through faith. And this is not your own doing; it is the gift of God."*[6]

Our faith is something that we have, but like grace and Salvation, it is not something that originates within us. It is entirely ours as a gift from our Heavenly Father. Unlike our trust, which takes active purpose on our part, faith is purely God's gift, and requires only that we accept His gift. Faith is an extension of His love for us as His children, and it returns to Him from an outpouring of our love for Him.

However, God also gives us the gift of free-will. It is possible for God to extend the gift of faith to someone, even demonstrate His loving presence in their life, and yet they choose not to receive it. They may hold fast to the belief that God exists, but they don't believe what He says.

Moses, and the first generation of Israelites out of Egypt, spent the remainder of their lives in a wilderness limbo between their Salvation and their Promised Land. They had seen and felt the mighty hand of God. They knew He was real. They believed in His existence. Yet, they still didn't believe Him. They would never dwell in the land of God's promise because of their unbelief.

True, when some devastation was brought upon them because of their unbelief, they cried out to God and promised their devotion. Being a Father who loves His children, He saved them time and again. It became the chosen cycle of their lives. For many Christians this is the cycle of their relationship with God. They have been freed from their bondage. Their Salvation and their eternal life have been bought and paid for with the blood of Christ. God wants to lead them to their Promised Land, but their unbelief is keeping them in limbo in the wilderness. They do not yet understand the difference between belief in God's existence and believing God.

To reach our Promised Land requires *believing* God, instead of simply believing *in* His existence. Believing God is not that complicated. Faith is the belief not only in the existence of God, but also in what He says and does. In its simplest form, it is the belief that…

God is who He says that He is.

God can do what He says that He can do.

God will do exactly what He says He will do.

We are who He says that we are.

We can do what He says we can do.

Trust

James 2:26 explains that faith without works is as dead as a *"body apart from the spirit."*[7] Faith without trust is also empty and doomed. Can any relationship function effectively without trust? If you believe that your spouse is a wonderful person who does incredible things for your family and the community, but you can't trust them on a personal level, what becomes of the marriage?

Faith and trust are what we rely on when our world is at its darkest. It is what keeps us grounded and confident when the winds begin to howl. Faith, emboldened by real and tangible trust, keeps us moving forward on our anointed path. If faith is the heart of a person, then trust is the mind. Together, they move the legs, feet, and hands, which are obedience.

We studied the meaning of the Greek word *pisteuó*. It is not a coincidence that this word is used often to mean both faith and trust. Each is a single side of the same coin. While faith is generated by our Father and bestowed upon us as a free gift, trust is our active and purposeful action to receive and use that gift.

It may be easy to believe that there *is* a God and He *can* do great things. It's often much more difficult to believe that He is *willing* to do great things in our lives. However, by God's own Word, we know that He desires the best for our lives. In Jeremiah 29:11 God says, *"For I know the plans I have for you, declares the Lord, plans for welfare and not for evil, to give you a future and a hope."*[8]

Following God without ever seeing the map or under-standing the plan is not easy. It can be deeply frustrating and sometimes terrifying. It's like jumping off a cliff each day and trusting that God will guide us safely to the ground because He did so yesterday and every day before.

It's even harder to trust another when we so often do not completely trust ourselves much of the time. How often have we let ourselves down? How often have we made bad choices and bad plans? Even the best and most successful among us still has a long list of times in which they have fallen short of the glory of God. Yet, God never fails us. He has, at every step, planned bigger and better things for our lives than any we could conceive. When we cooperate with God and place ourselves in a posture of blessing, He pours out that favor into our lives like a flood of blessings.

This doesn't mean that we will never have times of trouble and difficulty. No matter how perfect our coopera-tion with God may be, we live in a fallen world and times of trouble will periodically come. Such things come into the life of every person, believer and non-believer alike. How-ever, we know that God is with His children in every storm. Sometimes, He will quiet the winds, and sometimes He will teach us to walk with Him on the water.

It sounds pretty simple. Yet, most of us have failed at this more times than we can count. The good news is that ours is a God of second chances, even third, and fourth chances. His love for us is as great as it is stubborn. He will not fail us. He wants us to be abundant and victorious. When we *can't* walk, He will carry us. Where we *won't* walk, He will drag us. He will do this day after day until we finally learn to believe Him, trust Him, and obey Him.

The word *trust* can be defined as a "belief that someone or something is reliable, good, honest, and effective, etc."[9] If God is anything, I think we can all agree that He is reliable, good, honest, and most assuredly effective.

Obedience

I admit the hardheaded part of my spirit has always cringed at the word *obedience*. It instantly brings to mind the idea of an authority figure telling me that I can't do, or have, something I want. It feels restrictive, authoritarian, and controlling. These are all things of which I'm not very fond. Does the idea of obedience bring to mind similar ideas for you? If it does, you are not alone. The aversion to obedience has plagued humans since Creation.

To understand what it means to live a life in obedience and submission to God, it may help to understand the meaning of the original Greek words. In the New Testament, two of the most commonly used Greek words for obedience and submission are *hupakouó* and *hupotassó*. Strong's Concordance provides these definitions:

> hupakouó: "to *hear under* (as a *subordinate*), i.e. to *listen attentively*...to *heed* or *conform* to a command or authority: - harken, be obedient to, obey"[10]

> hupotassó: "A Greek military term meaning "to arrange [troop divisions] in a military fashion under the command of a leader"[11]

The word *hupakouó* is derived from two Greek words, *hupo*, which means "by, under,"[12] and *akouó*, meaning, "to *hear* (in various senses): - give (in the) audience (of)...be reported, understand."[13] We can think of *hupakouó* as *to listen under God*.

The word *hupotassó* also derived from the word *hupo*. This time in conjunction with the Greek word *tassó*, which means to "*arrange* in an orderly manner, i.e. assign."[14] Both *hupotassó* and its root word, *tassó*, were common military terms. Its emphasis is on a voluntary submission. In our New Testament world this means a voluntary submission to God as the ultimate authority, and to each other, in loving reverence to Him.

To live our lives in submission to God does not imply inferiority. God entered the world in the body of a fully human baby in order that we might be saved. Rather, obedience is an outward expression of a heart that is actively listening to and following after God. It is an acknowledgment that His plans are always best.

What I have learned through the many detours, ditches, and pits that blanket a path walked outside of God's plan, is that His desires for my life are so much better than mine. He has led me places I would never have dreamed of going and given me things so incredible I could never have even imagined them. My heart swells just thinking about His faithfulness and love. I say this with a humble heart. I have lost my aversion to the idea of obedience to our Father, not because I have somehow grown more holy, but because I love and trust Him, and His ways are better than mine. The best plan that I make is mediocre in comparison to what God has in store for me if I cooperate with Him.

Complete obedience is built upon a solid foundation of trust and faith in a God that is always faithful and always planning the best for our lives. Like any relationship, our trust in God is important and it is grown over time. If your walk with Him has been short, you need not worry. Whether you accepted Christ as Lord of your life yesterday or fifty years ago, He has always been with you.

If you are willing and obedient,
you shall eat the good of the land…
(Isaiah 1:19, ESV)

There are days and seasons in my walk with Him when my *faith, trust,* and *obedience* pivoted on a single fact – God has never failed to show up in my life in the past, so I trust He will show up now, and always. It is our faith and trust in God's love and His unfaltering faithfulness that keeps us walking in the direction He is leading, even when we don't have any idea where we are going. This is most beautifully illustrated in Hebrews 11:8: *"By faith Abraham, when called to go to a place he would later receive as his inheritance, obeyed and went, even though he did not know where he was going."*[15]

Abraham didn't know where God was leading. He hadn't seen the roadmap or the plans. It was by faith that he followed where God led. He trusted that God would keep His promise.

Our obedience to God is the fruit of our faith and trust in Him. Together with our love for Him, they form the very foundation of our walk with God. In our daily lives this means that if God is telling us to turn left at the next street-light when we planned to turn the other way, we turn left. If God is telling us not to do business with a certain person when we thought it was a wonderful idea, we obey. If God is telling us to walk a certain path or go out on a particular limb, our job is to obey. We are not looking at the map. We are not reading the plans. If God wants us to know His reasons He will share them, otherwise, our job is simply to have *faith, trust,* and *obedience* as we follow Him to the land of our inheritance. We are all imperfect creatures. Our *faith, trust,* and *obedience* will be far from perfect, but every day is a chance to serve Him better.

PRAYER

Father, I love You. I know that You have walked before me. I know that You have been with me every step of the way. Please fill me with Your Spirit. Guide me as I take this journey with You. Allow me to know You, draw closer to You, and have such mighty *faith, trust,* and *obedience* that my foundation is forever solid and sure. Let Your will be done in my life, my business, my church, and my family. Your plan is greater than mine. Lord, please let Your will always prevail in my life and in the lives of those I love. Amen.

CHAPTER TWO
MY SHEEP SHALL KNOW MY VOICE

My sheep listen to my voice; I know them, and they follow me. I give them eternal life, and they shall never perish; no one will snatch them out of my hand.
John 10:27-28 (NIV)

*O*ne night, during my first winter in the new house, I couldn't sleep. I had a terrible headache that was not going away. Afraid that it might turn into a dreaded migraine, I crept out of bed and walked downstairs to take an over-the-counter medication and grab an ice pack. Looking at the clock, it said 2:23 AM. I was less than thrilled and resigned myself to a fitful night and a drowsy day ahead. Walking down the hall to head back upstairs, I decided to peek out the front window. The sight that greeted me was pure beauty to behold.

It was the first snow of the season. Big wet flakes of snow fell from the sky and blanketed everything in a carpet of fluffy white. It looked like the inside of a magical snow globe. As they fell, the flakes were illuminated by the old-fashioned streetlights that dot the neighborhood, causing them to glow and sparkle as they danced in the gentle breeze. This is a big event in the South, where grocery stores sell out of bread and milk every time flurries are forecast on the evening news.

So faith comes from hearing, and hearing through the word of Christ. (Romans 10:17, ESV)

The land here is made up of rolling hills. It's not rural, but we are nowhere near an urban downtown. Sightings of foxes, hawks, deer, turkey, and coyotes are not uncommon, even in backyards. The rolling landscape has always made the sky my favorite part of this house. At sunset, there are few buildings to obstruct views of God's hand painted sky. On a clear night, thousands of stars are visible and a full moon can illuminate like a streetlight. On this night, the moon was nearly full, but hidden by snow clouds.

As I looked out the windows I saw Christmas lights and rooftops blanketed with glistening snow. It reminded me of winter in northern Italy, where the snow sparkles like diamond dust. If you climb to a peak that is high enough, you have an unobstructed view of the glowing houses that dot the hills and valleys as far as the eye can see.

One of the many beauties of Italy is the near impossibility of escaping the sight of a church or hearing the bells from their towers. All that was missing on this night was a church steeple standing atop a hill on the horizon. As the thought passed through my mind, the moon appeared from behind a snow cloud and illuminated the top of a church steeple in the distance. I had never realized the steeple was there. Trees normally obstructed the view, but tonight the last remaining leaves had fallen. Only evergreens remained, and their snow-covered boughs perfectly framed the majestic scene as the large white cross glowed in the moonlight amidst a sea of snowcapped roofs.

It was too beautiful not to watch. As I sat in the darkness, in my favorite chair, beside my favorite window, I watched the world turn white and relished the stillness and quiet of the moment. After a while, I noticed two big bunnies hop out of the bushes in our front yard. They danced, and skipped, and ran, and hopped. They weren't looking for food. They were playing in the snow.

The world was quiet. Everyone and everything was asleep, except for two bunnies and me. As minutes passed into hours, I lost all track of time. Any thoughts of pain were forgotten just as completely as any thought of the responsibilities of the day. In those precious moments all that existed were the dancing snow, the playful bunnies, the glowing cross, me, and God. It was in the quiet of that early morning that the idea of this book was born.

Not everything that we initially think of as *bad* is brought into our life by Satan. Not everything that God puts in our path is sweetness and roses. Not everything that He brings into our life will initially inspire an *Alleluia* and a *Praise Jesus*. Sometimes, God doesn't just allow something that we see as a negative. Sometimes, He is actually the one that delivers it, parks it in our driveway, and honks the horn.

In 2 Corinthians 11:2 the Apostle Paul writes, *"I am jealous for you with a godly jealousy."*[16] Our Father is not simply jealous. He is jealous *for* His children. Like any good parent He wants only the very best for His kids. Like any parent trying to motivate a willful child in the proper direction, our Father loves us enough to push, pull, nudge, encourage, direct, and inspire us to travel in the direction that He knows is best.

I didn't like the splitting headache. I liked it even less when it neared to the point of a full-fledged migraine. I didn't like the hours and hours of tossing and turning in bed, but it sure did get me up and out of bed that night. God wanted me to see the beauty of His Creation at that particular moment, so He did just about the only thing that would actually get me up to be a witness to His glory.

Sometimes, God, like a prodding parent, pushes us in the direction He wants us to go, using the only methods He knows will work for us at the time. You may have gotten up with the first pains of a headache or the first hour of sleeplessness. Alias, I am not such a person. So, God used a bit more prodding to get my cooperation.

Did God give me a headache that verged on a migraine? Now, if you ask some folks they will say, *'absolutely not!*

God doesn't bring bad things to good people!' They will argue, and they will never accept that they are wrong. However, they are indeed very wrong. Sometimes, *seemingly bad* things are the only way our Father can get our attention.

Sometimes, God will cause your car to break down on the way to work. On occasion, He will cause you to leave that important report for work on the kitchen counter. He can also bring you splitting headaches in the wee hours of the morning. Sometimes, He absolutely does bring us discomfort, inconvenience, and occasionally even pain.

However, I disagree that these are in any way *bad* things. Like a good parent, our Father knows His children and He deals with each of us individually. Also, like any good parent, His prodding is always for our greater good and usually because we didn't obey when He asked us nicely the first, second, or third time.

If your car breaks down it may seem bad, but if you avoid that drunk driver five minutes up the road, it is a blessing. It's frustrating to realize you forgot something important at home, but if going back makes you realize that you left the stove on, it is a blessing. A splitting headache is a miserable experience, but if it's the only thing that will get you out of bed to spend a few hours with God, it is most assuredly a blessing.

God doesn't just speak through Biblical prophets. He doesn't just talk to ministers and Sunday schoolteachers. God speaks to all of us every day if we listen for Him. God communicates with us through a variety of ways and circumstances. Here are a few:

Through His Word

God has given us a divinely inspired guide for living our lives. Second Timothy 3:16-17 says this:

> *All Scripture is God-breathed and is useful for teaching, rebuking, correcting and training in righteousness, so that the servant of God may be thoroughly equipped for every good work.*[17]

All Scripture is *God-breathed.* I love that phrase! If you ache, as I do, to know the mind and the heart of God, we need look no further than the very words He breathed into existence. Sometimes, the answers that we find in Holy Scripture are very straightforward, such as, *"You shall not murder."*[18] Sometimes, the answers that we will find are more nuanced and personalized.

If we turn to Scripture in prayer and contemplation for divine communication, God will eventually lead us to a chapter, a verse, or a story that speaks to our heart. Better yet, if we have spent time feasting upon Holy Scripture, our Father will bring to mind just the right portion of His Word to speak to our situation. If He doesn't direct you there right away, just keep reading and give Him time, He will. It may be through a verse or the story of a person's life, but He will reveal Himself within those pages.

Sometime, the words that He leads us to are long re-membered verses. Sometimes, they may be brand new to us. Regardless, they are always fresh and renewed. Don't you just love that about His Word? No matter how many times we read it, Scripture is always fresh and new. Verses that we have read a hundred times before still offer new insight, inspiration, and guidance to our lives each time they are read. His Word can be applied to every situation in our lives with new and fresh inspiration. All we have to do is turn to God and to His Word.

All seemingly divine communication should be filtered through His Word. God will never violate the Scripture that He breathed into existence.

When God leads me to Scripture as an answer to a question there is an incredible feeling of peace. It is the perfect harmony between the Holy Spirit inside me and His Word before me. Even when the answer is not exactly what I was hoping for, it still brings the peace and certainty that only comes from acting in unison with God. It is one way that we know we are cooperating with God.

The Bible is the standard through which every other communication must be compared. Any time you need to decide if a message from another source is truly a message from God, seek clarification in His Word. God will never violate His Word. Whether the counsel and direction you are receiving is coming from nature, other people, a seemingly divine inspiration you believe to be the Holy Spirit, or one of a myriad of ways God will sometimes use, it still should be filtered through His Word.

Through the Holy Spirit

At the moment we accept Jesus as Savior and set our lives to follow after God, the Holy Spirit comes to dwell inside of us. Whether we listen to the Holy Spirit's counsel or decide to ignore any communication, the Spirit is always with us. The Spirit is the voice in the back of our head and the source of that persistent feeling that will not go away. It blankets us with the serene peace that comes with thinking, feeling, and behaving in agreement with God. It is also the source of conviction when we have strayed from God's plans and are doing, thinking, or saying something that is contrary to God's plan for our life.

In John 14:26, Jesus referred to the Holy Spirit as the *Helper* when He says, *"the Helper, the Holy Spirit, whom the Father will send in my name, he will teach you all things and bring to your remembrance all that I have said to you."*[19]

For me, God speaks very often through the Holy Spirit. It takes time and experience to learn how to discern the voice of the Holy Spirit amidst our own fears, thoughts, and distractions. When in doubt, ask God for clarity. He is speaking in order to guide us. He wants us to hear Him and understand Him. If we truly do not understand, He will provide us with insight. However, if we are asking for continued clarity in hopes that God will change His mind and conform to our will, we will often hear only silence.

There is another thing that God will not always provide. He will not often explain His reasons or plans. In some cases the reasons will become clear over time. Other times, we will never understand the reasoning behind what He is asking of us, nor do we need to understand. To walk with God requires our trust and faith. There will be seasons when our complete *faith*, absolute *trust*, and blind *obedience* is based solely on the fact that God showed up in our lives unfailingly before and He will surely do so now.

Sometimes, the Holy Spirit speaks loudly. Oftentimes, we must find some quiet time to be alone with God, if we are to hear His gentle whisper. Whether a hike in the woods, time in the garden, sitting quietly in the kitchen, or an afternoon drive, it is vitally important that we spend one-on-one time with our Lord. It is how we help to grow our relationship to Him, train our ears to better hear Him, and center our lives on His peace and His purpose. Without the peace and purpose that come from the Most High God, our lives are left to scatter amid millions of distractions. Instead of walking with God on the path of our anointing, we will surely end up lost in the desert, or worse, descending into a muddy and mired pit.

Where we elect to spend our time reveals a lot about where our priorities reside. We often forget to make God a priority in our life, much less our first priority. As a result, the beautiful work of building and maintaining our relationship with Him is overshadowed by the demands and continual distractions of daily life. How easy we make the enemy's job when we make God a check mark on a to-do list instead of a living, breathing relationship that requires priority in our life. If Satan knows that all he has to do to distance us from God is toss pressing distractions into our path, we will spend the rest of our days putting out fires and juggling minor disasters.

Every good and godly thing flows through the Father. For every other relationship and responsibility to function as God has intended, we must first prioritize our relationship with Him. He alone will make our crooked paths straight and He alone will help us fulfill responsibilities and grow our earthly relationships. The moment that we place any relationship, any desire, or any obligation, above Him, we undermine its ability to flourish, and undermine our relationship with our Father.

God doesn't just speak to Christian leaders and teachers. He speaks to all of His children.

Baring a burning bush, He speaks to me most powerfully when the Holy Spirit leads me to a specific section of His Word. Whether I am actively seeking an answer or not, there are days I read His Word, and though I feast on it as food for my soul, there are no flashing lights and trumpets. Then, there are times when I read a specific passage and my world stops, time stands still for just a moment as my mind tries to catch up to the revelation my soul has made. His Word aligns in my soul with the Holy Spirit and reveals to me His guidance or instruction. Sometimes, I may have been seeking an answer for days or weeks. Sometimes, I haven't been seeking a specific answer at all. God will say what He needs us to hear, in His time.

Through Burning Bushes

Sometimes, God's voice isn't subtle at all. There are times when something is important enough, or we may be hardheaded enough, that He speaks to us in the only way that gets our attention. When I need a really clear and absolute answer from God, I often find myself asking Him, *"Lord, I might not need a burning bush, but I sure would appreciate a neon sign."*

I still vividly recall every burning bush and neon sign moment that God has given me. Though, I realize that most of them have been because I wasn't listening to His quieter messages, I still treasure every single one. Never discount the voice of your Father speaking into your life.

On one Friday, I sat quietly, in perpetual and fervent prayer. I had not budged from my seat. I had not eaten or drank a thing. Every single word from my lips and thought in my mind was devoted to my single petition. I heard the phone ring and I ignored it. I was not going to budge. The phone rang again, and again I ignored it. The phone rang a third time. I felt a pull to answer it, but started to ignore the ringing, yet again. About that time I heard a voice that left no room for my dismissal. The words were very clear: *I am trying to answer your prayer. Cooperate. Answer the phone.*

I did as I was commanded to do. The call began the process that answered my prayer and granted my petition ten-fold. God may not always speak in a booming voice from Heaven, but He does speak loud and clear. There is much glory and favor that we miss when we ignore Him.

31

Through Other People

I am always cautious when someone says '_God told me to tell you (fill in the blank)._' Just as with anything in life, people can use the name of God to justify and further their own agenda, their own emotions, and even their own sin. Just because someone writes the word _God_ across the front of their personal agenda, does not make it God sent.

However, God absolutely does use other believers, and even nonbelievers, to communicate to us. Oftentimes, the message He sends to us through other people is the same one He has been trying to deliver to us through the Holy Spirit, His Word, and many other ways. We either haven't been listening or we are in need of greater reinforcement. What makes these moments so powerful is that they often come as a lightning bolt from the sky. They startle us with the external voice of what the Holy Spirit has been counseling us for so long. When these moments are God sent, they often have the feeling of déjà vu.

When we experience these moments it is important to listen for what God is trying to communicate. Whether or not the words of others are reinforcing other godly communication, we should always filter them through His Word and seek counsel from the Holy Spirit. He speaks so that we will understand. He wants us to hear His message and understand it so that we may act upon it. When in doubt, just ask Him. He will help you receive His message. Don't stop at simply asking for clarification. Ask to hear His voice and receive His direction. He will provide!

Through Events and Circumstances

God's communication is not always verbal. Often, He speaks to us in divine circumstance. Nonbelievers sometimes call it *coincidence*. Merriam Webster's Dictionary defines the word *coincidence* in this way: "a situation in which events happen at the same time in a way that is not planned or expected."[20] Can you think of a better way to describe God's miraculous and supernatural intervention? The love, favor, mightiness, and faithfulness of God are beyond our comprehension. When He lays His hand upon our lives and purposefully orchestrates events and circumstances in a way that can only be the hand of God, we can only stand in wide-eyed wonder and cry out *Alleluia!*

Sometimes, God uses events and circumstances in ways that are less dramatic, but no less supernatural. You may think it is a *coincidence* that you run into someone you just thought about, or found the perfect house the first week of your search. If you are operating in harmony with God's will, He is orchestrating events that lead you where He wants you to be. God puts into motion events that lead you to His better plan. He can also block your path to a destination that is damaging to your faith journey.

God will sometimes cause things to happen that keep you from what you want and put you on the path to what He wants for you. Part of being sensitive to God's communication and listening for Him with an expectant heart is to constantly be aware of the fact that what others call *coincidence*, may actually be the divine hand of God.

Through Nature

Many of the moments in which I am closest to God have come while experiencing the majesty of God's creation. Whether it is the first snow of winter or a sunset hand-painted by God, I cannot help, but pause and breathe in the sheer grandeur of His creation. As God pointed out to Job, even the animals, the birds, the fish, and the plants of the earth know that they were created by the hand of the Most High God *(Job 12:7-10)*. In God's hand is, *"the life of every living thing and the breath of all mankind"*[21] *(v. 10)*.

The truth of His Creation is simple, but far from simplistic. It is designed to work in a certain way. Part of its beauty is the perfect balance of order and creativity.

Our Father established Creation with certain very particular rules. He invented the very notion of creativity, and then in His divine wisdom, established it between the framework of rules and order. He causes the sun to rise every morning in the East and set every evening in the West. Yet, between our dawn and our dusk, He allows glorious creativity in the beauty. Within each sunrise and sunset are perfectly painted scenes of blues, pinks, reds, oranges, purples, and yellows. No two are ever alike. God paints a different sunset each day, just as surely as He individually forms every snowflake.

If you have trouble clearing your mind and just being with God in conversation or meditation, there is no better place than outside in God's own handmade cathedral. Take a walk. Sit in a garden. Watch the unfolding a sunset.

When We Ask

A few years ago, a friend was in the hospital. Her family was deeply worried they would have to say goodbye. If there is ever a time for family and friends to be close, this was the time. So, a few friends and I packed our suitcases and headed south. When we arrived at the hospital, we understood the reason for concern. She was in ICU and looked like a woman who was being called home.

It was late at night when we finally got to the hotel, but I couldn't sleep. It was a warm night, so I headed outside to sit near the pool. I was all alone and the world was quiet. I implored God to lay His healing hands upon our friend and restore her to perfect health. I also asked to hear His voice in this situation. It was a voice that I longed to hear. The last time I had felt the guidance of the Holy Spirit was several days before when God led me to make this trip. As I finished the prayer and took a deep breath of humid air, a flash of lightning in the distance caught my eye. It was heat lightning, the colorful distant display of a far-off storm that lights the sky without the sound of thunder. For the next hour I sat, wrapped in the warm night air, alone with God, and watched as the night sky lit up in a show of blues, pinks, oranges, and reds. It was both startling and one of the most beautiful things I had ever seen.

I asked to hear God's voice and He answered me. Perhaps, not in the way I had expected, but in a glorious way nonetheless. Within twenty-four hours our friend was out of ICU, and within a week she was home.

Beloved, one of the most important things I pray you take from this book is the truth that God's voice is not reserved for teachers and preachers. God speaks into the lives of every single one of His children. He is speaking into your life right now. He wants you to seek Him every day and in every situation. Start by seeking Him with your words and thoughts. Instead of bringing all your worries, hopes, and fears to other people, bring them first to God. Bring it all to the One who can do something about it!

Our prayers do not have to be long and formal. Talk to God throughout the day. Thank Him when you merge safely into traffic. Acknowledge Him and talk to Him about your day as you talk to an old friend. Specific quiet times with God for prayer and meditation are important, but they are not the only way we talk to Him. Try chatting with Him. You might just be surprised to hear His answer.

When We Listen Expectantly

We know that God will speak whether or not we are willing or ready to listen, but if we're not listening for Him with expectancy, we may miss His message. Just like a parent speaking to a moody teenager, He is far more likely to speak to us if we are eagerly expecting His voice. If your teenager is irritable and not attentive, with headphones blaring music, how likely are you to interrupt and tell them there is chocolate cake in the kitchen? God often takes the same approach in speaking to us as His children. He still speaks, but unless it is vitally important, He will speak in a tone so soft that we are forced to remove our headphones.

God can surely swirl the winds and send down the lightning bolts. Sometimes, He will do just that. Though, often times He will speak in a whisper instead of a roar. His voice will often come in a gentle breeze, rather than a hurricane. If we do not spend time training ourselves to slow down and pay attention, we will miss the opportunity to hear the voice of our Lord speaking into our lives.

God is telling us to slow down, pay attention, and listen. He is reminding us that a relationship with Him, like all relationships, is a two-way street. We have to make an effort and pursue Him just as He is pursuing us. Our Father will not compete with our busy day, our important calls, or our urgent emails. He will not accept second place in our lives. We know that God will meet us at the level of our expectation, but if we expect Him to take second place all we are likely to hear is silence.

When We Obey

Here is a simple truth about God: He gives His most important assignments to those He can count on to do His will. We aren't doing God a favor when we accept our anointing and become His hands and feet. God spoke words and created the universe. He could accomplish anything He wants, at any time, just by speaking the words. Yet, often He does incredibly important work through the flawed earthen vessels of His Children. He allows us to come closer to Him as we serve His mighty mission. If you want to grow closer to God, to know Him, to serve Him, start by saying *yes* more often when He asks.

It is not always easy. We live busy lives. We struggle with our own issues and fears. Even Moses asked God *why me,* and actively encouraged Him to give the important anointing of leading the Israelites out of Egypt to someone else. I find it comforting when even God's best and brightest display the same reactions and struggles we all have from time to time. Their lives also clearly show that following the path to a Kingdom destiny begins by saying *yes* to God, and obeying His divine instruction.

PRAYER

Dear Lord, tune my ears to You. Give me a quietness and sensitivity to hear You amidst all that seeks to distract me. Give me discernment to understand what You are saying and a mighty *faith, trust,* and *obedience* so that You never need to use insistent methods to get my attention. Thank You, Lord, for speaking into my life and allowing me to hear Your voice. Thank You for every method that You use to direct me towards Your better plan. Even when I may not like Your methods at the time, I know that You are faithful. Thank You for showing me the light that I may follow. Thank You for loving me and using me as part of Your plan. Amen.

CHAPTER THREE
PREPARING THE WAY

For we are God's handiwork, created in
Christ Jesus to do good works, which God
prepared in advance for us to do.
Ephesians 2:10 (NIV)

orty-years elapsed between when God brought His Chosen People out of bondage in Egypt and when He delivered them into the Promised Land. David was a young boy tending His father's sheep when he was anointed by the Prophet Samuel, upon God's instruction. He was a man of thirty when he succeeded Saul as King of Israel. Forty years passed between the time Moses fled Egypt as a fugitive, and when he encountered God on Mount Horeb. There is work to be done before God can plant us in the field of our harvest. The years between our Salvation, our anointing, and our harvest are not lost years. Rather, they are seasons of preparation.

The Israelites may have spent forty years in the desert, but they were not wandering aimlessly. God was preparing them for the moment in which they could be brought across the river Jordan and into the Promised Land. Neither did God abandon them to their own devices. He dwelt amongst them as He prepared them, sustained them, and provided mighty evidence of His powerful, real, and active presence in their lives.

God instructed Moses to build an Ark of acacia wood, *"two and a half cubits long, and one and a half cubits wide, and one and a half cubits high"*[22] *(Exodus 25:10)*. God instructed that it should be overlaid with pure gold both inside and out. It would have two gold rings on each side so the Ark could be carried on two acacia poles. Inside, the Israelites were to place the testimony of God.

Atop the Ark of the Covenant was to be a *"mercy seat of pure gold"*[23] *(v. 17)*. Two gold cherubim were to be placed on each end of the mercy seat, with their wings spread upward, covering the seat, and facing one another. God said: *"There I will meet with you; and from above the mercy seat, from between the two cherubim which are upon the ark of the testimony, I will speak to you about all that I will give you in commandment for the sons of Israel"*[24] *(Exodus 25: 22)*.

When not in use, the Ark was placed in the Tabernacle Tent, which was to be made of fine linen of blue, purple, and scarlet color. God met His Children in the wilderness. They had made a home for their Lord, and He dwelled among them! He sustained them. He led them. He was with them as surely as He is with you! Perhaps, you are still in the wilderness in your walk with God. You have been freed from the bondage of your personal Egypt, but you have yet to cross the River Jordan and into your Promised Land. This is the season of your preparation.

The time between your anointing and
your harvest is not wasted.
This is the time of your preparation.

Some folks think of being a Christian as simply the acceptance of Christ and a list of things we should and should not do. It is true that our Salvation has already been bought and paid for in the blood of Christ Jesus. It is a gift that is freely offered, for which we cannot earn, repay, or qualify, but it is far from cheap. Its cost is the complete and unqualified surrender of our lives to the purpose and plan of the Most High God.

Our Salvation is far from the end of our walk with God. If we were to examine Exodus as a timeline, the Israelite's freedom from bondage in Egypt is far from the end of their story. It can be argued that it was really only the beginning. So too, is the timeline of our Salvation. The freedom from bondage it entails is only the beginning of our faith journey. It is the beginning, not simply of a new chapter in our life, but of a whole new book. There is so much that our loving Father has planned for us along this journey. His will is more incredible than anything we could imagine.

God does not ask us to go anywhere or do anything in which He has not already prepared and equipped us. Though, we may not realize that we are ready, God will know. He will inevitably ask us to tackle mighty assignments and traverse steep and difficult terrain, but we do so knowing that He walks ahead of us, preparing our path, and beside us ensuring we have the strength and power for the mission. In those moments when we simply cannot take another step, He will carry us. Rest assured that God will always be with us.

Therefore there is now no condemnation for those who are in Christ Jesus. For the law of the Spirit of life in Christ Jesus has set you free from the law of sin and of death. (Romans 8:1-2, NASB)

Through the death and Resurrection of Christ Jesus, we have been reborn anew. Our old life has died away and God has given us a resurrected life that leads both to His eternal promise in Heaven, and a very earthly Promised Land. To reach that land there will be work that God does in us, and there is work that we do as Christians to grow into ever maturing and mighty men and women of faith. As we journey ahead together we will examine the work that we must do in growing our relationship with God. For now, let's look at some of the work that God does in us as our Father.

God Removes Our Bondage

There is a video that has now gone viral from an animal rescue organization that saved a group of Beagles from a research laboratory. The dogs had been born in the lab and lived their entire lives in cages in sterile environments. They had never been outside, walked on grass, or felt the warmth of sunlight on their face. Partway in their journey from the only home they had ever known to their new foster families, the volunteers stopped at a dog park to let the dogs play outside for the first time.

Even when you may not realize it at the time,
God is still at work preparing you.

A few crates were brought out at a time and the doors opened. The volunteers lovingly encouraged the dogs to come out of their crate and be petted. Still, the dogs were nervous and reluctant. They sniffed and gently pawed at the blades of grass as they tried to adjust to the new surroundings. Finally, one dog worked up the courage to exit the crate and run towards his cheering rescuer. Then, one by one, the others slowly came out to join in the experience.

The moment we accept Christ as Lord and Savior, and begin to follow after God, He breaks loose the shackles of our bondage. Whether your captivity is sexual sin, addiction, abuse, deceit, divorce, abortion, shame, rebellion, or unworthiness, the Most High God sets you free.

43

It is not something for which we can ever earn or qualify. Rather, it is God's gift to us as His children. Though, just because our chains have been broken, and our cell doors sprung open, does not necessarily mean that we feel free to step out into the sunlight and toward the gentle, loving encouragement of the One who rescued us. Listen to these words from Romans 8:15. Absorb them and believe them as the divinely-inspired Word of your Father:

> *For you have not received a spirit of slavery leading to fear again, but you have received a spirit of adoption as sons by which we cry out, "Abba! Father!"*[25]

We have lived our entire lives in cages in a sterile environment. We have never before felt the warmth of God's love or the solid foundation of His strength beneath our feet. For some, it takes time for the mind to catch up to the sudden and drastic freedom.

However, our Father's love is stubborn. He does not want His children to live in shackles and be caged by the bondage of our past. He longs to set us free. Rest assured, God will continue to bring us through the wilderness, until our minds finally catch up to our souls.

We must be strong and never give up. It is nearly impossible to escape our cages by being timid and shy. Over time, God will help you build persevering strength and develop a permanent heart of valor. For now, all you need is one moment of insane courage. One moment of complete *faith, trust,* and *obedience* to the Father who is calling you by name and lovingly encouraging you to come out. In one brief moment you can cast aside the words of guilt, shame, and unworthiness that have been spoken over your past, and run into the sunlight. Don't stop to question. Don't even think. Don't consider anything except the words of the Father. Run into the arms of your *Abba*.

By His Word, God tells us that we are His beloved children, forgiven, redeemed, adopted, and blessed. Leave the cage and run, full steam, straight into your Father's arms. By the time your doubts, fears, and the whispers of the enemy catch up to you, you will already be basking in the warmth of God's love, and feeling His strength beneath your feet. He will have already begun to build in you a heart of courage. He has already begun to build your memory stones. If we trust in the Lord with all our heart, He will lead us – body, mind, and soul - out of bondage and into a glorious future in the land of His promise.

God Builds Our Memory Stones

Just before God led Joshua and the Israelites to the Promised Land, He brought them to the flooded waters of the Jordan River. If they were to take the land of Canaan, they first needed to cross the raging river and enter the territory. Where God led them, He provided them a way.

The Ark of the Lord would go ahead of them. As soon as the priests carrying the Ark dipped their toes into the very edge of the river, the water was cut off far upstream. The priests stood in the muddy riverbed, the Ark of God held aloft, as the entire nation of Israel hurried across to the other shore. God, Himself, stood still. For what must have taken hours, the priests carrying the Ark stood rooted in this strange place. Alexander MacLaren writes: *"through all the stir the ark was still. Over all the march it watched. So long as one Israelite was in the channel it remained, a silent presence, to ensure his safety. It let their rate of speed determine the length of its standing there."*[26]

Can you imagine crossing that riverbed, with a flooded torrent of water held at bay just up-stream? What a sight it must have been! How much easier it must have been to believe that God would not let them drown when all they had to do was look up and see the priests standing still in the middle of the riverbed, a visible sign of God's presence hoisted on their shoulders. The Ark did not hold that water at bay. The mighty hand of God did that, but the Ark was a very real sign of His presence with them.

Even the most *faithful, trusting,* and *obedient* amongst us still sometimes need a visible sign of God's real and active presence. This is especially true when we are walking through the muddy riverbeds of life whose flooded waters threaten to drown us in their raging rapids. God knew this then, just as He knows it now.

As soon as the nation had completed this miraculous crossing, God instructed Joshua to have twelve men place twelve stones at the site of their camp in Gilgal. Joshua obeyed and then he said to the people: *"When your children ask in time to come, 'What do those stones mean to you?' then you shall tell them that the waters of the Jordan were cut off before the ark of the covenant of the LORD. When it passed over the Jordan, the waters of the Jordan were cut off. So these stones shall be to the people of Israel a memorial forever"*[27] *(Joshua 4:6-7).*

God was instructing them to create a tangible reminder of their faith and of His faithfulness. The stones were physical markers of the many times God had shown up in the lives of these first two generations out of Egypt. These were physical memorials of the parting of the Red Sea, pillars of cloud and fire, the drowning of their enemies, the manna from Heaven, and the safe crossing of the Jordan.

Joshua also erected a second set of twelve more stones. These were placed in the riverbed, *"where the feet of the priests bearing the Ark of the Covenant had stood"*[28] *(Joshua 4:9)*.

Why would God want memory stones placed in a flooded river? Though Scripture doesn't give a reason for this second set of stones, based on all we have seen of God through our journey so far, let me suggest a reason.

The river wouldn't always be flooded. There would be periodic times of drought when this water would run low. During these dry seasons, the crops would be in danger of dying and the people would be praying for the rains to come. In these times, the stones in the river would be easily visible. They would serve as a reminder of God's love, faithfulness, and active presence even during the dry season. Our Father never wants His children to forget that He dwells among us. He sustains us. He leads us. He loves us. He alone is the source of all freedom and victory.

Ours is not a dead religion in service of a silent God. Far from it! Ours is a living faith expressed in a real and tangible relationship with our Creator. Relationships are not built, they are grown over time. They are watered with love, nourished with trust, and fed by faith.

Building our memory stones is one way God feeds our faith and nourishes our trust. If you are like me, you can point to events large and small, every day that demonstrate the real and active presence of God's hand in your life. You can look back over the course of your life and point to the times when God led you by pillars of cloud and fire.

He always stands by his covenant-- the commitment he made to a thousand generations. (Psalms 105:8, NLT)

For the first time in my life, I have an outside cat. He came with the house. Believe me when I say that he is not outside by my choice. He likes to come inside, but he will only stay for so long before the newness wears off and he's screaming to be let back out. This past winter, I let him outside on a particularly warm day. By late afternoon it was turning cold, so I opened the door and called for him to come inside. Surprisingly, he usually does. This time, he was nowhere in sight. For fifteen minutes, I searched and called for him, but to no avail. I grew more worried.

Finally, I prayed, *"Lord, it's getting colder and I'm worried. Please bring him home so he can be warm and safe. Amen."* No sooner had the words left my mouth than a happy, meowing cat came running up, ready to come inside. Some may call this a coincidence, but we know that God doesn't do coincidences. For me, this was a memory stone, deposited by God, into my life. It was a tangible demonstration that He heard my words and He answered my prayer.

Sometimes, our memory stones are as big as an illness that has been supernaturally healed, an accident that was divinely avoided, or a relationship that has been redeemed by the active intervention of God. Sometimes, they are as seemingly small as a cat coming home with the close of a prayer. They are all vital and massive in the growth of our relationship with God. Each one is erected in our life as a memorial stone. Every single one is tangible evidence of God's active role in our lives. They are real and profound reminders of our faith and of God's faithfulness.

They are the reminders that our Father holds back the flooded waters of our lives. When our dry seasons come, these stones serve as memorials so we will never forget that though the ground may appear parched now, our beloved Father will bring forth the healing rains and deliver an abundant harvest. He has done so in the past, He will surely do so in the future.

God Prunes Our Vines

In John 15, Jesus explains God's role as the gardener of our lives. We know that God will feed, water, and nourish His children. He certainly provided for the Israelites in the wilderness. However, God has another role as the gardener of our lives. He prunes our vines.

Every gardener knows that pruning a plant is just as important as watering, feeding, nourishing, and weeding. Pruning cuts away the dead, damaged, and unhealthy parts of a plant. It gets rid of unnecessary branches that block the flow of air, cut off sunlight, and lead to mildew. It cuts away dead flowers that if left alone will drain the plant of energy. Different plants are pruned in different ways and in different seasons. Some shrubs are pruned after their spring bloom. Many annual and perennial plants need to have their dead flowers pruned away throughout the year to keep the plant healthy and blooming.

He cuts off every branch in me that
bears no fruit, while every branch that does
bear fruit he prunes so that it will be even
more fruitful. (John 15:2, NIV)

Grapevines are usually pruned in the fall at the end of the growing season. Have you ever seen a grapevine after its end of season pruning? It's as startling as it is drastic. The plant looks more destroyed than pruned, but come spring, new branches will grow and the plant will produce more fruit than it ever would have without the careful attention of the gardener.

Perhaps, you have branches of attraction to destructive relationships, self-destructive behavior, addiction, or cycles of guilt and obligation. Perhaps, your branches are destructive people and places that sap your energy and draw you back into the life of bondage from which God has already set you free. Perhaps, your branches are not destructive at all, but there are simply so many of them that air and sunlight can't flow through. Maybe these are the branches of over commitment, over responsibility, or overextension.

The one common denominator is that each of these branches, if left alone, will drain your energy, inhibit your growth, and prevent your abundant harvest.

Our loving Father will prune away every branch that keeps us from the abundance He has planned. He will prune away our selfishness, ego, anger, doubt, bitterness, fear, envy, shame, gluttony, and impatience. He will prune away any negative emotions, damaging circumstances, bad habits, destructive people, or negative thinking.

Sometimes, the ending of a relationship, the loss of a friendship, or the termination of a job are examples of God's pruning of our branches. That which He prunes does not have to be outwardly negative. If we worship at the altar of our job, our school, a relationship, or even family or friends, God may also prune those branches as well.

He will prune away anything that prevents or hinders our growth and our closeness to our Father. God will never abide being second place in our lives. Ours is a Father who is jealous *for* His children to have the best…His best. Thus, He often prunes away those branches that get in the way of our highest Kingdom destiny and His eternal plan.

If you want to know what may need pruning in your life, begin with anything that doesn't first flow through the living vine of the living God. Determine what takes up all of your time and distracts you from your relationship with God. Look at what keeps your mind occupied and your heart troubled. Those may be the first distractions in need of pruning. If something does not honor your Father, bless others, and lift you to a higher destiny, it may need to go.

God Cuts Away Our Covering

Before God allowed the Israelites into the Promised Land, He instructed them to resume the Covenant of Circumcision. Joshua 5 tells us that all the men of military age, who had come out of Egypt had been circumcised, but those born in the wilderness had not.

After the entire nation had been circumcised, they remained in camp until they were healed. Afterwards, the Lord said to Joshua: *""Today I have rolled away the reproach of Egypt from you." So the place has been called Gilgal to this day"*[29] (v. 9).

Do not underestimate the danger that the Israelites faced even as they obeyed God. Once they had crossed the Jordan River they were in the land of Canaan. They were in enemy territory. The spies under Moses once said of this same place: *"the land we traveled through...will devour anyone who goes to live there. All the people we saw were huge. We even saw giants there, the descendants of Anak. Next to them we felt like grasshoppers, and that's what they thought, too!"*[30]

That report alone had so terrified the generation that followed Moses that most of them wanted to return to slavery rather than claim the land they had been waiting on for four hundred years. Now, the children of that generation were being given a vital requirement by God. Fulfilling that requirement would mean nearly all the men of military age would be incapacitated and recovering for days. As the entire nation of Israel camped at Gilgal, they would be completely defenseless against enemy attack.

God asked His Chosen People for their radical obedience and ultimate vulnerability. Before God ever gave the instruction to Joshua, He had already ensured their protection. Joshua 5:1 tells us this: *Now when all the Amorite kings west of the Jordan and all the Canaanite kings along the coast heard how the Lord had dried up the Jordan before the Israelites until they had crossed over, their hearts melted in fear and they no longer had the courage to face the Israelites.* [31]

How great is our God that even before He has asked something of us, He has already prepared for our victory and protection! Not even mighty kings and great armies can stand against the King of Kings! Nor are they a match for the children of God acting in obedience to His plan.

Our Father has equipped us with the shield of faith, the sword of His Word, and the helmet of Salvation. If you have the full armor of God, if the commander of His army is going before you, and His Holy Spirit is your rearguard, of whom (but God) should you ever have cause to fear?

Secrets, shame, and hidden sin distract us from God, protect our shame, and attract the enemy.

Gilgal comes from the Hebrew verb *galal*, which means "roll away."[32] Other words for reproach include, *shame, dishonor, blame,* and *scandal.* Only after God had quite literally removed their covering, did He roll away their shame. They had laid down their past before God and were ready to begin a new life in the land of His promise.

Covered secrets and hidden sin create very specific and dangerous results that will prevent us from entering our Promised Land. They distract us from our Father. They protect our shame and reproach. They also lure the enemy.

It is impossible to keep anything evil, negative, or shameful, hidden under a covering of secrecy that does not also hide what is good, pure, and godly. The act of hiding things and keeping secrets takes energy away from living a bountiful life. It does something even more destructive to our lives. It sidetracks us from a relationship with God.

Have you ever tried to keep a secret or protect a lie? Perhaps you are simply a fan of modern-day soap operas. Either way, you know that anyone keeping secrets and protecting lies will spend so much time worrying about their exposure that they are ultimately consumed by a state of fear and paranoia. This fearful state will leave them blind to everything else in life, including God.

God will not abide our divided attention. He will never accept second place in our lives. We cannot ever be fully *faithful, trusting,* and *obedient* to our Father, unless we are also completely honest and professing of our sin, failure, and our mistakes to Him. God is like a parent who already knows all of our secrets, but He wants to hear us profess them so we can move forward, and out of our place of hiding. His Word offers us specific counsel on this topic:

> **Hebrews 4:13:** *Nothing in all creation is hidden from God's sight. Everything is uncovered and laid bare before the eyes of him to whom we must give account.*[33]

Luke 12:3: What you have said in the dark will be heard in the daylight, and what you have whispered in the ear in the inner rooms will be proclaimed from the roofs.[34]

Just as any soap opera fan knows, lies and secrets will never stay hidden forever. They will eventually be exposed to the light of day. God will continue to bring us through the wilderness until we are finally able to be obedient to His instruction and remove our covering.

Secrets, lies, and hidden sin also have another, equally dangerous, consequence. They compound and intensify our feelings surrounding what we struggle to keep hidden. These emotions attract the enemy just as surely as a shark is attracted to the smell of blood.

It is important to remember that just as we can keep nothing secret from God, we can keep nothing secret from Satan for long. The enemy is as cunning as he is perceptive. Eventually, he will poke and prod, question and tempt, until he has discovered what we are hiding. It doesn't matter if what we are keeping secret is something we have done or had done to us. It doesn't matter if it happened yesterday or fifty years ago. Nor, does it matter if our secret is really all that bad, or if we simply perceive it with great shame and need for secrecy. Satan will use it!

He will also use every emotion we have attached to it in order to subvert us from our anointing and lure us away from our Father's love, grace, and mercy. Make no mistake, what we keep hidden we also give power. The danger occurs when the longer we have kept something hidden the more power it has, and the more power it has over us.

55

No matter how much strength, you think you have, this is a battle you will be fighting all alone. God doesn't want anything to be withheld from Him. Our *Abba* wants everything we have ever done, had done to us, and every single shattered piece of our heart to be swept up and brought into the light of His love, grace, and mercy. He is never going to help us hide anything from the only source in all Creation that can make us healed and whole...Him.

Without the mighty power of God, you are left to fight this battle alone and you will eventually lose. The increasing power that is naturally given to all that you try to keep secret and hidden, will build upon itself like a snowball rolling down a mountainside until you feel as though you are living your entire life under the threat of an avalanche. All of your energy is directed into keeping the ever growing secret and shame hidden from the light of day until you can no longer bear fruit. However, expose a hidden shame to the warmth of God's love, and you will watch it melt slowly before your eyes.

Everything that is hidden will eventually be exposed. It may be today or it may be next year, but it will happen. The only question is how long do you want to remain in the desert, separated from your Promised Land, and how painful will the final cutting away of your covering be? God's love is pure and it is stubborn. God wants us to dwell in the land of milk and honey that He has prepared just for us. He will continue to bring us around full circle, to our Gilgal, until we are ready to surrender our covering and allow Him to roll away our reproach.

God is not asking us to reveal our every secret to the world. In fact, there are things He will want to keep just between you and Him. However, He does require that we keep nothing hidden from *Him*. He requires that we bring everything to Him, without justification, excuse, hesitation, or restraint. We lay it all down before the One who makes our crooked path straight, who can forgive our transgressions, roll away our shame, heal our brokenness, and lead us to a bountiful and victorious life.

The Israelites had moved about in the wilderness forty years until all the men who were of military age when they left Egypt had died, since they had not obeyed the LORD. For the LORD had sworn to them that they would not see the land he had solemnly promised their ancestors to give us, a land flowing with milk and honey. So he raised up their sons in their place, and these were the ones Joshua circumcised. (Joshua 5:6-7, NIV)

After years in the wilderness, God had brought the Israelites to the edge of the Promised Land. He had freed them from bondage. He had pruned their vines. He had built their memory stones. He had cut away their covering. He had rolled away their reproach. Finally, after 400 years in slavery and 40 years of preparation in the desert, He had brought them to the very edge of the land promised to them as descendants of Abraham. By testing and refining He had prepared and purified them for their highest anointing – the conquest of the Promised Land. It is by these same methods that He prepares us today.

PRAYER

Dear God, I know that You walk before me and prepare my path. I know that You want the best for me and long for me to inherit the land You have promised and prepared just for me. Please prune away all that keeps me from a full and complete relationship with You. Bring into the warm light of Your love, mercy, and grace all the secrets, shame, and hidden sin that I have kept buried for so long. Free me from the shackles of all that bind me and roll away my reproach, so that I may be made whole, and healed, and righteous in the land of Your promise. Amen.

CHAPTER FOUR
REFINE US LIKE SILVER

For you, God, tested us;
you refined us like silver.
Psalm 66:10 (NIV)

*T*he United States Navy SEALS are known the world over as one of the most elite Special Forces units ever created. Name a high valued, and dangerous military operation the U.S. has undertaken in recent history and there were likely members of a SEAL team involved. They are called upon when an operation has to be accomplished at all costs and against all odds. They are the elite of the elite. Richard Marcinko, the first Commander of SEAL Team Six, offered insight as to how they acquire such skill: "We all knew there was just one way to improve our odds for survival: train, train, train. Sometimes, if your training is *properly intense* - it will kill you. More often – much, *much* more often – it will save your life."[35]

Only thirty-three percent of recruits will complete Phase One of the grueling SEAL training process, designed to test their physical, mental, and psychological endurance just to the point of breaking, and then a few steps beyond.

The purpose of this phase of their training is to instill important knowledge, skill, faith, trust, obedience, and enormous perseverance. It may seem punishing, but to accomplish and survive their future missions, it will take every ounce of what has been instilled and sharpened during this training and testing season. They will eventually utilize everything learned during this time.

We often think of our role as disciples in pastel shades of peace and submission, but His Word tells us that there are times in which we are called to fight. The Promised Land was not handed over peacefully to the Israelites. It was conquered with the help of God's army. Even when we are not called to active battle, we still must be able to stand against the slings and arrows of the enemy and of the world. Ephesians 6:13-17 puts it this way:

> Therefore put on the full armor of God, so that when the day of evil comes, you may be able to stand your ground, and after you have done everything, to stand. Stand firm then, with the belt of truth buckled around your waist, with the breastplate of righteousness in place, and with your feet fitted with the readiness that comes from the gospel of peace. In addition to all this, take up the shield of faith, with which you can extinguish all the flaming arrows of the evil one. Take the helmet of salvation and the sword of the Spirit, which is the word of God.[36]

To be the hands and feet of our Lord in the world is the service to which we are all called. To accomplish our anointing - the missions that God has personally appointed us to complete - we must also possess skill, knowledge, *faith, trust, obedience,* and enormous perseverance. Just as an elite soldier is tested and trained in preparation for their future assignment, so too does God test and train us. Our Father does not send us anywhere without first preparing us and preparing our way.

It is not a coincidence that everyone from Abraham to Jesus has been tested prior to God raising them to the level of their highest anointing and sending them out into the world to accomplish His works.

Consider it pure joy, my brothers and sisters, whenever you face trials of many kinds, because you know that the testing of your faith produces perseverance. Let perseverance finish its work so that you may be mature and complete, not lacking anything. (James 1:2-4, NIV)

By the testing of our faith, God grows us up into mature disciples, ready and able to fully step into our anointing and withstand the slings and arrows of spiritual warfare. It is a refinement not of our mortal state, but of our ability to put aside our human weakness and lead with the Holy Spirit that dwells inside us. This is the essence of a mature faith. For surely into the lives of every person will come moments of darkness and seasons of challenge. This is true for Christians and non-Christians alike. The difference between a child of God and our non-believing neighbors is that we have a loving Father who will sustain us and who has prepared us by testing and refining. Isaiah 48:10 says, *"See, I have refined you, though not as silver; I have tested you in the furnace of affliction."*[37]

This passage from the Prophet Isaiah is important because, here, God is describing for us exactly what testing is meant to accomplish. We often hear the word *test* and think of a distant headmaster handing out a pop quiz to see who is living up to set standards. That could not be further from the truth. Merriam-Webster's dictionary offers these definitions of the word *refine:*[38]

"to remove the unwanted substances in (something)"

"to improve (something) by making small changes"

"to free...from impurities or unwanted material"

"to become pure or perfected"

This is the very essence of God's testing and tempting of His children. Our Father doesn't test us just to see our grade. After all, Scripture tells us that God walks before us and knows us so well He can count the number of hairs on our head *(Deuteronomy 31:8 and Luke 12:7)*. If God were handing out a pop quiz, He would already know our grade before we even picked up a pencil. Rather, God is refining the last vestiges of unwanted impurities from our hearts, minds, and souls so that we may be pure and whole as we enter our Promised Land.

The transliterated Greek word for *affliction* is *kakopatheia*. It means, "experience of evil, suffering, distress, affliction, perseverance."[39] It is translated as "suffering affliction" in James 5:10: *"Take, my brethren, the prophets, who have spoken in the name of the Lord, for an example of suffering affliction, and of patience."*[40]

Sometimes, that which we perceive as bad from an earthly perspective is actually fulfilling and accomplishing God's greater plan. It is preparing and refining us for something better than we could ever dream.

Our Salvation was purchased with the blood of Christ, but the path to our Promised Land takes time, work, training, and effort.

During the most intense five and a half days of SEAL training, recruits will sleep no more than four hours. They will endure physical training more than twenty hours a day, and run a total of over 200 miles. That certainly sounds like suffering affliction and distress to me. How about you? However, the end result of perseverance through this affliction is the perfecting of an elite warrior who is able to accomplish any mission, their country calls upon them to complete.

Fleet Admiral Chester W. Nimitz, for whom the USS Nimitz is named, said of the men who fought on Iwo Jima, "uncommon valor was a common virtue." If you are fortunate enough to live in a country of freedom, then you must never fail to acknowledge that the freedom and safety you enjoy has been purchased and preserved with the honor and sacrifice of a solider. In my humble opinion, the only calling higher than service to country is service to God. If those called to the service of their country have been refined and tested into elite men and women, how much more so must be those called to the service of God?

The testing of our faith comes in many different ways. We will discuss a few of them.

By Temptation

When we think of temptation our minds often go first to the temptation of the flesh. Though, physical temptation is by no means the only way in which we are tempted. Testing by temptation comes any time we are drawn to replace God's desires for our lives with that which the world says we *should* desire.

His Word tells us that sometimes God doesn't simply allow us to be tempted. There are times when He leads us to the place of our tempting. Before Jesus began His anointed ministry, the Holy Spirit led Him into the wilderness to be tempted by the devil *(Matthew 4)*.

Satan's power is limited by God. The enemy can only tempt us within the limits God has established *(Job 1:12 and Luke 10:19)*. We can rest upon the absolute conviction that God is faithful and, *"will not let [us] be tempted beyond what [we] can bear"*[41] *(1 Corinthians 10:13)*. Satan can try his worst, but our Heavenly Father has our back! Even in the midst of our testing, God is still faithful!

God has given us the gift of free-will. It is through this gift that the enemy will seek to lure us away from our anointed path. It is also through this gift that we can fall victim to our own human weakness and self-destructive tendencies. Just because God has freed us from bondage, built our memory stones, pruned our vines, cut away our covering, and rolled away our reproach, does not mean that we are ready to withstand the temptations of a very cunning enemy, or our own weakness and self-destruction. Before we can be sent out to conquer our Promised Land, God will ensure that we are ready for the slings and arrows that will surely come our way.

Our victory in the midst of testing and temptation is best ensured when we are prepared and ready beforehand. Our temptation doesn't have to be as stark as sexual sin or deceit. Oftentimes, it's much more insidious and subtle. When the temptation is hidden inside something seemingly benign or every day, it can be very difficult to recognize.

Then Jesus was led by the Spirit into the wilderness to be tempted by the devil. (Matthew 4:1, NIV)

I love yard sales, estate sales, and antique shopping. You might call it a hobby, and on pretty weekends you might find my mother and me visiting more than a few of them. I am by no means an expert appraiser, but as a result of many years of shopping and collecting I have developed a pretty good eye for evaluating the value of a piece.

On one particular outing, we stopped by a yard sale held by an elderly woman and her daughter. A large set of china on a side table struck my eye. I love to entertain, so china and serving pieces always catch my eye. I recognized the pattern and markings. It was a large set of antique china, produced by a very collectible maker and each piece appeared in perfect condition. The entire collection was worth well over $5,000-$7,000, even at estate sale prices. They were selling the entire set for $125. The collection had belonged to the elderly woman's mother and they had no idea of its value.

Our tests ensure that we are prepared
to face all that the world and the enemy will
bring against us along our walk with God.

Now, I love both china and bargains. I could have been fooled by my own desires into thinking that God wanted me to have a great deal. However, I would have failed the test He had for me that day. When I told the mother and daughter the true value of their collection and gave them the name of an antiques dealer to contact, both women burst into tears. What I had not known was that the sale was to pay off the funeral expenses of the elderly woman's husband. The amount they lacked was $5,000. God had not sent me there to find a bargain, He sent me to be obedient and deliver the clear message: He is a faithful God and He will provide *(Psalm 33:4 and Philippians 4:19).*

By Eliminating Our Comfort Zone

In *'Comfort Zone to Performance Management,'* Alastair White describes a comfort zone in this way: "The comfort zone is a behavioural state within which a person operates in an anxiety-neutral condition, using a limited set of behaviors to deliver a steady level of performance, usually without a sense of risk."[42]

I don't know about you, but that sounds good to me. Anxiety-neutral, limited risk, and steady performance all sound like good things. Then again, I am a fan of my comfort zone. How about you? I don't just like it. I've painted the walls, put pictures up, and decorated the place. I've always liked this tranquil unchanging space. It may not be God's best, but it sure is comfortable. Perhaps, this is why God has so often selected this area in which to refine me.

During a particular season of my walk with God, I knew that He was asking me to step outside my comfort zone, but I had yet to perfect my listening skills when He spoke, or my obedience for that matter. God kept asking me to change things and step into something new. He kept patiently sending me easy opportunities. My answer was generally the same, *'Thanks, but I'm comfortable here.'* I may not have been deliriously happy with my comfort zone, but I was used to it and it was, after all, comfortable.

Has God been offering you a similar opportunity? Is He nudging you towards an unknown path? You may know that it's leading to a place so much better than where you are at now, but an unknown path is a scary thing.

The stronghold of my particular fear was finally broken – for the most part – when He fundamentally changed almost every aspect of my life within a year. In refining me of this particular unwanted substance, God was drawing me closer to Him, and building an entirely new section of memory stones to serve as an eternal reminder that my trust in Him will never be misplaced.

The changes He brings to your life may not be as drastic, but rest assured change will come. If we elect to obey the gentle nudges, shake loose the comfortable, and walk where God is directing, then He just might let us move at a more gentle and easy pace. However, if we force our Father to do the changing for us, our comfort is likely not going to be His first concern.

Perhaps, God is asking you to start a business, found a ministry, go back to school, take a mission trip, start a charity, adopt a child, or move across country. He is asking you to step out of the land that you have known and cross the parted waters of the Jordan. You may or may not be able to see the Promised Land from where you stand. You may have no idea that it is anywhere around. God is demanding your blind obedience, your unwavering faith, and your absolute trust.

Your Promised Land won't be the end of your journey. God will still have great wonders waiting for you. He wants to pour out His best into your life. He wants you to dwell in the land of milk and honey, but you will need all the *faith, trust,* and *obedience* you can muster in order to claim that land as your own.

By Daily Annoyance

The single most common way God refines us is with the affliction of daily irritation. I know that sitting in rush hour traffic may not seem like a Holy perfecting of our hearts, minds, and souls, but it may well be our most important and most difficult. Jesus said we would be recognized as His disciples by the way we love one another *(John 13:35)*. We are called to be vessels of Christ's love in the world. First John 2:6 says it plainly, *"Whoever claims to live in him must live as Jesus did."*[43]

Does this mean that how I respond to a flat tire, a rude driver, a pushy store clerk, an irritable child, a crashed computer, a nasty co-worker, an inconsiderate spouse, a missed opportunity, a sarcastic boss, a frustrating client, or a burst water pipe is a reflection of my relationship with God and part of my refinement in Him? Yes!

This is as difficult as it is important because our challenge is twofold:

1) How we act and react to the world.

2) The condition of our spirit during the experience.

How many times a day do we meet rudeness with at least irritated dismissal, pushiness with defiance, condescension with anger, rudeness with hateful words, or thoughtlessness with annoyance? Perhaps, you have gotten pretty good at controlling your outward response. You have perfected the cool, polite exterior that cleverly hides your impatience, anger, or bitterness. You may wish some-one a nice day with a warm smile, but in your head you are calling them things that are less than PG. I know that I am guilty of this from time to time, how about you?

We hope that if we can maintain the discipline not to allow our inner emotions to seep through, all will be okay. This may be a human way of handling such difficulty, but it is not God's way. We may think our *"own ways are right, but the LORD weighs the heart"*[44] *(Proverbs 21:2).*

To God, the emotions and motives of our heart matter just as much as our actions. To God, there is no difference between us seething on the inside because of other people's bad driving during rush hour traffic and venting our anger out the window at the top of our lungs. Just because we think it, but do not speak it, doesn't make us godlier.

My grandmother was the finest Christian I have ever met. I can't recall her having a negative word to say about anyone. Whenever someone was rude, she just let it roll off. Their behavior never touched her mood or determined her response. She'd continue to smile and treat them with the same warm southern manners with which she encountered everyone. I don't mean to imply that she allowed people to take advantage of her, but she simply refused to allow any situation to determine her mood or set the tone of her day. She refused to allow anyone or anything to steal the joy from her world. Even more importantly, she refused to al-low anything to interfere with her relationship with God.

It is often easier to rise to a challenge when there is an epic battle to be fought. Heightened emotions, adrenaline, and endurance take hold and allow us to rise higher and go farther than we thought ourselves capable. However, when we return to the everyday routines of life, we slip back into our old habits. It's those very same old habits from which God is trying to break us free.

To put feet to our faith and become the men and women God needs us to be, we must be able to naturally respond with the reaction of the Holy Spirit rather than ourselves. We are impatient, angry, jealous, and filled with a temper that is quick to judgment. However, the Holy Spirit is patient, kind, and filled with love and grace. In those times when we need to meet a situation with righteous anger or rebuke, God will let us know. The more we practice God's response to any situation the easier and quicker it will come, and the closer we grow to our Father.

By Troubles and Obstacles

Life is filled with pitfalls, snakes, sheer cliffs with no guard rails, and boulders that fall from the hillsides, or are pushed by the enemy, and sometimes by so-called friends. Our paths are almost always filled with obstacles. This is especially true of the path of our anointing. There is nothing that the enemy wants more than to stop us dead in our tracks and lure us away from God. We are the trophies on his wall and he loves collecting us. However, sometimes the mightiest, most seemingly insurmountable obstacles are not actually blocking our path, but preparing us for a higher calling. Throughout Scripture, God provides us with example after example of mighty men and women of faith, whose highest destinies and victories were reached not in spite of their obstacles, but because of them. In 1 Corinthians 10:13, the Apostle Paul wrote this: *"No test or temptation that comes your way is beyond the course of what others have had to face. All you need to remember is that God will never let you down; he'll never let you be pushed past your limit; he'll always be there to help you come through it."*[45]

The Greek word for temptation is *peirasmos*,[46] which in the context of 1 Corinthians, can also mean testing. We know from this passage, and from the story of Job, that God will never allow us to be tempted or tested beyond our level of ultimate endurance. He will either quiet our storm or He will teach us to walk on the water!

The Navy SEAL's training is designed to take them just past the point of breaking. It is done under the careful watch and instruction of trainers whose ultimate goal is for the good of the recruits so they may not only survive in difficult situations, but also emerge victorious. This is also the goal of God's testing and training of us as His beloved children. He wants His children to live victoriously.

Only when we have experienced testing and training, beyond what we thought ourselves capable, can we stand in a world outside our makeshift classroom. It is only when God has broken away our worldly supports that we have the faith, knowledge, skill, obedience, and perseverance to lean unto Him. God gives us strength to continue on our anointed path when the storm clouds come and have chased away all but a few who have also crawled through the testing season.

Even when Joshua and the Israelites had finally made it to the edge of their Promised Land, after forty years in the wilderness, it still wasn't theirs as a free gift. God had used their wilderness years to prepare them for the next season along their anointed path. They still had to conquer and claim the land of Canaan. Every day, and every testing along their path, had been leading them to the moment of their greatest battle and their greatest victory. God had been laying the groundwork for that victory not simply for years, but for generations.

God often gives His most important missions to those whom He can consistently count on. He uses our testing seasons to perfect so we will be ready and able to accept those mighty assignments in His Kingdom plan.

Think of everything that had to happen, not just in your life, but in the lives of your parents, grandparents, and great-grandparents, to lead you to this moment and this place. Think of all the stars that had to align, all the chance meetings that had to occur, all the obstacles that had to be maneuvered around or rolled away to bring you to this place in your walk with God.

Perhaps, the place where you stand today is not so good. You may be in the wilderness or even in the furnace of refinement with Job. You know that all things work for the good of those who love God and are called to His pur-

73

pose *(Romans 8:28)*, but the words don't speak truth into your heart. I dare suggest that even in the midst of darkness there are seeds of hope, *faith, trust,* and *obedience* in your heart.

God will faithfully fulfill His part. It is up to us to faithfully fulfill our part. However, there are times when the greatest obstacle in our path is us.

If we let Him, God will grow in us a mighty faith and unshakable trust. For now, we need only enough faith and trust to fill a mustard seed.

The black mustard seed was the smallest seed sown by first century farmers in the Near East. Yet, Jesus said, *"Truly I tell you, if you have faith as small as a mustard seed, you can say to this mountain, 'Move from here to there,' and it will move. Nothing will be impossible for you"* (Matt. 17:20).[47]

If we can find even the tiniest bit of faith and trust in God, He will not simply sustain us in the wilderness, but He will lead us to the land of His promise. If we look, really look, over the history of our lives, we will see that God is a promise keeper. He has been faithful to us even in times of our unfaithfulness. He has believed in us, though we have doubted Him. He has loved us even when we were not very loveable. He has not left us, though we may have left Him. We are the children of a God who keeps His word!

Can a good and loving parent ever be completely objective about their child? Can they ever separate their view of their child from their love of their child? Does a loving parent ever stop caring for their child, even in the face of rebellion or grave mistakes? Of course not. A parent's love of their child is not conditional on anything the child ever can or will do. Their love is based entirely on their outpouring of emotions towards their baby.

We are made in our Father's image. If the love you have for your child is absolute and unconditional, can you imagine the love that the Father has for you? You may have planned your children for years, but the Father has been planning for you since the very creation of the universe. When He opened His mouth and spoke light into existence, He had you in mind for this time and this place. It is simply impossible for God to separate His view of you from His unbridled love for you. He is your Father. No matter your age, you will always be His baby.

God is faithful. He has never left you and He is not about to start now. How many times have you experienced near misses and last-minute saves? How many times can you say that you are here only by the grace of God? He has made promises over your life and He is a Father who keeps His word. As long as you are alive in this world, God is not done with you yet. He still has amazing plans to fulfill in your life and through your life.

As I look back on the course of my life I see all the ways that God has sustained me, believed in me, pushed, pulled, and encouraged me just a bit further along the path He has planned for me. He has never abandoned me. He has never failed me. He has never stopped loving me. Even in the moments when I could not begin to imagine how God would transform a dire situation for the better, I still knew that He would show up. Though the water may have been at my neck, He has never allowed it to go over my head. He has never let me drown. Even when I could not believe that a God so perfect could love a woman as broken as me, I still had the solid rock of His promises. He has surprised and awed me in the most incredible ways. I know He has not led me this far to leave me now. He will never abandon you, either!

PRAYER

Dear Lord, I pour out all of me so You may fill me with all of You. I know that You loved me even before You formed in my mother's womb. My *Abba*, though the circumstances in front of me may seem dire and I may have no idea how You could possible redeem this for Your best, I know that You can and You will. I choose to see these circumstances as a chance to witness Your glory and watch You show up in a mighty way. Lord, I surrender my life to You. I ask only that You train me, teach me, refine me, and lead me so that I may be a humble servant of Your mighty Kingdom. Fulfill in me Your anointing. Show me Your will. Train me so that I may claim the land of Your promise. Amen.

CHAPTER FIVE
AN EXPECTANT HEART

*"For I know the plans I have for you," declares
the Lord, "plans to prosper you and not to harm
you, plans to give you hope and a future."
Jeremiah 29:11 (NIV)*

I am going to ask you a question. I would like you to give it some thought before answering. It is an important question. It is important to your relationship with God and to your journey towards your Promised Land. I would like you to think back and remember your emotional mindset surrounding the mile markers of your life as you answer this question:

For what do you believe God?

I am not asking *why* you believe Him. I am not asking *if* you believe *in* Him. I am asking whether you *believe Him*, and if so, how much? What do you believe the Creator of Heaven and Earth can and will do in your life?

Have you ever missed out on an opportunity and thought, *'Well, that's just my luck'*? Have you worked at a job you hate for years, but when a friend suggests that you apply for something else, your reaction is, *'Why bother, a new one probably won't be any better'*? Are you unhappy in your marriage, but think, *'That's just what marriage is like'*?

One of the most pervasive afflictions in the life of a Christian is a defeatist mindset. It is so insidious that even the most joyful and believing Christian can fall into its trap.

We ask God for only the barest necessities, and then we are disappointed when that's all He gives us. At one time or another, most of us have prayed a prayer similar to this one: *'God, please just let me get by. Just let me have enough money for the bills this month. Just let me stop fighting with my family.'* What is your *'Lord, please just let me _____'*?

God meets us at the level of our expectations. If we pray for just enough money to pay the rent that is all we can expect to receive. If we pray to just stop fighting with our family, silence is all we can hope to bring into our home. If we pray to just get by in life, God will let us do just that.

Throughout our journey together we will talk a lot about the importance of expecting God to do great things. I would argue that there is no better example in all the Old Testament of an expectant heart than the one demonstrated by Joshua in the Valley of Aijalon.

Joshua and his army had marched all night to rescue the city of Gibeon, from a coalition led by King Jebus. The Israelites were small in comparison to the many kingdoms surrounding them. If those other nations ever realized the

Israelites could be defeated, they might join together to re-take the land the Israelites had conquered.

Joshua rescued the city and pursued the coalition forces eastward, through Beth-Horon, then southward through the Valley of Aijalon. The Israelites needed a decisive victory and they needed to complete the march before the sun and moon shifted positions in the sky. In other words, they needed more hours in the day. Haven't we all prayed for such a miracle? Joshua needed the seemingly impossible, but he knew that nothing has ever been impossible for God. So, in front of his entire army, Joshua commanded the sun and moon to stand still. He knew that God was on their side. He knew that Israel had the favor of the Lord, who created the universe. He believed God would deliver a mighty miracle. Can you imagine asking God for such a thing and expecting Him to deliver? Well, Joshua sure did! He believed God for the miracle! The tenth chapter of the Book of Joshua records what happened:

> On the day the LORD gave the Amorites over to Israel, Joshua said to the LORD in the presence of Israel:
>
> "Sun, stand still over Gibeon, and you, moon, over the Valley of Aijalon."
>
> So the sun stood still, and the moon stopped, till the nation avenged itself on its enemies, as it is written in the Book of Jashar. The sun stopped in the middle of the sky and delayed going down about a full day. (v. 12-13)[48]

Joshua not only believed in God's existence, he believed God. He knew that God is faithful. He knew that God keeps His promises. He knew that God was fighting for His People. Because of this knowledge, Joshua had confidence in taking his greatest need to the Lord. With an expectant heart, he commanded the sun and the moon to stand still. God met him at the level of his expectation. *"The sun stopped in its tracks in mid sky; just sat there all day. There's never been a day like that before or since — God took orders from a human voice!"*[49] *(Joshua 10:13-14).*

Oh, to have the spirit of Joshua! We can have that same spirit! The same favor that was upon Joshua is upon us. The Israelites were God's Chosen People. Through Christ, we are God's adopted children. Our Father fights for us just as surely as He did for the Israelites who claimed the Promised Land. His Word is clear on who we are and who we are in relationship to Him.

> *It is not the children by physical descent who are God's children, but it is the children of the promise who are regarded as Abraham's offspring. (Romans 9:8)*[50]

Through the death and Resurrection of Christ, we are also the children of God. We are the children of the promise. We are the descendants of Abraham and heirs to the Covenant the Lord cut with him. We can and must expect the Most High God to do great things in our lives.

Every single day I pray this prayer over my family:

> *Lord, Thank You for the flood of obvious favor that You pour down over them. Thank You for holding them in the*

palm of Your hand and shielding them with Your love throughout the day. Thank You for enveloping them in Your Blessing. Please lift them up in every way and bring them closer to Your heart. Amen.

To believe in the mighty power, immeasurable grace, boundless love, and obvious favor of God, is not arrogance, it is faith. To have a heart like Joshua requires only that we trust God and believe what He says. To have a heart filled with such a faith and trust is a requirement, not an option, if we are to live victoriously.

Take delight in the LORD, and he will give you the desires of your heart. Commit your way to the LORD; trust in him and he will do this: He will make your righteous reward shine like the dawn, your vindication like the noonday sun.
(Psalm 37:4-6, NIV)

Some of God's beloved children simply do not believe that life will get any better. As they give voice to their negative expectation with complaints and defeatist words, their mindset gets stronger. They may know that God exists, but they do not believe Him for anything better. They have grown so accustomed to things not working out that this has become their expectation. They are trapped in the stronghold of defeat that sees only the fruit of mediocrity.

Have you ever met a person that seems to have a perpetual cloud over their head wherever they go? They could be standing on the most beautiful beach in the world, looking at the most beautiful sunset ever painted by God, and when they look up all they see is the gray cloud over their head. It is a cloud of their creation.

A defeatist attitude does not abide in the Spirit of God. However, it will certainly block us from receiving the flood of God's favor. Its constant rain will certainly keep us from hearing the loving voice of our Lord.

An expectant heart invites God's favor and receives God's best.

The Most High God is our *Abba*. He longs to give us His best. He continually says to us: *Trust Me. Believe Me. My plans for you are greater than you can imagine.* He wants to pour out the flood of His favor into our lives, but first we must believe Him for that best.

If what God has planned for us is simply beyond our imagination, how can we have expectation to receive it? How can we have expectation for the glories of God, if logical and rational facts tell us that it is impossible? If the doctors tell us that our diagnosis is terminal, how can we expect a miraculous healing? If our company has gone bankrupt or our jobs exported overseas, how can we expect God for an intercession? If we are elderly and childless, how can we expect God to miraculously deliver us a child? How could we possibly expect a miracle when the world says it's impossible?

Our human minds are limited. God knows this, which is why He often teaches by visual reference. The third Covenant God made with mankind, He made with Abram, son of Terah, the tenth descendant of Noah. God told Abram (later known as Abraham) that he would be the father of many nations. God instructed him to walk outside and look up at the stars. Then, God promised that Abram would have as many children as there were stars in the sky. The most astonishing aspect of this promise was that neither Abram, nor his wife, Sarai, was young. They were of very advanced years and Sarai had never borne a child.

He took him outside and said, "Look up at the sky and count the stars--if indeed you can count them." Then he said to him, "So shall your offspring be." (Genesis 15:5, NIV) (God to Abram)

Why did God ask Abram to go outside and count the stars? Because He knew that Abram could not conceive of the magnitude of His promise. For Sarai (who God later renamed Sarah) to conceive a child would be impossible by any worldly standards, but we know that nothing is impossible for God. The Lord wanted Abram to have visual reinforcement of the mightiness of His promise.

This isn't about having a positive attitude or New Age visualization practices. This is about trusting God to be God and accepting Him as the King of our lives. This is about unshackling our minds from the bondage of despair and mediocrity, and accepting the full and obvious favor of God. We miss out on untold wonders when we fail to fully accept our role as a child of the Most High God.

Let's answer a few more questions:

Do you believe…
God **is** exactly who He says that He is?

He **can** do exactly what He says that He can do?

He **will** do exactly what He says He will do?

You **are** exactly who He says that you are?

You **can do** exactly what He says that you can do?

If we believe the answers to these questions are *yes*, then why, do we try to put the Creator of Heaven and Earth in a box of our limited understanding?

When we talk about a relationship with God, it isn't a metaphor. It is an actual, real, and living relationship. As with all relationships, it goes both ways and takes both sides to fully evolve into something spectacular.

God gave us the gift of free-will. However, there are times that not even our own free-will can supersede God's will for our life. However, most of the time, God will allow us to use this gift of our own accord. Most of the time, God's favor will only flood into our lives if we decide to accept it. To receive God's best we must expect God's best. To be able to receive the flood of His favor we need an open heart, an open mind, and an expectant soul.

Often, not only do we fail to expect God's best, but we consciously envision Satan's worst. We brace ourselves by contemplating the very worst outcome possible of a situation for which we care greatly. Then, having spent so much time with the vision of disaster seared into our minds, we act as if the worst has already come to pass. Do you know someone who does this?

When a loved one is diagnosed with a serious illness, instead of expecting God for a miraculous healing they're already busy mourning. When a company announces the slim possibility of future layoffs, they are already acting as if they're unemployed and will be homeless and bankrupt.

Expecting the worst does many things. Probably the most frightening and dangerous consequence is that it shrouds us from receiving God's blessing and His favor. Assuming the worst and filling our time with negative expectations does nothing to prepare us for the road ahead. God, Himself, has already prepared the way. Our Father does not ask us to walk a path and then fail to provide for the journey. His Word is filled with reassurances:

> *Exodus 23:20:* *"See, I am sending an angel before you to protect you on your journey and lead you safely to the place I have prepared for you."*[51]

> *1 Corinthians 2:9:* *However, as it is written: "What no eye has seen, what no ear has heard, and what no human mind has conceived"* — *the things God has prepared for those who love him...*[52]

Deuteronomy 31:8: "The LORD himself goes before you and will be with you; he will never leave you nor forsake you. Do not be afraid; do not be discouraged."[53]

We cut ourselves off from God's best for many reasons. Each reason is often very personal and frequently based on our perception of events that happened long ago. As we develop greater *faith, trust,* and *obedience,* and learn to view our present and our future through the lens of God's truth, how many of us take the time to reexamine our past through the same filter? Yet, it is our past that has so often molded our perceptions and reactions in current situations. Oftentimes, our past is the very thing that is holding us back from a deeper and richer relationship with God.

We will examine some of the reasons we cut ourselves off from His best. Let's start with one of the most common.

Fear of Being Disappointed

There are times in everyone's life when we feel down hearted. Life doesn't always work out the way we had planned. Sometimes, it doesn't even look like it will work out for God's best. We have all been disappointed. We have all known times when we hoped for the something that never came. Sometimes, the plans that we have for our lives are simply not in agreement with God's plans.

Sometimes, if the experience is especially painful, we cut ourselves off from the possibility of hope. If we never want or expect too much, we will never again face the pain of disappointment. If you don't expect to get that promotion, you won't be disappointed or embarrassed if you are skipped over for someone else. If you don't expect your spouse to be sensitive or understanding, you won't be hurt if they lack thoughtfulness or consideration. How many people in your life fit this description? Perhaps, you see yourself in this just a little bit?

Let me ask you a question. Does this method of coping with life work for you? Does assuming that the desires of your heart will never be fulfilled really buffer you from the pain of rejection and disappointment, or has the pain simply shifted from a momentary agony to a dull sting that blankets your entire life? It may not be as sharp as the pain of temporary disappointment, but it never goes away.

We know that God meets us at the level of our expectation. We know that an expectant heart is not mere wishful thinking. It is built on the foundation of God's promises. We can assure ourselves that God is never in a hurry, but He is never late. Still, the remembered pain remains so fresh in our mind that it drowns out all we know of God and His faithfulness. However, if we assume the worst, how can we ever hope to receive His best?

If we decide to collect our disappointments, they will eventually knit together to form a covering that effectively blocks out the flood of favor that God wants to pour into our lives. This in turn creates even more disappointment. The end result is a vicious cycle that takes courage, discipline, and our mighty Father to break. At this very moment there are beloved children of God living in this cycle of defeat. It does not have to be this way!

If not broken, this cycle will eventually be handed down to future generations. By our example, we will teach new generations to collect their disappointments instead of their memory stones. We will teach them not to expect great things from God, lest they be further disappointed. Instead of giving your children a heritage of faith in a big God, you will give them a legacy of hopelessness in a God who seems tiny only because of the limits of your vision.

―――――――

Having a limited expectation of God's ability and willingness to bless our lives shrouds us from the flood of His favor.

―――――――

That which we give our attention is what grows in our life. Without even realizing it, we choose to feed, water, and nurture our fears, or we grow our *faith, trust,* and *obedience.* If we have spent time listening to our fears and acting on their behalf, we haven't shielded ourselves from pain. Instead, we have inadvertently grown a large boulder that sits squarely in our path to God's land of promise.

Believing God for great and mighty things after a lifetime of listening to our fears is not easy, but it is the one single shift in our perception that is guaranteed to alter the rest of our life for the better. It is a guaranteed game changer in our relationship with our eternal Father, and our journey to dwell in His promise. It is the one single shift that allowed an entire nation to move out of the desert wilderness and into the Promised Land.

Need to Be King of Our Life

This one is a little personal. We all like to feel in control of our life and on top of everything. It's why we have to-do lists for our to-do lists, email reminders programmed into our phones, and apps that help us manage our lives. How many of us can get through a dinner in a restaurant without seeing someone check their phone? We like to be in control, or at least *feel* that we are in control.

However, to walk with God means to hand over the control of our life to the one and only true King. It means to accept that while we may have an opinion, we do not get a vote. Our job is to go where God directs and do what He says needs doing. It means we must make decisions in accordance with His will and not our own. We are to follow God's plan even when it directly contradicts with our carefully laid plans…especially when it contradicts.

This doesn't mean that we forgo our responsibilities. It means our responsibilities and our priorities are set by God. It means that if we planned to leave the house at eight in the morning to head somewhere important, but the Spirit of God says to leave earlier, we leave earlier. It means that when we are rushing through our busy day and God says to stop and chat with the homeless woman we pass every day, we take the time to stop and chat. It means that if God tells us to pick up the check for someone else, we do it. It also means that unless you are a surgeon on-call, or have similarly critical job, you can sit the smart phone down for an hour to pray and eat dinner with your family.

Some things that God will ask of us may not necessarily make sense at the time. Sometimes, we will never know why He gave us the instruction. It's His better plan and He doesn't have to share with us His reasoning, although many times He will bless us with a glimpse. Sometimes, the requests will be easy. Sometimes, they will be difficult. If He's asking you to be kind to those you dislike the request may even be a little painful. No matter the request, what's important is our immediate obedience.

On the issue of our obedience, God is clear. Exodus 19:5 says that by obeying the voice of God and keeping His Covenant, we will be His *"special treasure from among all the peoples on earth."*[54] The Hebrew word for *special treasure* in this verse is *segullah,* meaning "possession."[55] First Peter 2:9 also uses the word possession in a significant way: *"You are a chosen people, a royal priesthood, a holy nation, God's special possession, that you may declare the praises of him who called you out of darkness into his wonderful light."*[56] We are God's special possession. We are His Chosen People *(Col. 3:12)*! Our Father is the Most High God. His plans are for our welfare, our hope, and our future *(Jer. 29:11)*. Alleluia!

All that is required of us is our *faith, trust,* and *obedience.* Still, that is not always easy for us. Loss of control is a scary thing. Obedience in these moments requires a monumental amount of trust bolstered by a monumental amount of faith. This is especially hard when our walk with Him has been brief. How can we trust someone we cannot see when there has been only limited time to collect the memory stones of His faithfulness?

No matter how young or old you may be, regardless of whether you accepted Christ yesterday or fifty years ago, God has always been with you. You may have just started your walk with Him, but God has been walking with you before you were even born. He knew you before He formed you in your mother's womb *(Jeremiah 1:5 and Psalm 139:13)*. He loved you before you were even conceived! The words God spoke to the Prophet Jeremiah still ring true to His boundless love and purpose for you. God told Jeremiah, *"Before I formed you in the womb I knew you, before you were born I set you apart"*[57] *(Jeremiah 1:5)*.

No matter what your past rejection, disappointment, abandonment, betrayal, or mistakes, the same God who can count every hair on your head, and who walks before you, is the Father who knitted you together in your mother's womb. He has been with you every step of your life. He has never rejected you. He will never abandon or betray you. His seal is upon your head. He has anointed you with a special purpose. He has set you apart from all the other people of the world. You are His special treasure.

Unworthiness

Another reason we cut ourselves off from God's best is a feeling of unworthiness. There is a big difference between godly humility, and outright insecurity or unworthiness. A humble spirit is a good and godly thing that helps us put God first in our life and receive His best. First Peter 5:6 says, *"So humble yourselves under the mighty power of God, and at the right time he will lift you up in honor."*[58]

To live in godly humility is to understand and acknowledge that all good things may flow *through* us, but they originate with the Lord. Our sense of self, our ego, our concerns for reputation and approval decrease, so that He may increase. When we have godly humility, our foundation rests on the One who formed the Heavens and the Earth. We are the creation of the Lord. His Word is filled with verses that attest to this truth, here is just one:

> *For we are God's masterpiece. He has created us anew in Christ Jesus, so we can do the good things he planned for us long ago. (Ephesians 2:10)*[59]

Godly humility does not equal low self-esteem or unworthiness. It's actually the complete opposite. People with godly humility have a great deal of confidence because they know from where their strength and victory comes. We are children of the Most High God. Our Father is the Creator of Heaven and Earth. Low self-esteem simply does not exist in the Spirit of God. How can it?

> ➤ **Godly humility** comes when we have placed our Father ahead of all else.

> ➤ **Unworthiness** comes when we place ourselves at the center of the universe.

A humble nature is God-focused. Low self-esteem is self-focused. To spend our lives concerned about what others think of us, even when we assume they think the worst, is the epitome of self-centeredness. To refuse to journey towards our highest Kingdom destiny because we doubt whether we are worthy is the essence of self-absorption. It is to refuse to trust God and His Word.

God has been very specific about who we are, what we are capable of doing, and what value He places on our lives. We have been fearfully and wonderfully made *(Psalm 139:14)*. We are God's masterpiece *(Ephesians 2:10)*. We are the apple of His eye *(Zechariah 2:8)*. Through Jesus Christ, we are all children of God *(Galatians 3:26)*. If God views us as His masterpiece, then what right do we have to claim that we are worthless or capable of only mediocrity?

Unworthiness and egotism are two sides of the same self-focused coin. We will never reach our Promised Land when we focus on ourselves instead of our Lord and King. To be free in the body of Christ means to have confidence in the source of all strength and all victory. It means to have confidence in ourselves as His masterpiece.

Need for Attention

Sometimes, people cut themselves off from God's best because they have a need for attention. It's a need that very often goes hand-in-hand with a self-focused life that fails to make God the Lord of their life.

Have you ever known someone who needs to be the center of attention? How many people have you known whose confidence changes with their number of social media friends and followers, or the number of people who *like* their pictures and posts? On the opposite end of this same scale, have you known someone who has a constant need to tell others all about their troubles? Even the lady at the checkout counter has heard all about their bad day and disappointing life. They seek the same attention, just in the form of sympathy. Perhaps you recognize these qualities in the people around you, or even yourself at times.

The need for attention is often closely associated with a feeling of unworthiness. When we are self-focused and we strive for the approval and attention of others, we are trying to fill a hole in our heart. It is a God-sized hole.

For am I now seeking the approval of man,
or of God? Or am I trying to please man?
If I were still trying to please man, I would not
be a servant of Christ. (Galatians 1:10, ESV)

If we try to fill this hole with a need for approval, praise, public accolades, and worldly successes, we are doomed to failure. We can never successfully fill ourselves with what can only be filled by God. There is no person or thing that will ever be able to fill a God-sized hole. When we try, we shut ourselves off to the best that God wants to pour into our lives. Only God can heal our hearts and make us whole. However, for that to happen, we must be God-focused instead of self-focused.

The only way to enter our Promised Land is to clearly acknowledge that we will never get there of our own accord. We must understand that we will only ever get there through the love, mercy, grace, and leadership of our Lord. We must weave this truth into our very soul.

To be God-focused is to demonstrate a godly humility that exalts Him as the center and head of our lives. It is to make ourselves, and our ego needs, in submission to our Father. This doesn't mean that we no longer have ego needs, but it does mean that we understand they can only be filled through God.

This is a hard thing for someone whose heart still has a God-sized hole. The pit of unworthiness, need for praise, and self-focus is an easy pit in which to fall. Everyone wants to be loved. We all like to feel the sympathy and empathy of others at times. We all like to know that other people feel our pain and understand our life experiences. Politicians, entertainers, and talk show hosts have formed entire careers out of their perceived ability to empathize, understand, and feel our pain. Marriages collapse and families break down when people lose the ability to empathize and understand those around them. Our empathy is an outpouring of our love. When we have stopped being able to empathize, we have stopped loving.

A person who feels unloved can dig themselves into a pit so deep that it is impossible to climb out of without the divine hand of a loving God. How many people do you know who have turned to food, shopping, alcohol, the need for attention, partying, sexual sin, or other self-destructive behavior in a failed effort to fill the hole left in their hearts? To feel unloved by a parent, a spouse, or the world is a deep and painful scar. However, no matter how unloved, or even unwanted you may feel by others, you are never unwanted or unloved by God.

Even if you were unplanned by your parents, you can still rest in the certainty that you were planned by God. He planned everything about you, down to the color of your eyes, the shade of your hair, and the location of your birth. He planned it all even before the world was formed.

The parents whose arms He delivered you into were specially selected because they had the specific genetic makeup needed to produce the beloved child He had planned. Even if your childhood was less than ideal, God was still there with you, planning and preparing for the abundant victory in which He can deliver you. You are His beloved child! You are the masterpiece of the Creator of Heaven and Earth! His is the only approval that you need!

We have examined some of the reasons that people cut themselves off from receiving God's best. Let's look at the rewards of developing a heart that expects God's best.

It Gets Us Out of God's Way

The single biggest obstacle in the path to your Promised Land is not Satan, a sinful nature, your family, your past, or your present circumstance. The single biggest obstacle in your path is you. No one can reject God's promise for your life, but you. No one can stop you from entering the land of God's promise, but you.

We spend so much of our time actively concentrating on how we believe a particular situation should work out that we actively shroud ourselves from receiving the many glories that God has planned for our lives. We limit God by our perceptions of the possible. An expectant heart is one that understands all things are possible with God. Something incredible can happen when we truly expect our Father to show up mightily in our lives – He will!

_____

Expecting God's best improves our relationship
with God and our relationship with other people.

_____

In our walk with God, He will ask and require different things of us in different seasons. Sometimes, He will ask us to run. Sometimes, He will ask us to be still. Sometimes, He will ask us to charge the walls of a fortified city with sword in hand. Sometimes, He will ask us to make peace. However, before we can do anything, He requires this of us: *"Be still, and know that I am God"*[60] *(Psalm 46:10).* I especially like the translation of this verse found in the Holman Christian Standard Bible, *"Stop your fighting--and know that I am God."*[61] Our Lord is the commander of our army, the professor of our classroom, and the leader of our anointed path. Before we can know whether to walk, run, stand still, fight, or make peace, we first must have conditioned ourselves to look towards Him in all circumstances. We must also have developed the patience necessary to wait for His direction and His better plan.

Much destruction has occurred in the life of Christians who simply fail to listen to God with an expectant heart and wait for His direction before deciding on a course of action. Every true victory and abundant harvest that we achieve is attained through the power of God acting through our lives. As Joshua and his army claimed Canaan, one city at a time, it may have been the Israelites fighting on the field of battle. However, it was God who delivered them into victory. The same is true for us.

To be victorious and reap the abundant harvest that God has planned for our lives, we must first get out of His way and stop interfering with His plans. We must learn to be patient and wait for His leadership. We must listen for God with a joyous and expectant heart and follow His direction wherever it may lead. To do this requires faith in God and His Word. It requires trust in His faithfulness and the bountiful fruit of obedience to His leadership. God will surely crumble the walls of our Jericho, but first we have to cooperate with His plan for victory.

It Improves Our Relationship with God and with Other People

If we have *faith, trust,* and *obedience* to God, then we free ourselves to accept His best for our lives. The end result of the flood of God's favor is our real and tangible witness to the active hand of God. With every witness of God's love and faithfulness, our collection of memory stones grow, and with them so does our *faith, trust,* and *obedience.*

The more we trust God with everything we are, everything we have, and every circumstance, we face, the deeper our relationship with Him grows. The closer we come to God the more He begins to grow in us a heart like His. As a child of God, you cannot aspire to a more life changing transformation than growing a heart like our God!

This is a powerful and blissful circle from which you will never want to escape. Those who have never freed themselves to receive God's best can never know the land of abundance that He has prepared.

To have a heart like God doesn't mean that we don't make mistakes. King David can be rightly called many things, but perfect would not be one of them. He made plenty of mistakes. Only one human ever walked this earth in utter perfection. His name was Jesus. How lucky we are that earthly perfection is not our goal. To have a real, living, and breathing relationship with our Creator is the goal of our life. That kind of relationship produces boundless *faith*, *trust*, and *obedience*. To have a heart like God is to have a heart that constantly turns towards Him.

The flood of His favor builds our memory stones and stretches our expectation of God. It is a never-ending cycle of God's love, faithfulness, and mighty power.

Having a heart that expects God's best not only improves our relationship with Him, but it also improves our relationship with other people.

There are conversations and disagreements that we continue to have with our co-workers, family, and friends. It seems that the encounters always go the same way and end up in the same place.

Albert Mehrabian, a pioneer of body language research, found that only 7% of our communication is through our words. The rest of our communication is either how we say something or our body language when we speak.[62] If every time we approach a difficult topic we automatically assume that it will end as badly as it has in the past, it likely will.

The next time, try this instead: Ask God to lay His hand on the situation and turn the hearts of all involved towards Him. Ask Him to pour into you the words that He wants you to speak and write. Then align your thoughts, words, actions, and expectations to God and His best. You may be amazed at the results.

Puts Us in a Posture of Blessing

Our *Abba* longs to pour out a flood of His obvious favor into our lives, but if we are not in a spirit of acceptance and expectation that flood of favor simply cannot reach us. If we are still shrouded with our limited expectations, tiny visions of God, and self-defeat we might as well be holding an umbrella over our heads while standing in the pouring rain of God's favor.

God will meet us at the level of our expectation. If we want God's best, then we have to believe Him for that best. We serve the God who created Heaven and Earth, then why do we expect from Him only small gestures? If a loved one is sick, we don't pray for them to just get a little better. We pray for a divine, miraculous, and supernatural healing that will leave them in better health than anything they have ever known before! We serve a big God who longs to do big and mighty things in our lives. To receive His favor, we first have to start believing Him for it.

Allows Us to Better Hear God

If our dog wants to come back inside, he makes a very specific sound at the door. It's not very loud and if we are not listening for it, we would never hear the sound. Still, no matter where I am in the house I can always hear it and know it's time to let him inside. I hear it because even though I am busy inside, I know he's outside, and I am listening for the sound.

God's voice is often just as quiet. We miss it in the course of our busy lives. If we aren't expecting it, His voice can be drowned out in the rush and chaos of our lives. If we listen with an expectant heart, then we consciously tune out the noise of the world and tune into His voice.

When we get in God's way we miss out on His best. Trusting our Father means getting out of His way and believing Him for His best.

Often times, God speaks softly, just so we *must* tune out the distractions of our everyday life and step closer to Him in order to hear His message. God loves His children and wants to keep us close, just like every parent does. He also desires to keep us close because the closer we are to God the more likely we can avoid the ditches that line our road.

God speaks, whether or not we are actively listening. He speaks even when we choose to ignore Him. However, our lives will get a whole lot easier when we actively listen and obey. God often saves His most important assignments for those He can count on to consistently listen for His voice and quickly obey His instructions. Demonstrating ourselves as people God can reply upon is another way in which we build our relationship with our Father and move towards our highest destiny. Our obedience to God starts with paying attention to His instruction. With every assignment in our Kingdom destiny, we get just a little closer to God and our Promised Land.

It Deepens Our Faith

The more expectancy that we have, the more we will see God's hand and His handiwork in our lives. That, in turn, leads to the collection of more memory stones of God's love and faithfulness. The collection of these stones reminds us of just how often God shows up in our lives, and it frees us to deepen our *faith, trust,* and *obedience.*

The more *faith, trust,* and *obedience* in Him we have, the more God will work in our lives and lead us on a path to the land of His promise. It is a cycle that lifts us closer to God. Our *faith, trust,* and *obedience* to our Father will allow us to take the most amazing adventure of our life. An adventure planned by the very hand of God.

So, the next time something happens in your life and you feel the pull to review your collected disappointments instead of counting your memory stones, do as Joshua did and shout to the sun, the moon, and the whole nation your belief in God's mighty power and faithfulness. Thank Him for all He has done, and all that He has yet to do. Believe Him for the incredible wonders He has waiting for you.

It Rebukes the Enemy

There is nothing the enemy hates more than seeing a child of God in a deep and intimate relationship with the Father, the Son, and the Holy Spirit. The deeper our love, faith, and trust in God grows the closer to Him we come and the more impervious to the enemy we become. It doesn't mean that he will stop coming. He will always come. It does mean that there is less and less room for him to gain a foothold. The more room we have made for the Holy Spirit, the less room there is for Satan and his forces to work their manipulative and evil plots.

Expecting God's best radically changes
our relationship with God and other people.
It also inhibits Satan's ability to manipulate us.

To live each day of our lives with an open mind and an open heart, expecting God's best in every situation, will radically transform our lives, our attitude, our future, and our relationship with God. In turn, that relationship will radically change every other aspect of our lives for the better. It will also radically change for the better the lives of the people around us. There is nothing more contagious than the Spirit of God poured out through the sacrificial love of one who lives in a deep and personal relationship with Him. It also undermines Satan like little else can. It's a good day when we are so close to God that our very relationship can sabotage the enemy!

PRAYER

Lord, Thank You for the flood of favor that You pour down over me and everyone I love. Thank You for holding us in the palm of Your hand and shielding us with Your love throughout the day. Thank You for enveloping us in Your many blessings. Please give us a heart like Joshua's, filled with the expectancy of Your mighty power and unending faithfulness. Please give us a heart like Yours that turns to You in every situation. Please lift us up in every way and bring us closer to Your heart. Amen.

CHAPTER SIX

I'LL TAKE THE BRICK, THANK YOU

Although the Lord gives you the bread of adversity and the water of affliction, your teachers will be hidden no more; with your own eyes you will see them. Whether you turn to the right or to the left, your ears will hear a voice behind you, saying, "This is the way; walk in it."
Isaiah 30:20-21 (NIV)

*T*he moment we accepted Christ Jesus as our Lord and Savior, the Holy Spirit began to dwell inside us. We may not know it. We may not feel it. Like David after his anointing, it may take time for the full fruition of our faith journey to be seen. Like the first generation of Israelites escaping Egypt, it may take time before we are mentally and emotionally free from the bondage from which God has just delivered us.

Though, make no mistake the Spirit of God is alive inside of you and me. The Spirit convicts us of our sin, guides us along our anointed path, counsels us, and teaches us along the way.

It is hard to say that there is one aspect of our walk with God that is more important to understand than the rest. If I had to choose, one of the places I would shine a big bright spotlight is this: *God doesn't just speak to ancient prophets, and modern day preachers, ministers, and bible teachers.* God speaks directly to every single one of us, nearly every single day of our lives. He counsels us, He teaches us, and if we would listen, He will direct us into abundant victory.

*The Father communicates using the
methods that work for each of His children.*

God's instructions to us are simple, but they are neither simplistic nor easy. He wants us to walk by *faith, trust,* and *obedience* to Him. In life that is often a lot easier in theory than in reality. No matter how faithful God has been in our lives, when faced with grave circumstances, we may forget. No matter how many burning bush moments we have had with our Father, in the chaos of life, we may not listen.

I must confess. I can be stubborn, hardheaded, and very strong-willed. Pick an adjective that applies to a Type A personality and I have probably been guilty of it at one time or another. Though, I haven't always counted this as bad. If you need something accomplished, give it to a Type

A personality. They will plan, navigate around, or bulldoze through any obstacle in the path of their declared goal.

However, it does have its drawbacks. Early in my faith journey, I was often too busy plowing ahead on my well thought out, predetermined path to hear God trying to tell me when the bridge had been washed out ahead of me. I was so focused on my goals that I often paid absolutely no attention to the gusty breeze pushing me in the direction of that bright shiny detour sign ahead.

God's communication methods will get persistently stronger, and sometimes more painful, until we pay attention.

I was too busy checking *my* time and staying on *my* schedule that the well-aimed bricks flying down from the heavens and hitting me square on the head were taken as signs of a bad day, but never did I relate them to the road I was traveling, or my plan.

Ten miles and a bottle of headache medicine later, I would be quite proud of my plan, my timing, and my ability to do what I thought needed to be done, even in the face of so many obstacles.

From past experience, this is usually the point when God often decided to dispense with the subtle hints and do just about the only thing that actually might get the attention of His hardheaded and inattentive daughter. He dropped the entire brick wall on my head. Sound familiar?

I suppose that I should be happy that He was always merciful and didn't let me plummet into the raging, icy waters that were ahead of me. Though admittedly, at the time, gratitude was rarely at the top of my list of feelings.

Often, we are so caught up in our daily lives, our individual desires, and our own thoughts that we fail to see the obvious and unmistakable signs that God is present in our situation, active in our lives, and guiding us in a specific direction – or away from one. He doesn't often call down in the echoed booming voice of a famous actor. He rarely sends us angels and a burning bush. Usually, God whispers, He nudges, He pushes, and if we are still too oblivious, He hits us over the head to get our attention.

Now I know what some of you are thinking: *God doesn't throw bricks! He loves us!* Yes, He absolutely loves us and because of that determined, stubborn, and faithful love He wants only the best for our lives. Most of the time what is *our* best and what is *God's* best are two very different things. I don't know about you, but I have seen my best, and I have seen what only God can accomplish. I will take God's best every single time.

Don't think the Father has ever used extreme measures to get the attention of His rebellious children? Let us look at Numbers 14. Even most non-believers know that the Israelites wandered the desert for forty years, but in the context and reasons we learn valuable lessons. God didn't free His Chosen People from slavery, save them from their enemies only to dangle the Promise Land like a carrot, and just to leave them in the wilderness.

The Israelites had done what many of us do from time to time, when faced with seemingly dire circumstances. They forgot God's faithfulness. They began to rely on themselves, instead of God. They questioned and rebelled against the Father who had brought them so far. Yet again, Moses asked God to forgive His people. Because our eternal Father is merciful, forgiving, and filled with more grace than we deserve, He forgave the Israelites for their persistent rebellion and unbelief. However, God had a warning that should give us all pause:

> The LORD replied, "I have forgiven them, as you asked. Nevertheless, as surely as I live and as surely as the glory of the LORD fills the whole earth, not one of those who saw my glory and the signs I performed in Egypt and in the wilderness but who disobeyed me and tested me ten times — not one of them will ever see the land I promised on oath to their ancestors. No one who has treated me with contempt will ever see it. But because my servant Caleb has a different spirit and follows me wholeheartedly, I will bring him into the land he went to, and his descendants will inherit it. (Numbers 14:20-24)[63]

God had given them every sign. The lives of this generation stood as a living, breathing testimony to God's love and faithfulness. God had removed every single obstacle from their path. He had even spoken directly to their leaders. Yet, when the situation grew frightening and uncertain, they doubted their Father. God had given them every reason to believe in His faithfulness, yet their own voices of doubt drowned out the still small voice of God *(1 Kings 19:12)*. They leaned unto themselves and not unto the Father, who freed them, delivered, and provided for them. They ignored the voice of God and as a consequence, they kept themselves from reaching the land of His promise.

But God is doing what is best for us, training us to live God's holy best. At the time, discipline isn't much fun. It always feels like it's going against the grain. Later, of course, it pays off handsomely, for it's the well-trained who find themselves mature in their relationship with God.
(Hebrews 12:10-11, MSG)

God did not keep them out of the Promised Land, their own unbelief and rebellious nature, driven by a lack of *faith, trust,* and *obedience,* kept them in the wilderness. God wants us to dwell in our Promised Land. He wants to lift us to incredible abundance and mighty victory. He wants to fulfill in our lives the Covenant that He cut with Abraham. However, that requires our cooperation. It requires our *faith, trust, obedience,* and our passionate love of the Most High God.

Like any parent, our Father will use whatever resources He knows will get our attention so that we may hear His voice and listen to the counsel of His Spirit. Sometimes, that means He whispers. Sometimes, that means He shouts.

Sometimes, that means He disrupts our path. Sometimes, that means He tosses a brick at our heads. Sometimes, that means He brings an entire brick wall down on top of us.

How many brick walls have been dropped into your life? Did you really have to find your spouse in bed with someone else to realize that your marriage was in trouble? Did you really have to catch your fiancé in a massive lie to realize that you had been dating a liar? Did it actually take having your job downsized to finally understand the job you've had for thirty years was not your true calling? Did your child have to get expelled from school before you decided to stop and reevaluate some things?

We are here to learn lessons, to draw closer to God, and to walk more confidently along the path of our anointing. True, we have free-will, but that free-will comes with a clause in tiny letters at the bottom of the page. We can choose to listen to God's soft voice and accept the guidance that He mercifully provides, or we can continue to dig ourselves out from under a pile of very heavy bricks for the remainder of our days. God's love for us is as boundless as it is stubborn. Our Father does not give up on His children. If after all of their rebellion, He did not give up on His Chosen People, He isn't going to give up on us.

When the Israelites, who had been children at the time of the Exodus from Egypt, had reached adulthood, God brought them back across parted waters, just as He had for their parents. This time, the water the Lord parted was the Jordan River and in God's beautiful scheduling, it was just in time for Passover, the feast which remembered God's faithfulness during the final plague that began their Exodus journey. He brought them to *Gilgal*, meaning in Hebrew to roll away and "circle (of stone)."[64] God had brought them full circle. He had given them a chance to rise out of the rubble of the previous generation and learn the lessons that He had been trying to teach all along.

Obeying God…
is always a more pleasant experience
when we do it the first time He asks.

God had given the children of Israel a *do over*. He gave them a second chance, but first He had to get their attention. Our God is a God of second chances, and third chances, and fourth chances. We are often as stubborn as we are broken. Our Father knows that it may take many tries for us to get it right. Even if we have learned to listen, to trust, and to obey in our walk with Him, we may still sometimes ignore the detour signs and end up in the ditch.

Many years and multiple concussions later, I have learned that sometimes flying bricks are the most generous and loving act God can provide. I thank Him and praise Him for each of them. They are His way of saying He has a better plan than any I could conceive on my own.

If we are to reach our Promised Land and walk closely with God, then we must pray for the sensitivity, wisdom, and discernment to recognize the first strong wind when it is ushering us to safety. It may seem like an unexpected detour, but it's a route straight towards our Father's better plan. When it comes, we must also have the obedience and humility to go where God is leading, even if it's in the opposite direction of where we intended to go.

If we want to reach our Promised Land and rise to our highest Kingdom destiny, then we must learn how to tune out worldly distractions and focus our attention on God's voice, with expectant hearts. At our Father's instruction, we will need to sacrifice our plans for those only the Most High God could ever create.

We must learn to make peace with the reality that God is not our co-pilot. The same God who created Heaven and Earth is never going to ride shotgun in our passenger seat. If we want the best this life has to offer, then we must acknowledge that what we desire is His best. To reach our Promised Land is going to require some sacrifices along the way. We will need to lay down some of our own wants and desires on the altar of sacrifice and take up the mantle of God's will and His better plans.

The Lord is our pilot, our co-pilot, our navigator, maintenance repairman, air-traffic controller, and design engineer. The God of Israel is our One and Only God. If we want to get to anyplace worth going we must remember that the road we seek is the one He has already made before of us. The best choice we can make in life is to surrender to the will of the Most High God. If we want the best this life has to offer, we must first stop and listen to a voice greater than our own, and then walk the path He anoints for us.

PRAYER

Dear Father, please tune my ears to Your voice. Make me sensitive and aware of Your gentle nudges as You guide me along the path of Your anointing. Draw me so close to Your heart that I need not doubt or wonder whether the gentle breeze pushing me in the direction of a detour is actually Your loving guidance drawing me to safety and leading me along a better path. Give me the focus to tune out worldly distractions and the strength to always remember that Your way is so much better than anything I could ever imagine. Amen.

CHAPTER SEVEN
JUNK IN YOUR TRUNK

*Get rid of all bitterness, rage and anger, brawling and
slander, along with every form of malice. Be kind
and compassionate to one another, forgiving each
other, just as in Christ God forgave you.*
Ephesians 4:31-32 (NIV)

*T*here are truck people. There are hybrid car people.
There are motorcycle people. I have always been a
four-wheel drive SUV person. I like SUVs. They can
do most anything a truck can do, but I have a safe, weath-
erproof place for my groceries. They also have really big
back seats, which are great for kids, pets, and everything I
tend to toss aside with the idea of sorting through later. A
few years ago, I decided to try something different. I
became a convertible person. It was wonderful. It also had
a big back seat and if I took the top down I could still haul
an eight-foot ladder. I loved it!

Well, I loved it until the very first time I drove on the interstate with the top down. Did you know that almost everything tossed into the backseat of a convertible will blow out of the car when traveling at interstate speeds with the top down? I faced a decision. I could change my habits, or I could find another solution. My solution was to take advantage of its really big trunk.

Don't panic. I'm with you. There's no need to fear
for I'm your God. I'll give you strength. I'll help
you. I'll hold you steady, keep a firm grip on you.
(Isaiah 41:10, MSG)

For the next six months this worked well. Everything I was accustomed to tossing into the backseat went into the trunk. Problem solved. At least, until I got a flat tire on the first snowy day of the winter season, and realized that the spare tire could only be accessed via a compartment in the bottom of the trunk. It only took fifteen minutes to change the flat tire. It took over an hour to clean out my trunk.

Can you relate? How much of our lives do we toss into our metaphorical trunk to be sorted through later? Perhaps, it is a previous divorce, an arrest, a bankruptcy, a series of lies, being fired from a job, being overweight, or a wayward child. Perhaps, it is not something that you did at all. Maybe, it is something that was inflicted upon you, such as abuse, rape, betrayal, abandonment, the loss of a child, or the sudden death of a loved one.

We all have experienced regrets, failures, and wounds. No one gets out of this life unscarred, but some folks go through life collecting them like memory stones. They carry them in special bags tossed over their shoulder. Every so often they sit down, take out a few stones and re-live the memories. Then, they carefully put them back, pick up the bag, and start walking again. Sounds painful on the back, doesn't it? It's even more painful on the spirit.

No matter how firmly we stand on faith or how passionately we follow after God, there are moments that we wish we could do-over. We all replay events in our minds when we long to have said or done something very differently. They are sandpaper to our soul.

When something is simply too overwhelming to deal with, like Scarlett O'Hara, we put it off until tomorrow. We carefully pack them up and lock them away in our emotional trunk. They are out of sight, but never far away.

Make no mistake. Our trunks will be cleaned out, our bags emptied, and our luggage unpacked. The only choice we get is whether we want to unpack them at a time and place that is convenient for us, or whether God will unpack them for us. God doesn't care about our convenience or what important agendas that we have for the day. He cares that we learn the lesson He is trying to teach. If we wait for God to do our unpacking, we may well end up in 20 degree weather, by the side of the road. He will keep us safe. He will guide us through the process. However, it likely won't be a pleasant experience. It will be intended to get our attention and make an impression.

117

SHANNON HOOPER

Ecclesiastes tells us that, *"God will bring every deed into judgment, including every hidden thing, whether it is good or evil"*[65] *(Ecclesiastes 12:14).* Why would God bring every good thing into judgment? Because it's impossible to hide what we believe to be sinful and shameful without also hiding what is good, and great, and righteous.

Our guilt and shame are two of the most potent weapons wielded by the enemy to distance us from God. Satan wants nothing more than to hurt our Father and absolutely nothing hurts the Father more than the loss of a child.

Secrecy and shame are cloaks we wear that blot out the light of God from reaching us. God already knows everything we have ever done, said, thought, or experienced. By His sacrifice, Christ Jesus has already washed us clean. If we hide beneath a cloak of secrecy and shame, we shut ourselves off from God, inhibit our relationship with Him, and willingly relinquish our right of inheritance as a child of the King. We also help accomplish Satan's goal.

There is a powerful difference between guilt, false guilt, and shame. We will examine them in the coming pages.

> **Guilt** is what we feel when the Holy Spirit inside us has convicted us of sin.

> **False Guilt** is what happens when we continue to meditate on our past sin, our past failures, and our past mistakes that have already been given over to God with a repentant heart and forgiven.

> **Shame** occurs when we have taken on our guilt and false guilt, and began to wear it as a cloak.

Guilt

The Holy Spirit that dwells inside us is also our moral compass. It is our instant gauge as to whether something is right or wrong. Some people devote entire careers to studying and writing about ethics and Biblical morality, but it can never match that quiet voice in the back of our mind that says *'don't do that'*. When we ignore that voice and move forward anyway, the Holy Spirit is also what convicts of us of the transgression. This is the essence of guilt. It is the Holy Spirit convicting us of missing the mark and being outside of God's will for our lives.

Guilt is a good thing and a godly thing when it leads us to turn to God with a repentant heart. By His Word, we know that our Father is faithful and forgiving. First John 1:9 says, *"If we confess our sins, he is faithful and just and will forgive us our sins and purify us from all unrighteousness."*[66]

Guilt is never meant to stay with us and be worn as a cloak. Jesus came to take away the sins of the world. We have been washed clean in the blood of the Savior. However, we still must bring our mistakes, our guilt, and our pain to God. Most of us would not be alive without the love, grace, and patience of our Father. Our *Abba* has a mighty love for His children! If we know He loves us, why would we be afraid to bring Him our mistakes?

Guilt is the fruit of sin and only God has the power to forgive us of sin and purify us from all unrighteousness. Left alone and unacknowledged before Him, guilt forms a cloak around our hearts and minds. It begins to cut us off from the goodness and grace of God, corrupting our hearts and our motives along the way. When done from a place of guilt, even our most selfless acts become selfish. When not brought before God with a repentant heart, guilt and sin cannot be forgiven. Unforgiven sin and guilt eventually turns to shame, and there are few more destructive forces in the human heart than the pervasive cloak of shame.

False Guilt

False guilt is the result of continuous meditation on our past sin and failures that have already been given over to God with a repentant heart and forgiven. It happens when even though we have taken our sin, guilt, and pain to the foot of the Cross and have been purified, we still choose to wear our guilt as a cloak that hides our hearts and minds from God's boundless love and grace.

Scripture tells us that God is faithful and if we confess to Him our sins, He will forgive us and cleanse us of unrighteousness *(1 John 1:9)*. We also know by His Word that we can have confidence in approaching God. He hears us. He loves us. He is a Father who wants to bless His children. First John 5:14-15 says: *"This is the confidence we have in approaching God: that if we ask anything according to his will, he hears us. And if we know that he hears us—whatever we ask—we know that we have what we asked of him."*[67]

So, we know that our Father wants us to come to Him with our sins, our mistakes, our troubles, our petitions, our joys, and our pain. We know that whatever we ask God that's in accordance with His will, it will be ours. We know that if we pour out our transgressions to Him and ask for His forgiveness we will be purified. If we know all of this, by His Word, why do we keep the cloak of false guilt?

Because We Lean Unto Ourselves

Have you ever confessed the secrets of your heart to God and still not felt washed clean? As Christians, we have accepted Jesus as our Savior and turned our life over to God. We may study our Bible devotedly. We may absorb His Word and commit it to memory. We may serve in our church and put feet to our faith. We may do all of this and still, from time to time, find ourselves leaning unto our own understanding rather than leaning unto God. We are human and at times, like the first generation of Israelites out of Egypt, we find letting go to be one of the toughest demands made by God.

We will come back to the Exodus story many times throughout our journey together. We do this because it so beautifully testifies to our own struggles as we get better at walking by faith with God. As Christians who have set our hearts toward God, we are like the Israelites led by Moses. We have been delivered from bondage and freed from our own personal slavery. Though, just because our souls are free does not mean that our minds are free.

When things became frightening and uncertain, the first generation out of Egypt longed for what was familiar. They cried out that it would be better to return as slaves to Egypt than face the seemingly uncertain future God was leading them towards in Canaan. They mistook what was familiar for what was safe. They opted for the devil they knew over a future with God that they could not see or imagine. They substituted the desires and commands of God with the fear driven desires of their minds.

―――――

Trust in the LORD with all your heart and lean not on your own understanding; in all your ways submit to him, and he will make your paths straight.
(Proverbs 3:5-6, NIV)

―――――

How often do we make the same choice? Have you ever stayed in a relationship that you knew wasn't what God wanted for you, but it was comfortable? Have you ever known that God wanted you to do something more with your career, but you kept the same old job because it was layoff-proof and allowed you to get by? Have you ever heard God telling you that you were His beloved, forgiven, redeemed, adopted, and blessed child, but you could not absorb it for all the words of guilt, shame, unworthiness, and fear that had been spoken over you in the past?

If you have lived most of your life in bondage, the boundless freedom that comes with being God's beloved child can actually be a frightening experience. It can be so unknown and unfamiliar that it's difficult to imagine. You may have physically stepped forward into a walk with God, but your mind takes time to catch up to your soul.

We Get Something Out of Being a Victim

Another reason folks continue to carry the cloak of false guilt is they actually get something out of the experience. It provides a well-reasoned excuse not to go too far out on a limb with God. It offers an instant response when God asks them to do something important. How can anyone start a business, repair a marriage, forgive someone, or shake loose their shackles, if they are guilty of so much? It gives a justification for claiming that God must somehow be mistaken. They have become a professional victim of their own guilt and shame. Anyone can become a temporary victim, but professional victims elect to remain in the experience and adopt a victim mentality in every aspect of their lives.

Being free of our shackles and standing firm on Holy ground as children of God can be a frightening concept. It is certainly a future we cannot begin to imagine. The cloak of false guilt provides many with just the right amount bondage to limit the scope of their horizon and keep them safely near the tree trunk and away from the branches.

Have you ever met a professional victim? Maybe, you have been known to take up the practice from time to time. Professional victims wear their guilt and victimhood as a badge. They happily recite all of their struggles and problems to anyone they meet. Even the stranger in the grocery line will know that their father was an alcoholic, they grew up in an abusive home, their spouse is a jerk, their boss hates them, and their mechanic just overcharged them. From the outside, it seems like choosing to live inside a cell, whose doors God long ago opened wide, would be a miserable experience. Still, that cell can be very familiar, and familiarity can be confused with safety.

Some carry the cloak of false guilt because it provides a justification for this victim mentality. Being a Christian is about a relationship with the living God. Like all relationships, our relationship with God is not a one way street. For the relationship to work, we have a responsibility to uphold our end and do our part. A victim mentality provides a moral justification for abdicating this responsibility.

If someone has failed, it's not because of disobedience to God's Word or His instructions, it's because someone else let them down, they weren't given a chance, or the deck was stacked against them. It allows for a *'why me?'* mindset that instantly puts a dramatic barrier between them and anything God asks of them.

We Are Listening to the Enemy

Guilt, false guilt, and shame are some of the most potent weapons used by the enemy. Sometimes, Satan works by speaking to us and tempting us directly, as he did with Eve in the Garden and Jesus in the wilderness. Other times, he crawls into our unguarded moments and uses what he finds against us. He wields the weapons of our own insecurities, doubts, fears, and guilt. Satan's voice can sound frighteningly familiar at times. One of the reasons this avenue of attack can be such a potent and insidious weapon is because we cannot tell the difference between our thoughts and Satan's work.

There is a voice that we hear telling us that we aren't good enough, we've made too many mistakes, our spouse doesn't love us, we are a failure, no one will ever want us, we shouldn't even try, or a million other lies that echo through our mind. Like a Mockingbird mimicking the songs of other birds, the enemy will mimic our voice, or that of others who have spoken negativity over us in the past. He will speak so often and so specifically to our most intimate pain and doubt that sometimes we allow his voice to drown out the voice of our Father.

As long as you did what you felt like doing, ignoring God, you didn't have to bother with right thinking or right living, or right anything for that matter. But do you call that a free life? What did you get out of it? Nothing you're proud of now. Where did it get you? A dead end. (Romans 6:20-21, MSG)

The longer we hold onto unconfessed guilt and unreleased false guilt the more of the enemy's work we are doing for him. He doesn't have to try hard to separate us from our eternal Father, because the cloak of shame we are hiding under is doing the job for him. All Satan has to do is push us further into hiding. That's where he wants us to stay because Satan can't do his evil in the bright, warm light of God's love. Satan cannot reach us when our ears are tuned only to the God who loves us.

Satan loses some of his mightiest weapons when we give everything over to God. When we surrender everything and keep nothing from Him, we can stand fully in His light. God will take everything we have and return to us only what is good, godly, healed, whole, and blessed.

We Carry a Guilt That Was Not Ours

Sometimes, the guilt we carry is not of our own making. We carry guilt for the deeds and decisions of other people. Perhaps, it was an unwanted divorce, the betrayal of a business partner, childhood abuse, domestic violence, or rape. It sure feels like the conviction of sin. We certainly feel the weight of guilt upon our shoulders. We may even feel responsible for what happened. We long to be washed clean. We yearn to be purified of all unrighteousness, but we cannot ask God to forgive a sin that we did not commit. This is what makes false guilt, not of our own making, so difficult to set down.

Sin and its fruit, guilt, result in a separation from God. Coming to God with a repentant heart, acknowledging our transgressions, and asking for His forgiveness, heals that separation and washes away our impurity. If the transgression was not committed by us, what do we have to acknowledge and confess?

There are beloved children of God who are living in cycles of misery and defeat at this very moment because they still carry the bondage of false guilt that was not of their own making. That is a misery that only drives bad choices and further separation from God.

A false guilt, not of our own making, produces the same feeling of guilt and separation from God. The difference is that it is not the Holy Spirit convicting us. It is the echoes of a past that we have refused to unpack. It is the words of a parent saying, *'you're not good enough'* or an abuser saying, *'you made me hurt you.'* Sins may indeed have been committed, but they are not ours. They are transgressions that we have taken on and worn as a cloak of false guilt.

Shame is not only the fruit of the enemy, it is one of the most powerful weapons in his arsenal.

False guilt, not of our own making, is not a fracture or separation in our relationship with God. It is a creation formed from the past that we refuse to set down and have projected onto our present and our future. When we ask God for forgiveness in these circumstances, we are asking for something that He simply cannot and will not give. It's not because He doesn't love us, or want us freed from this bondage. His love for us is boundless. However, we are asking Him for the wrong thing.

We are asking for forgiveness, when what we need is a mighty healing and a helping hand. We need a healing of the wounds we still carry. We need a healing of our own destructive thinking. We need our Father to take us by the hand and help us unpack the baggage we carry so that it may be laid down at the foot of the Cross.

We Have Defined Ourselves by our Baggage

If you asked me who I was at the start of my walk with God, I would have given you my name, where I grew up, the names of my parents and grandparents, and what I liked to do. Seems like a reasonable answer to the question, right? But it's not. I am not my parent's child. I am not the city where I grew up. I am not my education, occupation, or interests. I am not even my particular church or religious denomination. If you asked me the same question today, my first response is this: *"I am a child of God."*

A shroud of shame prevents us from fully being who God created us to be, fulfill our anointing, and claim God's promise.

We define ourselves by our past. It is natural. It is also potentially destructive. Maybe your past doesn't resemble a 1950's sitcom. Maybe your past involves abuse, mental illness, arrest, abandonment, rape, molestation, abortion, divorce, addiction, or any of a million other things.

Even if your past involves realities that are far less extreme, we all look back on parts of our lives with a heavy heart or a regretful mind. We all wish certain things had been different. We all carry with us our past decisions, our past experiences, and the past situations we had no control over, yet which marked us with their own particular brand. No one gets out of this life unscarred by pain and regret.

In spite of all of that, God is adamant that we are not the sum total of what has happened to us. We are not the end result of our victories or our defeats. Neither are we the sum total of the works we do or the mistakes we make. We *are* the sum total of whom God says that we are and He is very clear: **We are His Beloved children.**

God isn't waiting for us to get better so we can come to Him and serve Him. He isn't waiting for us to be fully healed or have our act together. He isn't waiting for us to get a degree, a better job, a nicer car, more time in the day, or have children that can keep their clothes clean.

So many sons and daughters of the King of Kings tell themselves that they will come and present themselves to God when they finally have everything pulled together, when they are not as messy, broken, disheveled, and distracted. They want to make a good impression to God and please Him. Yet, God knows every single thing we have ever done, whether it is good or bad. He knows the motives of our heart and the thoughts that run through our mind. He knows it all and He is saying: *Come to Me in your brokenness, your confusion, your hurt, your shame, your messiness, and your faults, bring it all to Me, My Beloved Child. I love you just as you are, more than you will ever know. I see all you are and I love you. Come to Me just as you are and let me make you whole and healed.*

If you take only one thing from this book, I pray that it is this fundamental truth: Whatever state that you find yourselves in, God is asking you to bring it all to Him. He is asking you to stop sweeping your broken pieces under the rug while you smile through hidden tears. He is asking you to sweep up all the pieces of brokenness and bring it all to Him. God will create a masterpiece out of a broken heart if only we give Him all the pieces. There isn't a mess that you can find yourself in that God cannot bring you through. There has never been a pit dug deep enough for which the hand of God cannot lift you out. There isn't a decision bad enough that God cannot forgive. There simply isn't a past sinful enough that God cannot redeem. In all of human history, there has never been a heart so broken that God's love could not heal.

God is not asking for your sacrifices or your offerings. He is asking for you! You are not your parent's child. You are not the city where you were born. You are not your job. You are not your worst mistake. You are not your deepest shame. You are not the sum total of the words others have spoken over you, the scars carved into your heart, or the messy broken pain that you hide behind a pleasant smile. You are the redeemed, chosen, adopted, blessed, favored, and anointed child of the Most High God. The Father who formed you and loved you even before you were born is the Creator of Heaven and Earth, and He is telling you:

Come to Me. Come as you are. Bring it all to Me.
Bring me your sin and your shame.
Bring me your brokenness.
Bring me your messiness.
You are My beloved child.
I know everything about you.
I love you more than you can ever know!

We Do Not Feel Worthy of Forgiveness

Another reason that we reject God's best is because we carry a guilt so potent and seemingly immovable that we do not feel worthy of forgiveness. Perhaps, others are still holding your past over you. Maybe, you refuse to let it go. There are a million reasons, each one as personal as it is ultimately destructive. The Most High God certainly believes you are worthy of forgiveness!

Instead of your shame you will receive a double portion, and instead of disgrace you will rejoice in your inheritance. And so you will inherit a double portion in your land, and everlasting joy will be yours.
(Isaiah 61:7, NIV)

When our guilt has metastasized and turned into a shroud of shame we do more than cut ourselves off from God. We make choices out of a place of self-defeat, shame, and self-destruction that can and will reverberate through every aspect of our lives until we have dug ourselves into a muddy and mired darkened pit.

Guilt left unrepentant, and false guilt still carried, will eventually turn into a shroud of shame. When it does, we surely will lose sight of the difference between who we are and what we have done, or had done to us.

Shame

In the Garden of Eden, Adam, and his wife, Eve, were both naked. However, Scripture tells us that they felt no shame *(Genesis 2:25)*. Upon eating the forbidden fruit, their eyes were opened to their nakedness and they felt shame for the first time. As a consequence, they covered themselves and hid from God.

Their first response was shame. Their second response was to hide themselves from God. Their story tells us some important things about the destructive nature of shame.

> ➤ **First:** Shame absolutely does not exist in the Holy Spirit. It is not a state or experience that God gives to us. It is quite literally the fruit of the enemy.

> ➤ **Second:** Shame is an external state that separates us from God.

Shame is built upon on a lie straight from the deepest pit of hell. There is nothing good or godly that dwells within its shroud. A spirit of shame cannot, and does not, dwell within the Holy Spirit. In fact, there are few paths that lead as quickly and directly to separation from God, as the path of shame. This creates a fierce and evil quagmire because our shame causes us to hide from God, yet He is the only one who can break us free from its bondage. Like a gardener pruning a vine, God wants to remove anything that separates us from Him, keeps us from His best, and prevents our claiming the land of His promise.

After the Israelites had spent forty years in the wilderness, God brought them back across the River Jordan to a place that would be forever known as Gilgal. He asked for their *faith*, *trust*, and *obedience*. Unlike their parents, who had questioned God, this second generation did as God commanded. Afterward, God said to Joshua, *"today I have rolled away the reproach of Egypt from you"*[68] *(Joshua 5:9)*. We know that another word for reproach is shame. Psalm 44:15-16 painfully articulates a life lived under the state of reproach: *"I live in disgrace all day long, and my face is covered with shame at the taunts of those who reproach and revile me, because of the enemy, who is bent on revenge."*[69]

A shroud of shame will separate us from God and hide all that is good.

Biblical scholars disagree on the ultimate definition of *Gilgal.* Some believe it refers to the circle of stones found there. Others believe it's from the verb *galal*, meaning to "to roll, roll way."[70] I like to think that it refers to both.

God brought His People full circle to roll away the shame and reproach of their former lives. He was giving them a new life in the land of His promise. However, before they could claim it, he helped them lay down the baggage, not just of their own past, but also that of previous generations. He wants to do the same for us. His promise to us is clear, *"Anyone who believes in him will never be put to shame"*[71] *(Romans 10:11).*

Are you still in the desert in your walk with God? Do you still carry the reproach of divorce, abuse, abortion, illness, depression, failure, bankruptcy, sexual sin, abandonment, or any of a million shames that the enemy whispers into your ear? Do you long for your Father to roll away the reproach of your past? We must reclaim the promises of God that the enemy has so carefully stolen. By His blood, Jesus rolled away the reproach of each and every one us. But like all of the glorious freedom that we find in the love of Christ Jesus, just because we are free, does not mean that we feel free.

———

The Most High God, the Creator of
Heaven and Earth, calls you His beloved child,
His masterpiece, and the temple of His Holy Spirit.

———

It does not matter what shame you carry around with you or how long it has been the weight around your neck. It does not matter what words of reproach others speak over your life. It does not matter what anyone thinks of you, as long as you understand what God thinks of you.

The Most High God, the Creator of Heaven and Earth, calls you His beloved child, His masterpiece, and the temple of His Holy Spirit. You are among His Chosen People and His Royal Priesthood. Then Beloved Child, why should you listen to the negative words of anyone who dares claim that you are less than what God Almighty says about you?

Every single person has been wounded in their own unique way. No one gets out of this life unscarred. Very little of the negative and defeatist words spoken by others have any reflection on us. More often they provide an insight into the speaker's unhealed heart. Why would you willingly surrender your inheritance as the child of God because of the negativity harbored in the heart of another?

We spend our lives meditating on things. We replay words, experiences, and conversations over and over in our heads until it is all we can think about. The one criticism, the negative words, or past defeat become the mantra of our daily thoughts. If we spend our lives mired in the murky waters of negativity, we will never claim the abundance and victory that God has planned. We will never reach the land of His promise.

Instead of replaying thoughts that bring us down and make us feel defeated, let's spend our day meditating on who God says that we are. Let's replay the Word of God through our minds so often that it absorbs into our very being. Let's embrace the incredible possibility and the mighty victory that God speaks over us. Let's walk with the faith only a child of the Most High God can experience.

All that is required of you is to believe God. Set your focus to Him instead of the world. Give Him your *faith, trust,* and *obedience*. Bring everything to the One who can actually heal you, guide you, and bring you to abundant victory. Bring all of those suitcases of past shame, defeat, mistakes, pain, and loss to Him. Pour out every last bit of it at the foot of the Cross and let God roll it away.

135

PRAYER

Dear God, help me to unpack the trunks I have carried for so long. Hold my hand as I place everything I find at the foot of the Cross. Envelope me in Your love and Your light. Bring into Your light all that I have tried to keep hidden from You, and even from myself, so that it can be laid down. Lord, I pour out my guilt, my sin, my mistakes, my failings, my hurts, and my shame before You. Please place Your healing hands upon me and mend all of the broken places that You find. Lord, help me take stock of my heart in these matters and please bring to my mind all the guilt, false guilt, and shame that You find there, and please help me to lay it all down at the foot of the Cross. Amen.

CHAPTER EIGHT

TRAINING FOR THE PROMISED LAND

Every athlete exercises self-control in all things. They do it to receive a perishable wreath, but we an imperishable. So I do not run aimlessly; I do not box as one beating the air. But I discipline my body and keep it under control, lest after preaching to others I myself should be disqualified.
1 Corinthians 9:25-27 (ESV)

*D*uring the recent Olympics I marveled at the enormous preparation that goes into acquiring and perfecting the technical skill and aerobic base necessary to become a world-class athlete. For a runner, it can take four to eight years just to build the lung capacity, heart strength, and endurance to compete at that level. Most Olympic athletes plan their training schedules and goals up to four years in advance.

In preparation for the London 2012 Olympics the average British athlete had trained six hours a day, six days a week, every month of the year. Each athlete had likely invested more than 10,000 hours of training into a moment that would last a few seconds to a few minutes. A canoeist may have lifted nearly 1,200 tons a month at the gym, the weight of six blue whales. An elite swimmer may have already swam over 1,800 miles in the previous year. That is the distance from London to China. An athlete can spend anywhere between $15,000-$250,000 on coaches, trainers, nutritionists, equipment, travel, and other expenses.

If an athlete and their coach must devote this much time, effort, energy, and expense into the preparation for a game, how much more preparation goes into training God's children for the harvest of their Promised Land? If we want to be a mighty man or women of God, then we have to train like it. Just as an athlete must train in endurance, strength, mental discipline, and skill using a variety of methods, God prepares us for our harvest in different ways, each equally as important.

If we want to reach God's highest anointing for our life, reap the harvest, and claim the land of our promise, then we have to be willing and able to do the following:

1) Persevere through the journey

2) Conquer our Promised Land

3) Defend the ground on which we stand

We know that God is training us, preparing us, and refining us. We know that God frees us from bondage, prunes our branches, cuts away our covering, and rolls away our reproach just as He did for the nation of Israel at Gilgal. Now, we come to the fifth chapter of the Book of Joshua where we find Joshua and the Israelite army at the edge of the Promised Land. It is here that we realize the arrival is nowhere near the end of their story. Here, we will come to understand some of the reasons for all of this training, refining, and preparation.

For we are God's handiwork, created in Christ Jesus to do good works, which God prepared in advance for us to do. (Ephesians 2:10, NIV)

Some four decades before, God had made a promise to Moses that was recorded in the Book of Exodus. He promised to deliver His Chosen People from bondage in Egypt and *"into a good and spacious land, a land flowing with milk and honey"*[72] *(Exodus 3:8).*

God had delivered an entire generation of His People out of bondage and sustained them in the wilderness. He had brought them right to the edge of the Promised Land, but they had rebelled. They lacked the *faith, trust,* and *obedience* to receive the fullness of God's promise. Because of their unbelief they would never inhabit this land. Instead, God brought up the next generation to take their place and appointed Joshua to lead them.

This generation learned from the mistakes of their parents. They believed God. They trusted Him. That *faith* and *trust* produced the *obedience* that would allow them to receive the full measure of God's promise and blessing. So again, God brought His People to the very edge of promise.

"So I have come down to deliver them from the power of the Egyptians, and to bring them up from that land to a good and spacious land, to a land flowing with milk and honey..." (Exodus 3:8, NASB)

After God stopped the waters of the Jordan River, so the people could cross on dry land, the nation camped at Gilgal, on the edge of Canaan. There, God rolled away their reproach. For the first time, the entire nation of Israel stood on the land promised to them as descendants of Abraham. They were ready to claim their inheritance.

There was only one problem - the land was already occupied by the Canaanites, Hittites, Amorites, Perizzites, Hivites, and Jebusites. If the Israelites wanted to claim their Promised Land, they would have to fight for it. This would be no small feat.

Not much had changed among the kingdoms of Canaan in a generation. They still had fortified cities and mighty armies. The people who lived there were much the same as their parents, who had so terrified the previous generation of Israelites, they cried out, *"wouldn't it be better for us to return to Egypt?"*[73] *(Num. 14:3).*

The previous generation believed that attacking Canaan would result in certain death by an enemy sword. Claiming this land would not be easy, even for a mighty warrior such as Joshua, and his army. However, Scripture tells us that because their battle was Holy and at the divine instruction of God, He sent along some immense help. As Joshua neared Jericho, the city where their first battle would be fought, this is what he saw:

> *Now when Joshua was near Jericho, he looked up and saw a man standing in front of him with a drawn sword in his hand. Joshua went up to him and asked, "Are you for us or for our enemies?"*
>
> *"Neither," he replied, "but as commander of the army of the LORD I have now come." Then Joshua fell facedown to the ground in reverence, and asked him, "What message does my Lord have for his servant?"*
>
> *The commander of the LORD's army replied, "Take off your sandals, for the place where you are standing is holy." And Joshua did so. (Joshua 5:13-15)[74]*

Why was this generation's relationship with God so vastly different from their parent's generation? Their parent's generation spent the remainder of their lives in the wilderness, never seeing the Promised Land. By contrast, God sent the commander of His heavenly army to fight for the children of those who had fled Egypt. The answer can be found in Joshua 1:16-18, which tells us of Israel's reaction to God's appointment of Joshua as the new leader:

Then they answered Joshua, "Whatever you have com-
manded us we will do, and wherever you send us we will
go. Just as we fully obeyed Moses, so we will obey you.
Only may the LORD your God be with you as he was
with Moses. Whoever rebels against your word and does
not obey it, whatever you may command them, will be put
to death. Only be strong and courageous!"[75]

"Whoever rebels against your word and does not obey it,
whatever you may command them, will be put to death."[76] That
sounds like extreme *faith, trust,* and *obedience* to me!

While God is doing work in us,
we must also be training ourselves.

That same extreme *faith, trust,* and *obedience* is exactly
what will be required for us to conquer our Promised Land
and keep it. Just as surely as we have won ground against
the enemy, he will come back and try to take every inch of
our conquest. This second generation understood this fact
and they did not remain passive. They had grown up in
their wilderness season. They had trained and prepared for
this conquest. If we want to seize the land of our promise
and defend that ground from the enemy, we must also be
active in our training and preparation. Just as God is at
work within us, we also have work to do. So, how do we
train ourselves to be increasingly stronger disciples?

We Retrain Our Mind

We retrain our minds by continuously and consciously judging our circumstances by His Word and the counsel of the Holy Spirit, and not by our own emotions. So much turmoil has been caused in the life of humans by allowing our emotions to judge our circumstances and lead our reactions. Counting our joys and God's faithfulness in the face of pain, fear, and trouble is not a natural response. It takes time and effort to train our mind for such a reaction.

We do not naturally look at a massive army standing in the way of our Promised Land and suddenly start listing all the times that God has shown up in the face of trouble before. Our natural responses are fear, anxiety, dread, anger, and despair. Counting our joys and God's faithfulness is a trained response. It is an active decision to look at a dire situation and refocus our mind on the history of our relationship with God. Whether your relationship with God is long or short, He has always been there in your life, even before you acknowledged Him or sought His path.

Our emotions ebb and flow with the changing winds and the shifting circumstances. If our view of our world and circumstances is formed through the window of our emotions we are left vulnerable and without defense against the attacks of the enemy. If Satan wants to divert us from our anointed path, sabotage our highest victory, and keep us from our Promised Land all he has to do is send a little anxiety our way. If he wants to keep us from hearing God's voice all he has to do is put a sales clerk, boss, or teacher in our path that will push our buttons and cause the rest of our day to be gloomy, annoying, and frustrating. If he's lucky we will pass along that emotionally charged mood to everyone we meet like a bad cold.

Retraining our mind and judging our circumstances by His Word and not our emotions means that we take a deep breath, a step back, and a bigger view...a godly view.

God's Word is solid. It is immovable. It is the foundation of all Creation. If our reactions - mental, physical, and verbal - are based on the solid foundation of His Word, it means they will not change based on the mood we are in at the moment. We are not called to show grace, mercy, love, patience, understanding, and forgiveness only when we are having a good day and can wrap our minds around the circumstance. We are called to show these qualities every day and in all circumstances. This doesn't mean that we are prohibited - or even cautioned against - standing up for ourselves and others. Nowhere, does God say we are required to let other people take advantage of us. God is not calling us to be a doormat. However, neither is He calling us to be a bulldozer for our faith.

'What would Jesus do?' is an often quoted question among believers. It usually elicits replies that lean towards the passive and the loving. Passivity can sometimes be very appropriate. Certainly, loving others is always our highest calling. However, if we take a Biblical view of what Jesus would do, we see that turning over the tables of thieves and chasing people with ropes made into whips is not outside the realm of possibility *(John 2:13-25)*.

Jesus wasn't above righteous anger. He was more than willing to stand up for what was right, righteous, and godly. Like everything about our walk with God, context and the motives of our heart matters a great deal. Jesus did everything in accordance with God the Father, and the Holy Spirit. He did nothing outside of that divine counsel. When we act in accordance with God, He will guide our response. In life, there will be times when we need to be quiet and perhaps even passive in a moment, a circumstance, or a season. There are also times when we are going to need to overturn the tables of some thieves and chase some people out of our temple.

We Collect Our Memory Stones

If you are like me, you can look back over the course of your life and pinpoint endless moments of God's handiwork, His faithfulness, His grace, and His intervention. They may be as big as a supernatural healing, as special as a person He put in your path, or as simple as a quick word from a passing stranger. His faithfulness has never left you. He has guided you by pillars of cloud and fire. He has fed you with manna from heaven. He has parted rivers before you. He has drowned the enemies that pursued you. If you look back over your life you are likely to see thousands of ways in which God has been real, active, present, and generous in your life and in the lives of the people around you. There are no coincidences, but there is most certainly the divine hand of a loving God reaching into your life for your good.

We have discussed how God uses these moments to build our memory stones of His faithfulness, just as He did with Joshua and the Israelites. My question to you is this:

Are you collecting those stones?

Are you writing them down and keeping them close? Are you preserving them so that future generations will be blessed with the lineage of faith into which they have been born or adopted?

The faithful love of the LORD never ends!
His mercies never cease. Great is his faithfulness;
his mercies begin afresh each morning.
(Lamentations 3:22-23, NLT)

Every single day of her life, for as long as I can remember, my grandmother read in the same well-worn Bible given to her by her parents on her eighteenth birthday. Each page was obviously well-loved and the binding was held together with duct tape. Without saying a single word, she handed down to me a lineage of relationship to God and to His Word.

Our memory stones are what help us to persevere through our seasons of trouble, testing, and refining. As surely as we live and breathe there will be times when we don't understand why something is happening in our life. Maybe it is an illness, the loss of a job, a death, or divorce. There will be times when the voice of God is silent in our world. Maybe our emotions are drowning out His voice, or maybe He wants us to remain still. Whatever the reason, these are frightening seasons that test our perseverance. Just like the Israelites who followed Moses, these are the seasons that cause us to doubt and to question.

We can read His Word. We can pray. We can have the support of faithful friends, family, prayer groups, and church family. Still, ultimately we need more. God knows this and it's why He gives us memory stones. He gives us the moments and even seasons that demonstrate that His presence is real, tangible, active, and purposeful. However, this only works if we can remember them and recall them in the seasons when they are needed most.

I do not always wait for seasons of trouble, testing, or refining to count my memory stones. Sometimes, during my quiet moments I take them out, one by one, and relive my moments with God. When I look through a beloved photo album, I can recall the location, circumstance, and feelings surrounding each snapshot. It is a similar experience when I take out my memory stones. I relive them as individual, tangible moments that are so much more than a chronology of my walk with God.

They are snapshots of my relationship with my Heavenly Father. I marvel at His faithfulness and His perfect timing, even when I could not see it at the time. I look back and see the seasons of my life and how they fit together as chapters in a book written by the most loving and beautiful Author the world will ever know. Sometimes, I laugh as I remember moments of God's humor and creativity. Other times, I weep as I remember His boundless love and devotion. Oftentimes, I simply marvel at His utter perfection. Always, I thank Him for showing up in my life in ways big and small, but certainly miraculous. These stones are more precious than diamonds or gold to me, and they are never far away from my heart, mind, or spirit.

For me, just as important as my time spent in prayer, meditation, conversation with God, and feasting on His Word, are the times I spend counting my memory stones and reliving how each one was collected along the path I have traveled with my Father.

We Empty Our Souls

I have lived enough to know that time spent living out my plans lead either to average mediocrity or to places I would rather not revisit. However, every moment spent living out God's intention for my life leads to wonders that are beyond my comprehension.

In 2 Corinthians 4:7, the Apostle Paul compares himself to an earthen vessel when he said, *"But we have this treasure in jars of clay to show that this all-surpassing power is from God and not from us."*[77]

These clay pots were fragile and broke easily. They were not necessarily something that a First Century Judean family would present to guests, if they could afford something better. Paul was making an important point. We are the common and fragile vessels. We have very little value in comparison with the Holy Spirit who fills us and works through us. Paul did not want his life to just be about superficial display. His life's mission and great desire was to be an instrument for the One who filled his vessel.

We are also called to be like earthen vessels, but it isn't as easy as it may sound. At the moment of Salvation, our clay pots do not magically transform into fine expensive china. They are meant to be clay pots with all of their chips, cracks, and fragile nature. It is not the pot that matters, but what delicious feast is prepared inside.

This brings us to our second issue. Often our pots are already full. We have already filled them with many things: defeat, ego, shame, blame, anger, depression, sin, fear, anxiety, desire, and self-destruction just to name a few. Each of these things is like sand poured into a jar. The more sand that we have, the less room there is for God.

God doesn't need us to accomplish His will. He could simply speak the words and supernaturally transform any situation. Yet, He often chooses to give us the privilege of serving Him and carrying out His will. Now, I do not claim to understand why God would select me to accomplish a Holy anointed mission, but He has. He selects you, too.

If you ask me who in Heaven and Earth I most desire to collaborate with my answer is God. Our collaboration is simple – He asks and I obey. It really isn't that complicated. The more I obey, the more my trust in Him grows and the more He helps me pour out my sand to make room for Him. The more of God that dwells inside of me the closer my relationship with Him becomes. The closer we become, the more faith and obedience I develop. The more obedience I demonstrate, the more He uses me as His hands and feet. Thus, the further along my anointed path He leads me and the closer to my Promised Land I venture.

Sounds simple right? Well, it is, and it is not. To obey God requires faith and trust. How do we have faith and trust if our walk with God may not have come that far? Sometimes, it requires a blind leap of faith.

Therefore, if anyone cleanses himself from what is dishonorable, he will be a vessel for honorable use, set apart as holy, useful to the master of the house, ready for every good work. (2 Timothy 2:21, ESV)

God speaks to us every single day. Each day He asks us to make a decision to say *yes* to Him. God doesn't always ask for something massive. Sometimes, He asks us to speak an encouraging word to a stranger or let someone cut in front of us in line. Other times, He may ask us to give of our time or resources. Though, He gives everyone a chance to serve Him, God gives His most special assignments to those He can count on to say *yes* consistently.

In my experience, most of the time I have no idea why God is asking me to do something when He first asks. Occasionally, the reason is immediately apparent, but much more often it takes time to discover. Other times, it remains a mystery forever. However, I have walked with God long enough to know that I don't need a reason to obey Him. The fact that He is asking is sufficient enough reason to say *yes*.

There are folks who will bristle at the idea of this kind of blind *faith, trust,* and *obedience.* It is a response that I understand. I used to be among them. It took this hardheaded woman many years to fully realize one important thing. While, I may have failed many times, God has never once failed me. His plans have always been perfectly devised and perfectly timed.

Claiming the Promised Land and defending it requires extreme faith, trust, and obedience to God.

Wouldn't you love it if your children simply took you at your word and trusted your wisdom? How much joy would it bring to your life if they simply did what you said the very first time because they love you, believe you, trust you, and know your ways are best?

I am convinced that our Father loves it when His children take Him at His word and display blind faith. When we trust and obey our eternal Father simply because He is our Father, I believe that it warms His heart. God wants His children to have the faith and courage to come out, onto the furthest limb with Him. When a child of God who has found that kind of blind faith and trust, unites with the Spirit of God, miracles happen in our average human lives. If you have had the chance to feel the presence of God and witness the wonders that He can and will do through your life, you will never want to be apart from Him.

151

If you have never had that chance, what is stopping you? Ask Him for the opportunity. Ask your Father to use you in service to His Kingdom.

Every time you and I say *yes* to God, we draw closer to Him. I don't know about you, but any chance I get to have a closer, richer, fuller relationship with God, I am going to take it. How about you?

We Step Out of Our Shackles

Just because God has freed us from the shackles of our personal bondage doesn't mean that we feel free. To live as free men and women of Christ requires us to claim our freedom and rebuke any attempt by the enemy to shackle us again, or to push us back into a cell of Satan's creation. It also means refusing to ever again step back into a cell of our own creation.

How often do we perform the enemy's job for him with our self-destructive and self-defeating thoughts, words, and actions? We limit the scope of our own possibilities and deny ourselves the boundless potential that resides within our Kingdom destiny. Whether it is bondage to a specific source, or the prison cell called our comfort zone, we seek to limit what God has declared limitless.

The Israelites under Moses stood at the edge of one of God's most magnificent promises. Everything they had longed to attain for generations was finally within their grasp. Not only was it attainable, but God, Himself, had promised to help deliver them to victory. Yet, they chose to mentally and emotionally remain imprisoned to a bondage from which God had long since set them free. They used their gift of free-will to remain inside their prison cell, unable to conceive of a reality different than that tiny box.

We read their story and wonder how anyone could make such a decision. What more assurance do we need than the Lord's own words promising victory? Yet, how often do we do the same thing? By His Word, God is assuring us of victory in the land of His promise. He is asking us to come to Him and dwell in a land of abundance that was created especially for us. Instead, we elect to remain in our small, dark cell because it is familiar.

The prison cells that we occupy are often unique and highly personalized. However, each has three very important things in common.

1) They limit our view of what's possible through God.

2) They keep us separated from God and His best.

3) By His death and Resurrection, Christ has already flung open the cell doors.

Maybe your cell is childhood abuse, the shame of an unwanted divorce, the stronghold of addiction, or the bondage of unworthiness, failure, or past sin. Regardless of what or who has built your particular cell, it cannot erase the eternal truth that you are the beloved child of the same Father who breathed life into Heaven and Earth. You are loved, redeemed, chosen, adopted, blessed, favored, and anointed. Not even Satan, himself, can bind you in shackles or cage you in a cell that God has freed you from. Not even you can slam the doors of your Redemption and Salvation shut again. Your choice is clear. You can step out into the limitless horizon of God's possibilities or you can sit in a familiar cell whose open doors you choose to ignore.

We Learn From Mistakes

Let me just state an unwelcome truth. God will continue to lead us around in circles, back to the place of our mistakes, until we have learned and absorbed the lessons He is trying to teach. The scenery may be different. The people may not look familiar. Though, as surely as we live and breathe it will be a déjà vu moment.

It's true that He does give us free-will, but our free-will extends only to whether we decide to follow His instructions. We only get off the merry-go-round of a particular training or refinement when He is certain that the lesson has been learned.

Do you feel like you are going around in circles? Does every guy you meet turn out to be the exact same model of jerk as the last guy? Are you constantly dealing with the same issues at home, at work, in your social life, or in your financial life? Perhaps, God is leading you around in circles for a reason. He can't introduce you to the partner He has selected just for you until He has first freed you from your current attraction to jerks. He can't pour out a flood of financial favor into your life until you have been refined into a good shepherd of the resources He has already given you. He can't give you better co-workers until you have fixed whatever is causing the rift with your current ones.

We leave behind this unpleasant series of circles when we start to examine our motives and actions with God's help. Chances are you knew the choices you were making were wrong, or at least outside God's plan for your life. That *"still small voice"*[78] *(1 Kings 19:12)* warned you against it when the thought first crossed your mind or fluttered across your nervous stomach. However, you ignored them and followed a familiar pattern to a very familiar place.

Changing our patterns of thought and behavior takes a very conscious effort. It calls for us to examine our choices, motives, and the underlying reasons behind each of them. Sometimes, there are changes that we can make on our own. Other times, it requires the help of a godly counselor. Always, always it requires God.

Understanding where we are going requires us to understand where we have been. Most every habit, behavior, thought-process, attraction, and pattern of our life is rooted in our past. We may be fully grown and otherwise functioning adults, but we are oftentimes making decisions rooted in decades old experiences. The same logic that once determined our choices at age six is influencing many of our decisions today. We cannot afford to let the negative history of our lives determine our future.

The negative patterns of thought and behavior we have established in our past must be radically changed. If these patterns are allowed to remain, they will drag us around in continual circles in the wilderness for the rest of our earthly lives. They will prevent us from ever walking closely with God or reaching our earthly Promised Land.

Just as scary, they are easily manipulated by the enemy and provide him with an open door into our lives. They act as a neon sign welcoming him into our lives.

We are not headed back towards our past. We are walking towards the future that God alone has prepared for us. This requires tossing out the negativity of our past and embracing God's best for our future.

We Get Out of God's Way

One of the single most important things we can do in our walk with God is simply to get out of His way and let God be God. Some of us don't even realize that we are in His way. Though, every time we try to solve a problem or fix a circumstance without first bringing the situation to Him, we have placed ourselves smack in the middle of His way. As they conquered the land of Canaan, Joshua and the Israelites would learn this lesson the hard way.

We train to ensure that we are prepared to claim and hold the land of God's promise.

The Gibeonites had heard all that the God of Israel had done for His people, including the Israelite victories at Jericho and Ai. They were afraid, so they developed a scheme. They sent a delegation to the Israelite's camp to make a treaty. Posing as messengers from a faraway land they loaded their donkeys down with worn-out sacks, moldy bread, and cracking wineskins (*Joshua 9*).

The Israelite elders were new to this land. They didn't yet know the entire geopolitical layout. The Israelites saw the messengers worn out clothes and depleted food rations. They were convinced that these men had journeyed a great distance. Believing the Gibeonite territory was nowhere near the Promised Land, Joshua and the elders made a peace treaty with them and swore an oath. However, they did not bother consulting the Lord. If they had, they would have discovered the men of Gibeon were deceiving them.

The Israelites soon discovered that the Gibeonites were actually their next door neighbors. Their land was smack in the middle of the Israelite's Promised Land. The Israelites willingly gave up a portion of God's promise and agreed to defend these deceivers simply because they elected to substitute their discernment for God's better judgment.

If we have learned anything in our journey so far, it is that God's results are always far superior to anything that we can ever achieve alone. God is not asking for our well thought out strategies, He is demanding our *faith*, *trust*, and *obedience*. Trusting God also means trusting Him to *be* God.

We cannot fix a circumstance, solve a problem, or tackle a mighty plan alone. When we fool ourselves into believing that we have the solution, instead of taking the issue to God and waiting for His better answer, we not only get in His way, we surrender our right to His best in the situation. In addition, we also undermine our relationship with our Father and inhibit our ability to achieve our highest destiny. We trade the mighty plan of a faithful God for defeat, destruction, and mediocrity when we fail to trust Him, believe Him, and come to Him. Taking everything to God, holding nothing back, and laying absolutely everything down at the foot of the Cross requires us to bring to Him every…single…thing.

PRAYER

Father, Thank You for the work You are doing in my life. I know that it is leading me to be a better servant of Your Kingdom. Please give me the *faith, trust, obedience,* strength, discernment, and sensitivity to persevere through this journey, claim the land of Your promise, and defend the ground upon which I have claimed from encroachment by the enemy. Tune my ears to Your voice. Center my mind to Your will. Search my heart for hidden motives that lead me around in circles. Grow in me a heart like Yours, so that with each passing day, I can grow in Your glory. Amen.

CHAPTER NINE

LISTENING TO YOUR FATHER

But people who aren't spiritual can't receive these truths from God's Spirit. It all sounds foolish to them and they can't understand it, for only those who are spiritual can understand what the Spirit means.
1 Corinthians 2:14 (NLT)

Earlier we saw *how* God speaks into our lives, now we examine how we perfect not only our ability to hear Him, but also to understand His message. This is another important way in which we train ourselves to be ready and able to fully claim God's incredible promise in our lives. Our ability to hear and understand our Father forms the bedrock of our entire spiritual life and our walk with Him. Before we can ever fully obey our Lord, we must first learn to hear Him and discern His instructions.

We Listen To God's Voice

There are a great many Christians who believe in Jesus Christ and Him Resurrected. They go to church, tithe, and read their Bibles. They believe in God as Lord of their life. They try to do good works. They may accept that God speaks through the Holy Scripture. They may even accept that God actually speaks to pastors, ministry leaders, and good Christian teachers, but they don't necessarily think that God would waste His time speaking to them. You may be among them, and if you are, I tell you this: The idea that God does not speak to you is a lie from the pit of hell. Don't take my word for it. Listen to God's Word on the subject, *"My sheep listen to my voice; I know them, and they follow me. I give them eternal life, and they shall never perish; no one will snatch them out of my hand"*[79] *(John 10:27-28).*

Not only does His Word proclaim that He speaks to us, the very fact that He speaks to us is one way in which we know that we are His children. Saint Paul wrote in Romans 8:14 that those who are *"led by the Spirit of God are the children of God."*[80]

In Luke 6:46 Jesus asks a question that I think He must ask us often, *"Why do you call me 'Lord, Lord,' and not do what I tell you?"*[81] I particularly like the translation from The Message Bible: *"Why are you so polite with me, always saying 'Yes, sir,' and 'That's right, sir,' but never doing a thing I tell you? These words I speak to you are not mere additions to your life, homeowner improvements to your standard of living. They are foundation words, words to build a life on"*[82] *(v. 46-47).*

Jesus goes on to give His disciples an allegory to demonstrate why we should listen to His Word:

> *As for everyone who comes to me and hears my words and puts them into practice, I will show you what they are like. They are like a man building a house, who dug down deep and laid the foundation on rock. When a flood came, the torrent struck that house but could not shake it, because it was well built. (Luke 6:47-48)*[83]

We know that in the moment of our acceptance of God as the Lord of our life, the Holy Spirit is deposited in us. The Spirit continues to grow as our faith matures and we pour out more of ourselves and our human brokenness to make room until eventually, and hopefully, we are earthen vessels filled with only the Spirit of God.

We know that the Holy Spirit guides us, convicts us, and gives us counsel. We know that as Christians we are supposed to listen and obey the Holy Spirit, but how do we distinguish the voice of the Holy Spirit from instinct, or worse, the voice of the enemy? Jude 1:19 says that our *"mere natural instincts"*[84] are different from the voice of the Holy Spirit.

In and of themselves, natural instincts are not bad, nor are they evil. Oxford Dictionaries describe the word *instinct* in this way: "An innate, typically fixed pattern of behavior in animals in response to certain stimuli."[85] We all have innate patterns of behavior. Some are knitted together in us at the moment of our creation. Others are embedded into us by our experiences as children and young adults.

A bird has a natural instinct to build a nest. A bee has a natural instinct to be attracted to certain flowers. Natural instinct causes a mother bear to protect her young. We also have natural instincts. These are all good things, and as God makes clear to Job they are godly things *(Job 38-39)*.

However, we must never confuse natural instinct with the will of God as expressed through the Holy Spirit dwelling inside us. So, how do we discern the origin of that quiet voice or the strong feeling that is leading us one way or another? In our walk with God, we must carefully evaluate each one. In the pages to come, we will discuss some of the questions that will help you make that evaluation.

Is It Consistent With His Word?

The single most important way to differentiate the voice of God from natural instinct, or the enemy, is whether it's consistent with His Word. God will never lead us in any direction that is contrary to the Holy Scripture that He breathed into existence. Before God revealed Himself in human form, He revealed Himself in His Word *(John 1:14)*. Nothing in His Kingdom can be separated from His Word.

John 1:14 says this about Jesus: *"And the Word became flesh and dwelt among us, and we have seen his glory, glory as of the only Son from the Father, full of grace and truth."*[86] The New Testament as a personal testimony to the glory God revealed through His One and Only Son. Through every page of Scripture we come to know God and His heart. Through those precious words we come closer to the heart of God and deeper in relationship with Him.

The transliterated Greek word used for flesh in John 1:14 is *sarx*. It literally means "flesh...the *body*...a *human being*."[87] *Sarx* is the same Greek word used in John 6:53 when Jesus tells His disciples, *"Truly, truly, I say to you, unless you eat the flesh of the Son of Man and drink His blood, you have no life in yourselves."*[88] The transliterated word for *eat* in this verse is *phago*, it means "to eat (consume) a thing to take food, eat a meal metaph. to devour, consume."[89]

A God-sized future requires aligning our thoughts, decisions, habits, and behavior with God.

In a manger in Bethlehem, the Word of God became flesh and blood in the form of a very special baby boy. God had revealed Himself to humans in many ways since those first words were spoken to Adam in the Garden. However, for the first time on earth, men and women could stand face to face with the living God. Moses may have talked to God as a friend, but he never saw His face. Exodus 33:20 tells us that no one could see the face of God and live. With the birth of Christ Jesus all that would change forever. They could see Him, touch Him, and even hug His neck!

If we want to spend all of eternity, close to God and His heart, we must feast upon His Word and devour every syllable. The Apostle Paul urged his brothers and sisters in Christ to be, *"steadfast, immovable, always abounding in the work of the Lord, knowing that in the Lord your labor is not in vain"*[90] *(1 Corinthians 15:58).*

The Greek word translated as *abound* in this verse is *Perisseuo*. It means "a thing which comes in abundance, or overflows unto one."[91]

In God and His Word our feet are placed on solid ground. When we abound in Him we overflow with the Spirit of God. We are like the ancient willow tree whose roots have dug so deep into the bedrock that even when the high winds come they cannot be moved or toppled.

Do We Feel At Peace?

Even if you accepted Christ as Lord of your life five minutes ago, you have within you the Spirit of God. One very reliable way to know if you should be doing what you are doing is whether you feel at peace upon consulting the Holy Spirit. That sense of internal calm that we experience comes when we act in alignment with the will of God. It is a fruit of obedience that lets us know we are walking a path that our Father has anointed just for us.

If you are agitated, fearful, anxious, or uneasy about a subject, it doesn't necessarily mean stop, abort, or go back. It may mean God wants you to pause and ask for His guidance, clarity, and discernment. It also means that your mind, body, and spirit are likely not operating out of a place of alignment with God and His Spirit.

In times of certain testing, it's natural for fears, anxieties, and uneasiness to surface because God is refining us. We are flawed creatures filled with fears, brokenness, and insecurity. When God asks us to do a mighty thing, like Moses on Mount Horeb, we may feel anxious and fearful.

However, when we stop and align our thoughts with the Holy Spirit, we feel peace over the path we are about to walk. It just simply *feels* right. You may not be able to logically say why, but it does. As strange as it may sound, there are times we can experience both anxiety and peace over a decision or circumstance at the very same moment.

Have you ever been asked by God to do something big and mighty? Perhaps, He asked you to leave a successful job, make a big move, or undergo a major surgery? It would be unusual for us not to feel a certain level of anxiety over such an important decision, but we know that our choice is right if when we stop, take a deep breath, and align ourselves with the Holy Spirit, we feel an inner calm that comes with being aligned with the will of God. It is a peace that transcends all understanding *(Philippians 4:7)*.

Is It In Context?

There are many times when we will have absolutely no idea why something has been placed on our hearts. Sometimes, this becomes apparent in time, but often we may never know. This is where our complete trust joins with our complete faith to produce complete obedience. However, context is often readily apparent.

We have seen, in our walk with God, that context often matters a great deal. One way to evaluate if what we hear, feel, or discern has a godly origin, is whether the message is in context to the situation happening in our lives. Have you been praying for God's guidance? Do you have a life decision to make? Is something being asked of you?

If neither the reason, nor even the context, is readily apparent, then it's worth considering whether your Father is showing you something that you might not otherwise be noticing. We live busy lives. Sometimes, God's communication is drowned out by the pressing demands of daily life. Every circumstance that we encounter has ripple effects through our life. Each is worth examining in context to God's communication. When in doubt, ask Him and listen expectantly. He wants us to come to Him with everything.

Is It Repetitive?

God knows that we are imperfect, inattentive, and often possess short attention spans. Thus, He often repeats His message. In the Bible, anything that is repeated usually has special significance. If He wants you to contact that friend you haven't spoken to in a while He may place it on your heart to call. If you still don't, He may have another friend mention them in conversation. If you still don't, He may have you run across an old photo of them. He will continue to place His request not only on your heart, but also in your path until you finally get the message and call.

God does not do coincidences. If we are experiencing a recurring pattern, there is a reason. Not all recurring experiences are from God. However, every one of them is worthy of examination. When in doubt, bring it to God. He communicates with us so that we will understand. He will find a way to help us discern His message. All we need is to simply come to Him with our uncertainty, and then wait patiently and expectantly for His answer.

We Feast Upon His Word

If you long to hear God speaking into your life and discern His message, there is no better place to begin than the Word He breathed into existence. It's the basis by which we can compare every other communication.

"When your words came, I ate them; they were my joy and my heart's delight, for I bear your name, LORD God Almighty." (Jeremiah 15:16, NIV)

In my home, we elevate food to a beloved pastime. We love to cook and create new recipes. We look forward to trying new dishes and new restaurants. We can spend hours browsing the cooking section of department stores picking out new gadgets and cookware. Some people have stamps, or quilting, or golfing. We have food. It shouldn't come as a surprise that I can actually list the top ten best meals of my life in descending order. I can tell you where I was, how it was served, and who joined us for the meal.

These were not meals that were devoured quickly. They were savored over the course of hours. As a result, whether they were enjoyed in a small Tuscan village or in our own kitchen, the memories of those meals are burned into the fabric of my mind as beautiful remembrances of an incredible experience. To this day, I can still taste the Sicilian cannoli picked up at a tiny bakery in rural Italy. I've tried many delicious cannoli since, but none ever comes close.

If we simply look at the food, admire it, compliment the chef, and upload photos of it to our social media accounts, but never actually take a bite, we will forever remain hungry. The same is true of God's Word. Think of the Bible as the most delicious meal you will ever enjoy. Jeremiah 15:16 compares God's Word to food and says that it provides both joy and our heart's delight.

Nowadays, we have so many ways to absorb the Bible: traditional printed version, apps, computers, and readers. Many Bible websites even have spoken versions free of charge. Regardless of how His Word comes to you, spend some time feasting. Take a few moments before you begin just to be with God, centering your mind and heart with the Holy Spirit. Ask God to open your heart, mind, and spirit so that you may hear Him and know Him better.

Oftentimes, we read other books for fun and the Bible for obligation. When we read great and entertaining novels or biographies, we see the characters and scenes come alive in our minds. We do not simply read the words on the page. Instead, they come to life inside the confines of our imaginations. By the time I have turned the last page of a beloved book, the characters have become life-long friends with which I have shared an amazing journey.

The next time you pick up your Bible, instead of seeing it as a bland book of instruction, or even God's Word put to paper, try reading it as the greatest story ever told. It is a love story, a drama, an adventure, a mystery, and a great epic all rolled into one. It is filled with romance, plot twists, heroic action, murder, and espionage. Can you think of a more exciting and compelling story than all of this set against the boundless love of God for His children?

The story of God's love for us is even more spectacular because we know that it's true and has been recorded just for us. When you pick up your Bible, try picturing the words coming alive like a movie in your mind. Envision what it was like to hear Jesus speak. Imagine Abraham staring up at a blanket of stars. Feel the pounding of David's heart as he faced Goliath. Journey with the men and women described within its pages. Commit their words and actions to the fabric of your mind and heart. Envision it through the wide-eyed wonder of a child.

We are called to have childlike faith. Luke 18:17 says, *"anyone who doesn't receive the Kingdom of God like a child will never enter it."*[92] If you have ever spent time around small children you know that they will pepper you with all sorts of questions. *Why is the sky blue? Why do fish have fins? Will there be animals in Heaven?* By the time they can talk, children have mastered the what, why, how, and who of conversation. They aren't being defiant or disobedient. They are questioning everything out of a passionate and childlike curiosity about the world around them.

This is the mindset in which we are called to approach God and His Word. The next time you are reading His Word, pepper Him with childlike questions so you may come to know Him more fully. Search the literal and the context to see what God is trying to convey and how it can apply to your life. I am convinced such childlike curiosity delights God. After all, He gave us the gift of curiosity.

Exodus 33:7 tells us of the Tent of Meeting, that Moses erected outside the Israelite camp in the wilderness. His Word specifically says, *"Anyone inquiring of the Lord would go to the tent of meeting outside the camp."*[93]

It doesn't say that only the priests or elders could encounter God. It says that anyone wishing to inquire of the Lord could go to the place of meeting and speak with the One True Living God. All they had to do was go.

As New Testament believers, we do not need a special tent outside of town. We are the temple of God's Holy Spirit. A Spirit of the Most High God dwells inside all of us. We are His children. We can encounter God at any moment. All we have to do is to seek Him. If we desire to claim God's promise for our lives, then seek Him we must. Only by seeking Him often, and listening expectantly, do our skills at hearing God's voice and understanding His message become perfected.

PRAYER

Father, Thank You for speaking into my life. Thank You for giving me the right to be called Your beloved child. Please give me ears that are tuned to Your voice, the discipline to tune out worldly distractions, and the discernment to understand Your message. Let me hear You loud and clear so that I may walk where you tell me to go, serve You in mighty ways, and claim the land of Your promise. Amen.

CHAPTER TEN
IT TOOK A GOLIATH

Do not be conformed to this world, but be
transformed by the renewal of your mind,
that by testing you may discern what is the will
of God, what is good and acceptable and perfect.
Romans 12:2 (EVS)

*I*n 2010, the city of Nashville, Tennessee experienced its worst disaster since the Civil War. Within approximately thirty-six hours, record rainfalls caused waterways to overflow their banks and surge towards nearby homes. Rivers that were once only a hundred feet across soon stretched for nearly a mile in width. Within hours, and sometimes minutes, entire neighborhoods were submerged in the muddy waters of a thousand-year flood.

Some residents were able to escape with only minutes to spare. Others were left to cling to their attics and roof-tops, praying for rescue. Roads and interstates turned into raging rivers as the muddy waters swallowed cars, trucks, and even tractor trailers. The portable classroom from a nearby school floated down the interstate, crashing into submerged vehicles as it moved with the rapidly flowing water. It was a scene repeated in counties throughout Tennessee, Kentucky, and Mississippi. In the end, the flood claimed thirty-one lives and caused $2.3 billion in damage.

Now it is God who makes both us and you stand firm in Christ. He anointed us, set his seal of ownership on us, and put his Spirit in our hearts as a deposit, guaranteeing what is to come.
(2 Corinthians 1:21-22, NIV)

Thousands of gripping and shocking images remain from those thirty-six hours. Not a single one of them will show National Guard troops, federal evacuations, or national search and rescue operations. However, what you will find are thousands of regular people who chose to step into the midst of a crisis and help others. Neighbors braved the rushing waters, one house at a time, to rescue friends and strangers alike. Truckers who stopped on the interstate to rescue motorists from rapidly submerging vehicles knowing full well they risked being swept away themselves. Families who opened their homes to perfect strangers, giving them shelter in the storm. Thousands of volunteers showed up at makeshift shelters asking one simple question, *"How can we help?"*

Very few of these men and women had any special training or experience. They were carpenters, bankers, truckers, mechanics, parents, and grandparents. Very few of them would fit into our view of an archetypal hero from a movie, but they became heroes, nonetheless. They changed the course of tens of thousands of lives, and forever impacted an entire city, and an entire region. They did it all because they saw a crisis and they chose to step into it with faith, instead of running from it in fear. The legacy they created in those thirty-six hours will be felt in ripples, large and small, for generations to come.

To experience God's abundant victory we need only have faith and trust enough to obey Him.

We would like to think that it is the everyday moments of our lives that determine our futures. Those moments are indeed important, but it's often in the crisis moments of our lives that we come closest to God and realize our individual anointing. It is often when we experience the blackest darkness, stand before the fiercest enemy, or face the greatest obstacle that we are called to a new level of our own God ordained destiny. These are often the moments that God uses to shape our future.

David was a young boy, caring for his father's sheep when God used a giant to create a future King. Moses was a fugitive and an aging shepherd, when God sent him to challenge a brutal Pharaoh and lead His Chosen People towards the Promised Land. Noah was likely a middle class merchant when God sent a great flood and charged Noah with the mission of repopulating the world.

It took a Goliath to make a David. It took a brutal Pharaoh to make a Moses. It took a flood to make a Noah. These were men of average means who ascended to their highest destiny only when they answered God's call to tackle a seemingly insurmountable obstacle. They may have been anointed and chosen by God years before, but it was not until the moment of their greatest challenge that their God ordained destinies were reached.

Scripture speaks a lot about anointing. We often think of ancient kings and prophets as being anointed. Perhaps, we think of modern day ministers and missionaries as living anointed lives. We do not always think of ourselves as God's anointed. However, His Word makes clear that we are also His anointed. In 1 John 2:27, the Apostle John tells us that as Christians we have been anointed by God with the Holy Spirit: *"But the anointing that you received from him abides in you, and you have no need that anyone should teach you. But as his anointing teaches you about everything, and is true, and is no lie—just as it has taught you, abide in him."*[94]

In its original Greek, the word used in this verse for anointing is *chrisma*, which literally means "anointing."[95] It derives from the Greek word *chrió*, meaning, "through the idea of *contact*; to *smear* or *rub* with oil, i.e. (by impl.) to *consecrate* to an office or religious service: - anoint."[96] Merriam-Webster's dictionary defines the word consecrate as "dedicated to a sacred purpose."[97]

As Christians, we have been anointed by the Holy Spirit and dedicated to God's sacred purpose. Saint Paul says this beautifully in his Second Epistle to the Corinthians:

> *Now it is God who makes both us and you stand firm in Christ. He anointed us, set his seal of ownership on us, and put his Spirit in our hearts as a deposit, guaranteeing what is to come. (2 Corinthians 1:21-22)*[98]

We have been hand-selected by God. He has set his seal upon us and placed His Spirit in our hearts, *"as a deposit, guaranteeing what is to come."*[99] He claimed us. He adopted us. He chose us. He redeemed us. He blessed us. He said to the entire world that we are His, and we shall dwell forever in the Kingdom of the Most High God. Each of us has a unique and mighty purpose to fulfill in His Kingdom and we do so through the power of the Holy Spirit. It is God doing what only He can do, but doing it through the flesh and blood earthen vessels of His children.

As Christians, we are disciples of the ultimate Anointed One, Christ Jesus. In Greek, the word *Christós*, from which the English word *Christ* derives, means *"anointed, i.e. the Messiah…Christ."*[100] It also shares the root word of *chrió*.

As Christians, we are redeemed by the death and Resurrection of Christ Jesus, we are filled with the power of the Holy Spirit, and we are anointed by the hand of God. Our Salvation has been secured by the blood of a Savior. While Heaven is the ultimate destination of God's promise, I submit that He has real and mighty plans for us right here on earth. Like David, Moses, and Noah, the level of our highest Kingdom destiny will not be completed until we answer God's call to tackle that, which is so enormous it can only be accomplished through the power of God acting through us as earthen vessels. We stand on the shoulders of the mighty men and women of His Kingdom who have gone before. Their lives are a testimony and an instruction.

If you think that giants, pharaohs, and mighty floods are only found in the pages of Scripture, think again. If you have yet to face your flood moment, just wait, it will come.

God uses crisis moments as opportunities for us to fulfill our Kingdom destiny.

The times in our life when we face the greatest obstacle, or the darkest moment, are the times when we have the greatest opportunity. It might not feel like an opportunity if you discover your marriage is ending, your family business is facing bankruptcy, your child is failing school, or your job is downsizing.

It does not always feel like a blessing when God asks us to leave the comfort of our everyday world and accept a mission so big that it is doomed to failure unless God shows up. Peace is rarely what we feel when God tells us He wants us to start a business, give a public testimony, found a charity, lead a mission trip, adopt a foster child, move across country, or transform our lives. Most of us like the quiet, predictable bubbles of our comfort zones and we are not eager to leave.

It is hard to see God's favor at work when He is asking us to leave behind that, which is comfortable in order to face a mighty challenge with a frightening leap of faith. Moses didn't seem to view it as an opportunity when he stood on Mount Horeb and heard the voice of God telling him to return to the land of Pharaoh. He was happy living in Midian, going about his day tending sheep, when the Lord spoke to him from the flames of a bush. God anointed Moses for a mighty mission. There are few moments more Holy than hearing the voice of God, proclaiming that you have been selected to deliver His Chosen People from slavery and lead them towards the land promised to them as descendants of Abraham. Moses listened to God's request, and his initial answer has probably crossed our lips once or twice: *"Who am I that I should go…?"*[101] *(Exodus 3:11). "Please send someone else"*[102] *(Exodus 4:13).*

How often is that our answer to God? We pray for Him to use our lives for His purpose. We speak beautifully about our desire to be the hands and feet of God, but when He calls us to step forward in our anointing, we answer Him as Moses did – *'Why me? Can you send someone else?'*

Our faith tells us that God will be with us, just as He was with Moses. Still, how often is our answer to God: *Why me? Why should I forgive the people who hurt me? Why should I stop to help that person? Why should I be kind to that perpetually hostile co-worker? Why should I leave my comfort zone? Why should I brave dangerous waters to rescue people? Lord, can you send me a different request? God, I've been a good Christian, why are you asking this difficult thing of me?*

Our Father is not punishing us by asking us to step up to a difficult challenge. After all, He is not only there with us as we face the challenge, He has already walked before us to ensure victory. God was not being harsh to Joshua by anointing him to claim the Promised Land. The Lord was not punishing Moses by asking him to return to Egypt to lead His People out of slavery. These may have been difficult challenges that He was asking them to tackle. They were surely doomed to failure unless God, Himself, was present and active in the situation. In the midst of this challenge, God gave them the opportunity to rise to their highest Kingdom destiny, and in doing so, to come closer to Him. God is giving us this same opportunity now.

God walks before us to ensure our path,
and with us to ensure our victory.

We can give God excellent reasons for resisting His call: *I have a mortgage, kids to pick up from school, and a demanding job. I'm not special enough, good enough, talented enough, or strong enough to be God's earthen vessel. I have no special skills to offer. I'm not a doctor, or a teacher, or a minister. My anger and bitterness is justified. It doesn't matter what I do. I have all kinds of special sin in my past, and even in my present.*

At the heart of all our well thought out, logically and worldly reasonable excuses is this question:

How can God possibly use someone like me
to accomplish anything Holy?

God's final Covenant was created for the Redemption of all mankind. Jesus was born without sin, so that He could take away the sins of the world.

God used a fugitive and killer to lead His Chosen People out of bondage. He used an adulterer and murderer to unite the tribes of Israel and usher in a time of peace. God loves nothing more than the redemption of His children. Not only can God use the fallen, the broken, and the sinful to serve as His anointed earthen vessels and accomplish His Holy purpose, often that is exactly who He selects.

The first person to whom Jesus openly revealed Himself as the Messiah was not especially pious or holy. She was a Samaritan woman who had been married five times and was currently living with a man who was not her husband. Yet, Jesus offered her the *"living water"*[103] and told her all about her life. She believed Him when He told her *"I AM the Messiah!"*[104]

This woman was unworthy in the eyes of many of her contemporaries. Times have not changed much. There are some people who would see her as unworthy even today. However, the Son of God found her worthy. In fact, that which made her unworthy to others provided her with the ability to encounter Jesus with confidence.

Great tensions existed between the Judeans and the Samaritans. Violent confrontations were not unheard of even during the lifetime of the first Apostles. Few women of the time would have been willing to speak to a strange man from a foreign land. In fact, few Samaritans would have been willing to speak to anyone from Judea.

This woman was different. With five husbands and a boyfriend, she was obviously accustomed to men and comfortable in their presence. This man from Galilee did not frighten her, nor was she afraid to testify to others in her village about her encounter with the Messiah. This woman, who was otherwise looked down upon, ended up becoming one of the first evangelists. John 4:39 says that, *"many Samaritans from that town believed in Him because of what the woman said when she testified."*[105]

God did not simply use this woman for His better plan. Our glorious Lord elected to use the very thing that likely caused her the greatest shame and stigma, to bring Redemption and Salvation to her, and her entire community. God can and will use everything and everyone to accomplish His divine plans.

Moses was a fugitive. The previous Pharaoh wanted him executed for killing an Egyptian soldier in a fit of rage after seeing the soldier beating a Hebrew slave. Moses had barely escaped Egypt with his life, and yet, he was handpicked by God. As king, David had the husband of his mistress killed in battle. His own son died en route to kill him. When your own child believes that you have become so dangerous and morally bankrupt that your death is the only solution, you know there isn't much further you can fall from the righteousness of God. Yet, in all of Scripture, David is the only person to whom God refers to as a *"man after my own heart."*[106]

God knew the sin David would one day commit, even before He anointed the boy as the future king. Psalm 139 tells us that God is always with us and foresees everything about us. He knows every word that we will speak before it crosses our lips. Yet, even the worst thing David would one day do could not erase God's seal from his head.

***

Your eyes saw my unformed body; all the days ordained for me were written in your book before one of them came to be. (Psalm 139:16, NIV)

***

God redeems the broken and He lifts the fallen. As long as you live and breathe on this earth, it is impossible for you to fall far enough from the glory of God that the grace of God cannot redeem you, heal you, adopt you, choose you, and anoint you. The mistakes and burdens of your past will not disqualify you from the anointing of God. The scars that you carry in your heart will not preclude your chance to serve God as His earthen vessel. The very same events, choices, and circumstances that you try to hide away from public view, are eventually what God will use as your testimony to the mighty power that resides at the foot of the Cross.

We know that our past does not preclude God from asking us to accept mighty challenges in His Holy name. What about the reasonable excuses that prevent us from saying yes to God? After all, we do have lives, children, families, and jobs. We have very well-reasoned justifications for our reluctance, our fears, anxieties, insecurities, and even our hatreds.

Deuteronomy 34:7 tells us that Moses was 120 years old when he died, making him about 80 years old when he was anointed by God on the side of Mount Horeb. I don't know about you, but I'm not sure that I want to challenge a Pharaoh when I'm 80 years old. I think I would rather watch my grandchildren play. If I am truly industrious, perhaps I could watch the sheep graze in the fields.

Every valley shall be exalted, and every mountain and hill shall be made low: and the crooked shall be made straight, and the rough places plain: And the glory of the LORD shall be revealed, and all flesh shall see it together: for the mouth of the LORD hath spoken it. (Isaiah 40:4-5, KJV)

David was only a boy when he received the anointing of God. First Samuel 16 describes him as having a ruddy complexion with bright eyes. Think of the red-headed boy in geometry class with the freckled face and rosy cheeks. David was the youngest son of Jesse, a sheepherder. When God called for him, he was tending his father's sheep in the fields, and he probably smelled like them, too.

David was not a solider. His defensive skills were limited to scaring off wild animals from the flocks. In quieter times, he mastered the flute and the harp. He was an afterthought, even to his own father. If we were choosing a future king of Israel and the person to save God's Chosen

People from a fearsome army, most of us would select a great warrior, perhaps the eldest son of a great nobleman. How many of us would select the freckled face, harp playing, youngest son of a sheepherder?

These men bore little resemblance to hero archetypes. They were at best, average, and at worst, filled with flaws, self-doubt, insecurity, and failings. Few people around them believed that they were born to do great things.

Whether we are young or old, married or single, wealthy or struggling, many of us look at our lives and think: *I would love to do great and mighty things in this world. I would love to be the hands and feet of God…if only. If only I were a little older or a little younger. If only I didn't have children or a demanding job. If only I had more money and fewer bills.*

We look at the Bible as a testimony of great men and women called to do great and mighty things by God. We sometimes forget that we too, have the same calling today. These men and women were not necessarily great by their birth, or even by their upbringing. They became great by answering God's call in their lives and refusing to be daunted by the obstacles in their path. They became great by saying *yes* to God. Their voice may have trembled. Their body may have shaken. '*Why me,*' may have been the first words out of their mouth. Still, their ultimate answer to God's request was *yes*.

Has God ever asked you to do something so big, so seemingly insane that to say *yes* would be ludicrous to the outside world? What did you say? To say *yes* and to trust Him, is all that God asks of us.

We know that God walks before us and makes our crooked paths straight *(Luke 3:5)*. We know that He went before Moses into the land of Pharaoh and made the *"Egyptians favorably disposed toward this people"*[107] *(Exodus 3:21)*. It seems so simple in theory. Yet, we know from our own experiences and by His Word that it may be simple, but it is far from easy. Trusting God and saying *yes* to His request, seems easy enough, but like Adam and Eve in the Garden of Eden, simple choices prove not to be so easy. Our fears, insecurities, desires, and past experiences get in the way of our ability to hear God's voice, and trust His words. Oftentimes, at the moment of our greatest victories, the voice we hear the loudest is not that of God, but of the enemies.

To reach the highest level of God's divine plan for his life, David had to say *yes* to the Lord's request that he go to serve the King. He had to say *yes* to the Lord's request that he walk into a field of battle and kill a giant with just a sling and a stone. He would be called to say *yes* to God repeatedly throughout his life. So are we.

God uses us right where we are, and with the tools and skills that we have at that very moment. David was not a soldier. He had no armor. He had no special training or weapons of war. As it turned out, a soldier was not who God needed in that valley on that day. He had plenty of soldiers. King Saul's entire army stood on one side of the Valley of Elah, facing the Philistine army.

The earthen vessel God chose for this assignment was a young boy experienced only in a sling and a stone. God did not want a fearsome battle. He did not want the earth of that valley to be stained with Israelite blood. God walked before David and He prepared the path. For David's part, he saw a need, he heard God's calling, and he said *yes*.

Scripture tells us that Noah was a righteous man with a wife and three sons. Researchers tell us that he was likely a shipping merchant of upper middle class status. God spoke to him and instructed him to prepare a boat of specific wood and specific dimensions. He was to bring upon this boat his wife, sons, daughters-in-law, one pair (male and female) of all the animals of the world, and food for all of them. God told Noah that He would soon bring about a flood to cover all the earth and rid the world of evil. How bleak and frightening a moment that must have been for Noah and his family? Yet, Noah said *yes* to God.

For Moses, the path to God's appointed destiny began at the moment of his birth. Moses was born in a time when an Egyptian Pharaoh had ordered the deaths of all the Hebrew firstborn male children. The story of one of God's great men almost ended before it even began.

Not only did Moses have to say *yes* to God on the side of Mount Horeb, but all those years before, his mother had to look at the dire reality around her, and believe that this would not be the fate of her son. By the strength of her faith in the divine hand of God her son was saved.

God uses everyone to fulfill His purpose. In the land of Egypt, he used a Pharaoh to create the future leader of His Chosen People. He used a flood to create the shepherd of God's Creation. In the Valley of Elah, on that fateful day, He used a Philistine giant to create a future king.

God did not create us to be spectators in life. He created us to move mountains, to be greater than even our own expectations, to make a difference in the world around us, to make a difference that we have lived at all. It is in the crisis moments of our lives that the hero within us emerges and we realize that we are capable of feats that only moments before, were beyond our imaginations.

"It is the Lord who goes before you. He will be with you; he will not leave you or forsake you. Do not fear or be dismayed."
(Deuteronomy 31:8, ESV)

The floods of our life may be small, or they may have the power of a thousand oceans. It may be the loss of a job, the ending of a relationship, a divorce, an illness, a bankruptcy, the death of a loved one, the start of a ministry, the founding of a business, the adoption of a child, or the move to a faraway land. Those are the days when our insecurities, fear, pain, and desperation are so deep that no words, no medication, no drink, or worldly hope will ever deliver us. Only God can deliver us, if we only cry out to Him. Yet, that is often the last option many will utilize. They complain to friends and take it out on family, all the while, sinking deeper into sadness and struggle as they try to handle it all on their own. If we know that God loves us and wants the best for us, why in the world are so many of us, often so reluctant to come to Him?

David understood the power of faith. Even when King Saul tried to dissuade him from facing the giant, David still had faith. Just as Noah before him, David trusted the Lord. He knew that the Most High God stood with him on that field as he faced Goliath. That is what God tries to teach each and every one of us. It is by *faith, trust,* and *obedience* that we shall slay giants, stand against Pharaohs, and ride the floods of the world. God loves us beyond measure and He wants to be our first stop, not our last resort.

Whether it is cancer, divorce, or rescuing strangers in a flood, God is going to ask you to slay some giants. He is going to ask you to walk into a valley and face something so big it would leave an entire nation shaking in its boots. We may be shaking too. It is fine if your hands are trembling, do it anyway. It's okay if your heart is pounding, follow God anyway. It may take all your strength just to put one foot in front of the other, but take your Father's hand and trust Him anyway. God is not asking you to be unafraid. He is asking you to trust Him even in the midst of your fear. Take His hand and follow where He leads.

Nothing is wasted in God's Kingdom.
Everything can, and will be, used for His purpose.

What are you capable of doing and accomplishing? What magnificent feats of wonder can you create, build, invent, or inspire? How do you reach the highest level of your God ordained destiny?

The answer is simple – it's in the crisis moments of your life. The moments filled with blood, sweat, and tears. It's in the moments when we are left with nothing to hold on to, but the knowledge that God is real, and present, and active beside us. These are the moments when we have the ability to change and shape the course of our lives and the course of the world. What great and mighty thing is God calling you towards? Will you answer Him in faith or in fear? Will you respond to His request with a resounding *yes,* or will you bury your head in the sand and ignore Him?

PRAYER

Father, I know that I am Your beloved child. I am not what I say that I am. I am not what the world says that I am. Rather, I am what You, my Creator, say that I am. Please lift me up to soar at the level of my highest destiny. Take away my spirit of fear, anxiety, and insecurity, and grow in me a heart like Yours. Use me as Your earthen vessel and use my life to accomplish mighty and wondrous things through the power of the Holy Spirit. Bless me with the opportunity to be Your hands and feet in the world. Make my ears sensitive enough to hear Your still quiet voice as You guide me along this path. Give me the courage to say *yes* to You and to run, not walk, in the direction You are leading me. Amen.

CHAPTER ELEVEN

DOING WHAT GOD IS BLESSING

"I will make you into a great nation, and I will bless you;
I will make your name great, and you will be a blessing."
Genesis 12:2 (NIV)

We know that God desires to bless our lives. We know that we are loved as His children *(Galatians 3:26)*. Our Father longs to give us the desires of our heart *(Psalm 37:4)*. He wants to pour out His favor into our lives, but to receive His blessing we must first put ourselves into a posture of blessing.

The transliterated Hebrew word for *blessing* is *berakah*.[108] It comes from the root word, *barak*, which means "to *kneel*; by impl. to *bless* God (as an act of adoration), and (vice-versa) man (as a benefit)."[109] We may kneel before God in church or in occasional prayer, but how many of us live our lives knelt before the Lord? How many of us adopt a spirit of humility before our God that takes joy in all He bestows upon us as a child looks to their Father?

We come before the Lord with many petitions. We ask Him for this thing, and that thing, until our prayers resemble a Christmas list of requested blessings. Before God can grant any of the desires of our heart, we must first acknowledge that we are unworthy to receive a single one. We are unworthy of the blessings and favor He has already bestowed upon us and our family. We are unworthy of the Salvation Jesus bought for us with His life.

First and foremost, we put ourselves into a posture of blessing by adopting a spirit of humility. Let's look at the other ways we put ourselves into a posture of blessing.

Knowing Who God Is & Who We Are In Him

In order to adopt a posture of blessing we must stand on His Truth. If we believe God, then we have to believe these five fundamental things: 1) God is exactly who He says that He is. 2) God can do exactly what He says that He can do. 3) God will do exactly what He says that He will do. 4) We are exactly who God says that we are. 5) We can do what God says that we can do.

Before we can understand who we are in God, what He can do, and what He will do, we must first understand who God says that He is. This is a powerful question. Moses was not the first person to whom God spoke, but He was the first person who asked God for His name *(Exodus 3:13-14)*. God replied, "I AM WHO I AM."[110]

English Translation:
"I AM WHO I AM"

Hebrew Transliteration:
"EHYEH ASHER EHYEH"

Hebrew:

אהיה אשר אהיה

Ehyeh is a verb that is often translated as *I Am,* but there is also so much more behind this word.

Hebrew verbs have no past, present, or future tense. Their tense derives from the placement of other words or letters before or after the root of the verb. The conjugation of the word *Ehyeh* indicates an action that is unending. It has always been and will always be. In Exodus, God is not just saying His name is *"I Am,"* He is saying that He was, and is, and ever shall be the absolute, immutable, unending, timeless, giver of life. He doesn't need anything else to sustain Him. The Lord simply *is.*

Hebrew is written right to left. If we take a look at the words *Ehyeh* and *Asher,* we see their first letter is א. It is the *Aleph,* the first letter of the Hebrew alphabet. The *Aleph* also carries with it important significance in traditional Jewish lore. It makes up the first letter of the Hebrew word *emet* (sometimes spelled *emeth*) meaning "truth."[111]

According to Jewish folklore, this word was carved into the forehead of a *golem,* a creation kneaded together from mud and dust, signifying an unfinished vessel. To deactivate the *golem,* the letter *Aleph* was scratched off, changing the word from emet (אמת), to *met* (מת) meaning "dead." The mere presence of this one letter gave life, and its absence brought death.

———

God created us to be a blessing to others,
as He has first been a blessing to us.

———

In perhaps His darkest moment, just hours away from the arrest that would lead to His torture and death, Jesus walked into the garden at Gethsemane, fell to the ground, and cried out to God: *"Abba, Father...everything is possible for you. Please take this cup of suffering away from me. Yet I want your will to be done, not mine."*[112] (Mark 14:36)

Abba means "father."[113] It comes from the Aramaic word *'ab*, which also means "father."[114] It is a familial name. We can think of a small child running into their father's arms excitedly yelling, *"Abba, Abba."* We can also think of it in today's terms as *Papa* or *Daddy*. We are also God's beloved, children. Our God is not aloof. He is not a distant headmaster handing out tasks to humankind. Far from it! He is our *Papa*. He is our *Daddy*. He is our *Abba*.

This brings us to our second question: **What can God do?** To answer this question we need look no further than the first lines of the first chapter of His Word: *"In the beginning God created the heavens and the earth. Now the earth was formless and empty, darkness was over the surface of the deep, and the Spirit of God was hovering over the waters. And God said, "Let there be light," and there was light"*[115] (Genesis 1:1-3).

Our *Abba* spoke the words and breathed life into the Heavens and the Earth. If we actually need a reminder of the mighty hand of God, we need only step outside and look around. Every bird, every animal, every person, every blade of grass was especially created by the God who is our Father. I don't know about you, but that continual revelation never ceases to take my breath away.

We'll come back to our third question. For now, let's look at questions four and five: **Who are we in God and what can we do?** Ephesians 2:10 says that we are, *"his workmanship, created in Christ Jesus for good works, which God prepared beforehand."*[116] Romans 8:16 says, *"the Spirit himself testifies with our spirit that we are God's children."*[117]

Psalm 139:13-16 beautifully expands on this truth. It testifies that God knitted us together in our mother's womb and we are *"fearfully and wonderfully made."*[118] It goes on to say, *"My frame was not hidden from you when I was made in the secret place, when I was woven together in the depths of the earth. Your eyes saw my unformed body; all the days ordained for me were written in your book before one of them came to be."*[119]

The original Hebrew word from which *"unformed body"* was translated is the noun *golem*.[120] We are the children of God, hand-knitted by His hand in our mother's womb. We are God's workmanship and His masterpiece. We are His unfinished vessel being made perfect and righteous in the Lord Jesus Christ. His mark of truth and life is emblazoned on our forehead with anointing oil. He has chosen, claimed, adopted, anointed, and blessed us. We are His. We are children of the King. We belong to our Father...our *Abba*!

We can do exactly what our *Abba* says that we can! When we act in accordance with our Father's will, we are able to move mountains by our faith, slay giants with a simple stone, bring down the walls of a city with our shout, and crush the enemy under our heel. When we stand with our Father, the impossible becomes possible! Alleluia!

Now, let's look at our final question: **What will God do?** The root word of golem is *galam* which means "to wrap up, fold, fold together."[121] The word *galam* is used in 2 Kings 2. The prophet Elijah was about to be called home to the Lord. He was traveling with the man who would succeed him, Elisha. Elijah is instructed by God to travel from Gilgal to Bethel, then to Jericho, and finally to the Jordan. At the water's edge, Elijah folded (*galam*) his mantle and struck the surface of the water *(v. 8)*. The Hebrew word for mantle is *addereth*, meaning, "glory, cloak...splendor... prophet's garment."[122] A prophet's mantle was a real and tangible symbol, not only of God's presence in their life, but also of their holy anointing.

As he struck the water, the river divided into two parts, just as it had done for Joshua and the Israelites years before. Elijah and Elisha were able to cross on dry ground. In Joshua's time, the waters were held back by the hand of God, so that His Chosen People could be delivered into Canaan and a very earthly Promised Land. For Elijah, the waters parted so that he could be delivered into the eternal land of God's promise, Heaven. Afterward, Elisha *picked up the fallen mantle* of his mentor *(v. 13)* and carried on in his role as a chosen prophet of God.

If we are following the divine purpose that God has planned for our lives nothing can stand in our way, not a giant, not Satan, not a fortified city, or a flooded river. As New Testament believers, God has given us the *mantle* of His Holy Spirit. It is much more than a tangible symbol. It is His real and active presence in our lives. From the time God *knits us together* (*golem*) in the womb to the time we cross into the land of His promise, our *Abba* will continue to part the waters before us, drawing us closer to Him.

There is nothing that can take His love away from us. No one can stop Him from being our Papa. He is our Father and we are His beloved children for all eternity! He wants to pour out the flood of His favor onto us.

We position ourselves to receive His favor…

By Believing God

Our *Abba's* love for us is boundless. He is a Father who is passionate about His children. Because His is a power beyond our understanding, He shares with us only what is within our grasp to conceive and receive. God will meet us at the level of our expectation. From Abraham, to the Israelites of the Exodus, to Job, Holy Scripture is filled with examples of great men and women of faith who were asked to continue believing God for mighty miracles even in the face of the impossible.

God does not speak just to hear His own voice. Our Father speaks to share important information. In His Word, He shares with us the stories of these great men and women so that we may draw hope, inspiration, and instruction from their lives. God had great things in store for Abraham, Moses, and Joshua, but first He asked them to stay in faith and continue believing Him even in the face of the impossible. God also has great things in store for His children right here on earth, but first He is asking us to stay in faith and continue believing Him.

―――――――――

For those who are led by the Spirit of God are the children of God. The Spirit you received does not make you slaves, so that you live in fear again; rather, the Spirit you received brought about your adoption to sonship. And by him we cry, "Abba, Father." The Spirit himself testifies with our spirit that we are God's children.
(Rom. 8:14-16, NIV)

―――――――――

If we want to be in a posture of blessing, then we have to first believe God for the miracle. We must first believe that He is capable and willing to bless our individual lives, to pour down a flood of His obvious favor, to heal our hurts, to lift us up, to cure our minds and our bodies, and redeem our souls. We must believe this just as Abraham believed for a son; as Moses believed when he raised his arms above the Red Sea; as the Israelites believed while they marched around Jericho; and as Joshua believed as he commanded the sun and moon to stand still.

I am certainly not suggesting that we ignore the obvious, but there is a difference between acknowledging what the world says is obvious, and accepting it. Both Moses and

Joshua sent spies into the land of Canaan to survey the terrain and its people. The facts on the ground had not changed much in a generation. The land was still abundant and the people still had mighty armies and fortified cities. The only thing that had changed was the Israelites. They had faith and trust that if God had led them to this place, then He would lead them to victory. They acknowledged the obvious, but they refused to accept it. Instead, they kept their belief and their focus on God's promise. That one, single, pivotal difference is what kept one generation from ever reaching the Promised Land, while another claimed it with the help of God's army.

There will be times when no matter how hard we pray, the outcome is not what we envisioned. There are times when our prayers are simply not in accordance with God's will. It does not mean that He arbitrarily denies His children the desires of their heart. It just means that His plans for us are something different and better. God has a plan and we don't always get to see the blueprints or understand His ways. Our job is simply to keep believing Him.

We may pray for a friendship to develop into something more, but God may have someone else picked out. We may pray for a business venture to bring fruit, but God may have an entirely different job in mind. There will be times when we pray for the healing of a loved one with all our heart, but they are called home anyway. There will also be times when we pray and God grants our petition tenfold. Did God answer our prayers in one case and ignore our prayers the second time?

Absolutely not! God delivered Joshua into a temporary earthly Promised Land. He delivered Elijah into the eternal Promised Land. Make no mistake. Each man was indeed delivered, just in a different way. These fragile earthen vessels provide our temporary home. Our ultimate citizenship is in Heaven *(Philippians 3:20)*.

Sometimes, the way God answers our prayers may bear little resemblance to the picture in our mind. It doesn't mean that God is ignoring our prayers. He is a Father who loves to bless His children. It just means that He has a better plan in mind and we don't always get to see blueprint.

By Adopting a Spirit of Appreciation

If you are a parent, do you give your child a bigger, better, and cooler toy if they were never appreciative or happy with the old version? God will never lift us up into another level of our journey if we cannot bring ourselves to acknowledge aloud our heartfelt gratitude that He has gotten us this far and sustained us this long.

It is easy to give thanks to God in the good times, when things are going our way and we seemingly have the world on a string. It's a lot harder when we hit the bumps in the road, the detour signs, and boulders that block our path. Inevitably, obstacles will come. Our challenge as Christians is to discipline our minds. If we want to claim the victory and inheritance God has waiting for us, and experience a fresh explosion of faith, we need to start behaving more like Caleb and Joshua. We need to keep our eyes focused on the size of our God, not the size of our problem.

Still, that is not always easy when things turn difficult, especially when our hearts and our minds have so strongly believed that God would deliver the desires of our hearts. Sometimes, it is those moments when the sting of pain, loss, and disappointment hurts the most that we desperately need to turn toward God with thankful and joy-filled hearts. First Thessalonians 5:16-18 says this: *"Rejoice always, pray continually, give thanks in all circumstances; for this is God's will for you in Christ Jesus."* [123]

How can we rejoice and give thanks when we have been left at the altar, when a loved one has died, when we've lost a job, or when our marriage is ending? Oftentimes we can't. Praise be to God that we are not required!

First Thessalonians tells us to rejoice, pray, and give thanks *in* all circumstances, not *for* all circumstances. There are times that we will stumble and fall along this path. Though God walks before us and fights at our side, sometimes we will still be beaten and bruised by the battles we fight. The only certainty along our walk is that no one will leave this life without scars, either visible or invisible. For most of us, our hearts, and sometimes our bodies, will be a living testimony to the battles we have fought and the wars we have survived.

God does not ask or expect us to be grateful in times of despair and pain. David, the man after God's own heart, was not always able to rejoice and give thanks in his moments of despair, and there were many. Though, we can always be grateful for the God who loves us and is faithful even in the midst of our troubles.

In Psalm 18 David wrote this:

> **Verse 1-2:** *I love you, LORD, my strength. The LORD is my rock, my fortress and my deliverer; my God is my rock, in whom I take refuge, my shield and the horn of my salvation, my stronghold.*[124]

> **Verse 6:** *In my distress I called to the LORD; I cried to my God for help. From his temple he heard my voice; my cry came before him, into his ears.*[125]

My strength. My rock. My fortress. My deliverer. My refuge. My shield. My Salvation. My stronghold. These are the names by which David called God. David suffered the pain of rejection, the pain of loss, the pain of persecution, the pain of betrayal, and the pain of self-destruction. Still, he did not allow his broken heart to become a bitter heart.

How do you describe God's presence in your life?

With each joy and each pain, he continued to turn towards God. In his brokenness, he poured out his heart to the Lord he loved, who loved him unceasingly. He cried out to the Father who heard his voice. David was certainly not happy for the circumstances that caused him so much pain, but he never stopped being joyful in his absolute and unshakable confidence as God's beloved, chosen, adopted, anointed, and blessed child.

By Working Hard

God led His Chosen People to the edge of the land He had promised to their forefathers. It was indeed a land of milk and honey. Though, God did not simply banish the inhabitants of the land and hand the Israelites the keys to the kingdom. If the nation of Israel wanted their Promised Land they would have to claim it. God would help them, but only if they were willing to march forward in *faith, trust,* and *obedience,* coupled with a lot of hard work. They were going to have to fight for their land.

---

*Sometimes, our desires or plans may
be honorable and even godly,
but they are not His plans for us.*

A lot of folks expect God's blessings to be delivered on a silver tray floating above a burning bush as they watch reruns of reality television. If that ever works for you, please let me know. It has never happened for the majority of us. We all want an easy fix. We want to lose weight, but not give up cake and donuts. We want to have a more affluent life, but not the long hours of hard work. We want a more God-centered family, but we also want to sleep in on Sunday mornings. We want a better marriage, but not the massive effort it takes. We often want the end result without the work. We want the Promised Land without the battle scars it took to claim that land.

SHANNON HOOPER

Let us come back to the description of God as the perfect loving Father. A wonderful father will sit with his children each night helping them with their homework, but he won't do their work for them. The lessons contained within each page are for his children to learn. If he completes their work, his child may be temporarily happy, but they have learned nothing. When the major test comes, his child will fail and he will have done them no favors. So a good father encourages, he helps, he prods, he refocuses his child's attention, he tries to help them digest the lessons of their work so that later they will ace the test. This is also true of our relationship with God. He is our loving Father.

―――――

Work willingly at whatever you do, as though you were working for the Lord rather than for people.
(Colossians 3:23, NLT)

―――――

In our walk with God, we will have many tests and many lessons. He will encourage us, help us, prod us, refocus us, and try to help us understand the lesson. God will do more than help us. He will send the commander of His Heavenly army to fight by our side. He will part the waters before us. He will turn the fortified walls of our enemies into crumbling rumble at our feet. He will do all of this and more, but first, we must have the courage of our faith. We must be willing to march into enemy territory and claim the land. We must be willing to trust our *Abba*.

By Becoming a Blessing to Others

Our job as Christians is as simple as it is sometimes very difficult. The late Dr. David Foster, author and beloved founding pastor of *The Gathering Nashville* church identified the *"four great to-do's,"*[126] in our life. He listed them this way: *"knowing God, loving God, loving what He loves, and doing what He's blessing."*[127]

"In everything I did, I showed you that by this kind of hard work we must help the weak, remembering the words the Lord Jesus himself said: 'It is more blessed to give than to receive.' " (Acts 20:35, NIV)

We put ourselves in a posture of blessing by keeping our focus on God and His desires. There is nothing that God loves more than His children. Our Father's heart longs most especially for those of His children who are broken, messed up, hurting, wayward, and fallen. Like a parent who loves all of their children, but secretly longs for their lost child to come home, God has a special place in His heart for those who have wandered far from the warmth of His love. If we want to adopt a posture of blessing, there is no better way than to step into the wilderness where an enormous piece of God's heart resides. Volunteer for a ministry at your church, tutor children at a community center, spend a few hours a week at a homeless shelter, or help out at a local charity. Pick a cause, an organization, or a ministry that speaks to your heart and soul, and spend some time there putting feet to your faith.

Serving God in such formal ways is not all that we are called to do. In John 13:34-35 Jesus says this: *"A new command I give you: Love one another. As I have loved you, so you must love one another. By this everyone will know that you are my disciples, if you love one another."*[128]

We serve God, and each other, when we look for opportunities throughout our day to pour out onto others the love that God has first poured onto us. If we slow down and really pay attention we can find dozens of ways to be a blessing and shower the overflow of God's love onto friends, family, and strangers.

Some days it is making a special meal for your family. Some days it is helping out an elderly neighbor. Some days it is paying for a stranger's groceries. In the course of your day tomorrow, pay attention and see just how many ways you can find to fulfill the commandment of Jesus, and show the world that you are His disciple.

Still, sometimes even after we have done all that God has called us to do, fulfilled our task, followed God faithfully and obediently, and placed ourselves into a posture of blessing, our plans may not work out quite the way we hoped. Though the goal we choose may be godly, it may not necessarily be God-intended.

After years on the run from his enemies, David had finally fulfilled God's plan. It had been a long road, filled with many twists, turns, and obstacles. Now David was finally King. He knew that God had blessed him greatly. The Lord had given him peace from his enemies and a palace made of cedar wood, a wood that was highly prized amongst the people of the ancient Near East. David suddenly realized that while he lived in a palace, the Ark of God still lived in a tent *(2 Samuel 7)*. A desire formed in David's heart to honor God in return for such blessings. He planned to build a great Temple for God.

---

*A posture of blessing requires a
humble and appreciative spirit.*

This was a mighty and honorable goal, but it was not God's goal for David's life. The Lord had other plans. He intended for the Temple to be built by David's son, Solomon. At night, the Lord gave a message to David through the Prophet Nathan. God's words are recorded in 2 Samuel 7:5-7:

> *"Would you build me a house to dwell in? I have not lived in a house since the day I brought up the people of Israel from Egypt to this day, but I have been moving about in a tent for my dwelling. In all places where I have moved with all the people of Israel, did I speak a word with any of the judges of Israel, whom I commanded to shepherd my people Israel, saying, "Why have you not built me a house of cedar?"'*[129]

Not every idea that we have is a God-intended plan. Not even everything we may want to do to honor Him is God-ordained. Sometimes, even the best, most honorable plan is not God's plan for our lives. He may appreciate the desire, but He may be telling us that He has other things in store for our lives and His Kingdom. In David's case, God appointed him to unite Israel and Judea into one kingdom under God, and bring peace to the Promised Land.

PRAYER

Dear God, I bow down before You as sovereign Lord and King of my life. I pour out all of me, so that You may fill me with all of You. Lead me on the path that You have anointed for me. Make me a blessing to all who cross my path. Lead those I love on the path that You have anointed especially for them. Let me serve You in all that I am and all that I do. Let me love others in the overflow of Your boundless love for me. Thank You for all that You do, and all that You allow me to do in service to You, and to Your Kingdom. Amen.

CHAPTER TWELVE
THE ILLUSION OF CONTROL

Many are the plans in the mind of a man,
but it is the purpose of the Lord that will stand.
Proverbs 19:21 (ESV)

*T*here is nothing in all the world that can, ever, match the presence of God in our lives. Moses was willing to trade all the milk and honey in the Promised Land, if only the presence of God remained with him and the Israelites *(Exodus 33)*.

Like every good father, our Lord's active involvement in our lives isn't always designed to make us happy. A good parent desires to help their children grown into good, honorable, and mature adults who are willing and able to have productive and fruitful lives. Our Father's goal is the same for us as His children.

This leads us to three aspects of our walk with God that is not talked about much in many churches today. You won't find them prominently displayed in many Christian books or Sunday school lessons. It's not something that many folks like to hear, but if you know Him, trust Him, and believe Him, you will be pretty glad for these truths. Here are the first two:

> God does not exist to please us. He is not a genie in a bottle. He will withhold just as many of our petitions as He will grant. His goal is to make us Holy, not necessarily always happy.

> If we want to live in true relationship with God, then we have to accept that our lives no longer belong to us. We don't set the priorities, terms, and conditions of our lives. We get an opinion, but not a vote. God alone sets the terms of our life.

Neither of these is a problem for me. Rather, they bring me great comfort. They should do the same for you.

In Exodus 32:9, God called the rebellious Israelites who fled Egypt a *"stiff-necked people."*[130] Some translations use the word stubborn or obstinate. Can you relate to that description? I sure can. We all have a stubborn, obstinate, and sometimes rebellious thread running through our nature. Some folks are just better at controlling it than others. However, despite my *stiff-necked* nature, I have eventually come to understand that my life gets better the closer I am to God. He always has something better in store for me than anything I would ever imagine myself.

Biblical truths become clearer when we stop and remember that God is not some distant king sitting upon a throne judging humankind. He is a loving Father trying to teach and lead His children on the right path. Just as a loving earthly father must sometimes put aside the desires, and at times even the temporary happiness, of his children for their betterment, so too, does our eternal Father.

Looking back over your life, how many prayers are you glad went unanswered by God? *'God please just let that cute boy with the dimples and cool motorcycle like me.'* *'Lord, please let the baby turn out to be a boy.'* *'God if you will just grant me this one thing and I will never ask you for anything else ever again.'* Any of these sound familiar?

For I know the plans I have for you, declares the Lord, plans for welfare and not for evil, to give you a future and a hope. (Jeremiah 29:11, ESV)

Like any good father, God does delight in giving us the desires of our heart *(Psalm 37:4)*. However, sometimes those desires stand in the way of our relationship with Him and the plans He has for our lives. In those times, God has a choice to make. He can either say *'no,'* or *'not now,'* to His beloved children because He has something far better in store, or He can give to us the desires of our heart knowing they fall miserably short of His glory. That is a hard choice for any parent to make. If we want to see an example of this in living color, we need only look to His Word.

From the time of Joshua's conquest of Canaan, the tribes of Israel lived in a kind of confederation of sorts under the leadership of wise and godly men and women called judges. Eventually, the Israelites decided they wanted a king and they made this demand to the Prophet Samuel, who had served them well as their judge. They desired this for reasons we may understand all too well in our own lives: everyone else had a king so they wanted one. This displeased and worried Samuel greatly and he turned to God. The Lord responded this way:

> *"Listen to all that the people are saying to you; it is not you they have rejected, but they have rejected me as their king. As they have done from the day I brought them up out of Egypt until this day, forsaking me and serving other gods, so they are doing to you. Now listen to them; but warn them solemnly and let them know what the king who will reign over them will claim as his rights."* (1 Samuel 8:7-9)[131]

If you're a parent, have you ever allowed your child to make a mistake so they learn a lesson the hard way, remember it, and hopefully never again repeat it? This is what God was doing with His children. What His children believed would make them happy, God knew would only end in misery and fall horribly short of His best. Still, the Israelites were determined their way was best and they had no interest in waiting on God. They got their King and he was Saul. He was a self-centered, egomaniac who would bring much misery to the kingdom of Israel.

Before we go any farther down this road, let us start by taking a look at happiness. Merriam-Webster Dictionary defines the word *happy* as "feeling pleasure and enjoyment because of your life, situation, etc."[132] What life situation makes you truly happy?

But the LORD is the true God; he is the living God, the eternal King. When he is angry, the earth trembles; the nations cannot endure his wrath. (Jeremiah 10:10, NIV)

I knew a woman, a faithful Christian, with a successful job. She had a good life, but more than anything else she wanted to be married and have children. Every day, she prayed for that hope to become reality. She dreamed of the children she would have, what their names would be, the flowers at her wedding, and the house where they would all live. Every day that passed was a reminder to her that she was single and childless. She looked around at her empty high-priced condo and felt alone.

Still, she kept praying, believing, and searching for her happiness just a little further down the road. Finally, she met a very fine man and began a serious relationship. He was handsome, good with kids, a Christian with a good job, a stable life, and from a good family. He clearly liked her, but he also clearly was not in love with her. She felt the uneasiness that comes with following a path that might be good, but not the one that God had anointed for her life. Her friends told her to wait. That *still quiet voice* said the man was not *the one*, but did I mention he was handsome? She became pregnant and while the man wasn't ready to be married, he did what he thought was right, and they married.

God's desire is to make us Holy and lead to the Promised Land. This means that sometimes He must sacrifice our temporary happiness to give us something enduringly better.

Flash forward ten years, and four children later. She had the husband, the children, and the beautiful home that she prayed for all those days and nights. She also had a husband who was rarely home and had grown more resentful of their marriage with every passing year. She had children who, for the most part, preferred to be with friends. She had a hundred extra pounds from depression that found temporary relief with chips and chocolate. She finally had everything she thought she had always wanted. However, she never dreamed that for much of the time, she would occupy that big, beautiful house all alone.

She paid a high price for tethering her happiness to the desire she had created in her mind, instead of waiting for God's best. She made the same mistake the Israelites made in demanding a king. The same mistake many of us make today. She rejected God as the King of her life and forgot that living in relationship with Him means surrendering our lives completely to His plans. We get an opinion, but not a vote.

If you are like most, these last few sentences may irk you a little bit. *'I am a Christian,'* you say, *'of course God is the King of my life!'* Have you ever taken a job that you knew was probably not what God had sent, but your checking account was overdrawn, the rent was due, and you had few other prospects? Did you marry a spouse that you knew wasn't God's selection for your life, but they seemed like the only option? I am sure at some point the Holy Spirit was tapping that handsome Christian man on the shoulder and saying *'you need to wait.'*

———

...but they who wait for the Lord shall renew their strength; they shall mount up with wings like eagles; they shall run and not be weary; they shall walk and not faint.
(Isaiah 40:31, ESV)

———

At one time or another we have all accepted less than God's best. This brings us to the third aspect of our walk with God that isn't much talked about:

> ➢ Sometimes, following the counsel of the Holy Spirit means accepting what appear to be dire circumstances, and continuing to trust God even in the face of the seemingly impossible.

Last year, my mother was diagnosed with five heart blockages. One was thirty percent blocked. The remaining four, including the notorious *Widow Maker* artery, was blocked at 99%. She was rushed, by ambulance, from her doctor's office to the main cardiac care hospital in the city and was told that without quadruple (possibly quintuple) heart bypass surgery she would not survive the month. In fact, her situation was so dire that she could have a massive, and likely fatal, heart attack at any moment. My mother has never been good during surgery. She had almost died from complications in recovery years before, but there were no other options, so the surgery was scheduled for first thing the next morning.

To reach our Promised Land requires extreme faith, trust, and obedience even in the face of seemingly dire circumstances.

As I prayed over her the next morning, kissed her goodbye, and watched them wheel her to surgery, I knew on a visceral level that without God's intervention this would be the last time that I would see my mother, this side of Heaven. Have you ever just *known* something? You may not have concrete proof, but you just *know*?

I sat in the waiting room with our family, Bible in hand, and I prayed for God's supernatural intervention. Without ceasing, I prayed that God would lay His hand on this situation and proclaim that not only would she live, but that she would be stronger, healthier, and more filled with Him than ever before. Thirty minutes turned into an hour. An hour turned into six hours. While I believed God for a mighty miracle, six hours is a very long time, and I am human. Finally, the cell phone that the hospital had given us for updates began to ring. There was another surgery that had become very complicated. All of the cardiac surgeons on duty were trying to care for that patient. My mother's surgery had yet to begin, but it wouldn't be long. Another thirty minutes passed, and another call came with the same message. It won't be long now.

Finally, a third call came with the same message. This time, while I heard the words of the nurse, I heard the voice of God louder. It was not a whisper. It was not a subtle hint. It was the booming voice of God. Though the room was filled with people, His words were meant only for me. He said: *You prayed for a miracle. I am answering your prayer. Accept my favor and wait.*

At the beginning of my walk with God, I might have been foolish enough to argue with Him. Waiting presented a problem. Every doctor involved with her care said that she could die at any moment without this surgery. However, if there is one thing I have learned in my walk with God is that when He speaks, my job is to obey. I told the doctors I wanted to postpone the surgery until the following day when the surgeons would be rested. This presented another problem, it was a Friday and no surgeries were performed on the weekends. It would be Monday before her surgery could take place. Did I still want to wait?

God is the King of my life. Everything that I have, everything that I am, and everything that I ever will be, is surrendered at the foot of the Cross and to the plan He has for me and my family. I get an opinion, but not a vote. If God says wait, then we wait. I would be less than honest if I said that the last vestiges of my old heart did not scream with worry about this decision. Still, I have gathered enough memory stones in memorial of God's love and faithfulness over the years to know, without reservation, God will provide for the path He asks us to walk. Even though I was worried, I felt the peace that comes with being aligned with the Holy Spirit and the will of God.

*We must trust God for the victory
even when we can't see how it
could possibly happen.*

The wait was not without bumps and downright scares. At one point her chest pains grew so strong, persistent, and untreatable that her room was filled with medical staff trying to decide if they should call in the emergency surgical team. While God is never in a hurry, He is never late. Just as the call was being made, the final dose of nitroglycerin medication began to work.

I had many emotions over this long weekend, most of them at the same time. However, I clung to one eternal truth: every emotion, good or bad, is subordinate to the will of God. On the decision to wait, the Holy Spirit gave me the sense of peace that comes with acting in unison with God's will. My job was to obey my *Abba*, and keep my mind focused on that peace.

---

*God alone sets the terms
of our life. We may get an opinion,
but we do not always get a vote.*

When Monday came, we were told that a brand new surgeon, who had just arrived in town, would be doing the surgery. As a faithful daughter, I did not like to hear that a brand new surgeon would be operating on my mother's heart, but I saw the hand of God too clearly to doubt. God asked me to wait on Friday, and a brand new surgeon started work on Monday. For whom had God commanded me to wait? Who had He sent as His earthen vessel? Whose hand would repair my mother's heart? These questions and more eagerly swirled in my mind.

As it turns out, God didn't just send us any heart surgeon. For the woman with four major blockages, who has never done well in surgical recovery, He sent the former Chief of Heart Transplant and Cardiac ICU of a major hospital, with more than two decades of experience. For what did I receive for having extreme *faith, trust,* and *obedience* in waiting for God's best? My mother's life.

There is victory awaiting our radical *faith, trust,* and *obedience*. It's the victory that only God can bring. We praise Him! Ours is a God who accomplishes mighty things!

PRAYER

Dear Lord, I surrender my entire life to You. Please guide the decisions that I make so they align with Your will for my life. Give me courage in the face of dire circumstances. Allow me to feel the overwhelming peace that comes from making decisions in unison with Your divine will. Thank You for building my memory stones and developing my faith as I draw closer to You. Give me a radical *faith, trust,* and *obedience* to You so that I may turn to You. Grow in me a heart of courage that turns to You in the face of every situation. Let my thoughts, words, and actions never cease to acknowledge and praise You as the Lord of my life. Amen.

CHAPTER THIRTEEN
MOTIVE MATTERS

Every way of a man is right in his own eyes,
but the Lord weighs the heart.
Proverbs 21:2 (ESV)

There was a food ministry that served a great need in their community. They bought food in bulk from national suppliers, packaged it in boxes, which they sold at nearly half of retail costs to a network of churches throughout the country. At the height of their ministry, they sold nearly 600,000 boxes of food per month, helping an untold number of needy families. On its face, it sounds like a brilliant plan to serve the less fortunate. Helping the poor is a fundamental aspect of our faith. In Mark 10:21, Jesus says, *"Go, sell everything you have and give to the poor, and you will have treasure in heaven. Then come, follow me."*[133]

The ministry grew from a back porch operation feeding unemployed mill workers to a $140 million a year non-profit with 300 employees. All seemed wonderful, until one day when agents of the FBI and IRS came knocking with search warrants and a forty-nine count indictment charging a variety of offenses, from fraud to money laundering. Prosecutors said the ministry founders used money from the nonprofit to buy cars, jewelry, and even a jet for personal use.

God searches the heart and
discerns the hidden motives.

While your situation may not be as stark as this one, it still brings up a powerful dilemma that many children of God find themselves. If our actions are accomplishing good in the world, do our motives actually matter?

The answer is that our motives matter a great deal to God. We all know that if we do the wrong thing, even for the right reasons, the consequences can be dire. However, often doing the right thing, for the wrong reasons produce the same results. How dire? Ask Cain and Abel.

Genesis 4 tells us the story of Cain and Abel, the two sons of Adam and Eve. Cain grew up to be a farmer and Abel a shepherd. Each brought an offering to the Lord. Cain brought the fruits of the soil, while Abel brought fat portions from some of the firstborn of his flock. Each offering was of great value. Upon receiving the two offerings God looked favorably only upon the offering of Abel. When Cain grew angry, God said to him:

"Why are you angry? Why is your face downcast? If you do what is right, will you not be accepted? But if you do not do what is right, sin is crouching at your door; it desires to have you, but you must rule over it." (Genesis 4:6-7)[134]

If both offerings were of similar value, why did God look favorably only on the offering of Abel? Motive! Cain did what was right, but he did it for the wrong motive.

Motive is something that not every person will care about. If you donate a large sum to a charity, they will likely be happy to accept the offering without concern for your motives. If you commit a crime, the judge may not care about the secret motives of your heart when he or she hands down a sentence. Your creditors probably will not care about why you maxed out all of your credit cards and now cannot pay them. Divorce attorneys don't really care about your motives for ending your marriage, unless they are applicable to the case. However, God cares about our motives very much. To God, the *why* is equal to the *what*, and the *how*. God's Word is very clear in this matter. Proverbs 21:2 says, *"A person may think their own ways are right, but the LORD weighs the heart."*[135]

How often are we guilty of doing good things, but for the wrong reasons? How often do we even examine our motives when making a decision? I believe if we examine our hearts, as God does, we will find that every single one of us has made decisions and choices that were motivated by reasons other than the service of God. How many marriages have been entered into out of a sense of debilitating obligation? How many jobs have been accepted because the money was great, not necessarily because that was the field where the Holy Spirit was leading? How much volunteer work or church service is done out of a sense of religious performance or desire for worldly praise? How many requests and invitations are accepted out of a simple desire not to hurt anyone's feelings?

"But I, the LORD, search all hearts and examine secret motives. I give all people their due rewards, according to what their actions deserve."
(Jeremiah 17:10, NLT)

Christianity is not simply a doctrine of laws and dogma. It is a real and personal relationship with the living God. I will dare to say that God does not care whether we read the New American Standard Bible, the New International Version, or the King James Version. I will also dare to ruffle some feathers by suggesting that neither does He care whether we sing from a hymnal on Sunday morning or from a big projector screen. Nor does He likely care whether we stand in prayer to Him during worship service or kneel down. The Bible isn't a social contract meant to keep us in line and make us socially responsible. God cares that we worship Him, love Him, believe Him, trust Him, follow Him, and obey Him. He cares whether we read His divinely inspired Word, feast upon it as our daily bread, and bring everything to Him.

Our lives get a lot more productive and a lot less stress-ful when we realize that we are here on the planet to do one thing and do it to the best of our ability. We are here to serve the God who created us. It really is that simple. We are created beings. Our Father created us for this time and this place for a mighty purpose in His Kingdom. The sooner we wrap our fully human minds around the need to be God-focused, instead of self-focused, the sooner we can embrace the breathtaking victory that resides in His plan.

God cares as much about why we do something as He does about what we are doing and how we are doing it.

We can spend our entire lives being bitter, angry, un-forgiving, and self-motivated. We can spend a lifetime in the wilderness, just getting by every day. However, this is not the life that our Father created us to live. We are called to be His Chosen People, His Royal Priesthood, His Holy Nation, and His beloved children. This requires a close walk with God and a spirit of sacrificial service to the One who has already sacrificed so much for us. The Apostle Paul wrote: *"I urge you, brothers and sisters, in view of God's mercy, to offer your bodies as a living sacrifice, holy and pleasing to God—this is your true and proper worship. Do not conform to the pattern of this world, but be transformed by the renewing of your mind. Then you will be able to test and approve what God's will is—his good, pleasing and perfect will"*[136] (Rom. 12:1-2).

What does this mean in our everyday lives? It means that as Christians, our worship of God does not end at the church doorsteps. Everything, from our actions and thoughts, to the words that we speak are not simply a testimony to Him, but also an act of worship to Him. They are our living sacrifice. Let that sink in for a moment. Think back over your day. Has your life been a living sacrifice?

I certainly feel the conviction of this, don't you? We all fall short of the glory of God, but that shouldn't stop us from getting up every morning and trying hard to be His beloved and anointed child. To be a living sacrifice to the Lord we love means that we must be humble and wise enough to stop and consider whether our words, thoughts, actions, and motives honor Him.

Your boss may never notice if you take a few office supplies, but God will notice. Your spouse may ignore the harsh words said during a fight, but God will hear them. You don't have to be a minister to serve God in your work, any more than you have to be a stay-at-home parent to find the time to make service to your family an act of worship to your Father. Get into the practice of running your thoughts, words, actions, and motives through the filter of one question: *Does this honor God?*

When our hearts lose their focus on God, we risk undermining our relationship with God and sabotaging our journey to our Promised Land. We also risk inviting the enemy into our lives. No matter how subtle or slowly pervasive, when our motives shift from the sacrificial service of God, to any other reason, they become debilitating.

Debilitating motives will eat away at our spiritual foundation, knock us off our anointed path, and shroud us from God's best as surely as any attack from the enemy. Shifting our motives also shifts our focus away from God, thus making it a favorite tool of the enemy. It is also an easy pit for us to fall into ourselves.

By no means is this an exhaustive list of debilitating motives. I am certain that you can add many more: guilt, obligation, worldly praise, unworthiness, people pleasing, greed, religious performance, pride, anger, desire to get even, lust, self-righteousness, or hopes of material return. Regardless of their origin, all debilitating motives have several things in common:

Debilitating Motives Are Self-Focused

The service of God means the surrender our lives to the will, plan, and purpose of God. It is to understand that we can never get from someone else what we can only get from God. It doesn't matter if that person is a spouse, pastor, friend, or even a business, a cause, or a project. God may allow some of our needs to be fulfilled by other people or things. However, He will make absolutely certain that *all* our needs will *never* be filled by them because He wants us to seek Him and only Him to fill our needs.

Take another look at the list of debilitating motives. Every one of them, from guilt, to anger, to people-pleasing, is self-focused rather than God-focused. Each one seeks to fill a need by worldly means that can only be filled by God.

Others may have greatly wronged you, and perhaps they deserve every bit of your anger and your desire for revenge, but we cannot usurp God's role. Romans 12:19 tells us to leave revenge, *"to the righteous anger of God."*[137] Revenge is not ours to take, it is God's place. Just as He promised Abraham that He would *"bless those who bless you and curse those who treat you with contempt,"*[138] He makes the same promise to us as Abraham's descendants. When we turn to God, even in our moments of frustration and anger, He will take care of the situation according to His will. When we try to take the place of God and do what only He has the authority to do, we undermine our relationship with Him and our path towards the land of His promise.

*But if we hope for what we do not
yet have, we wait for it patiently.
(Romans 8:25, NIV)*

This is also true for other debilitating emotions. We are as good at making ourselves feel guilty and obligated, as others are at trying to make us feel that way. However, His Word says clearly that there is *"no condemnation for those who belong to Christ Jesus"*[139] (Romans 8:1). By His blood, Christ rolled away our reproach and covered our sin in His sacrifice. When we continue to wear the yoke of guilt, from which He has already set us free, we are usurping the role of God and failing to make Him Lord and King.

Debilitating Motives Seek Quick Return

Over time, one of the unproductive branches that God has mercifully trimmed from me is the negative burden of impatience. Of course, the method He used to prune away this particularly fruitless stem was to make me wait, and wait, and wait. Eventually, even my hardhead accepted that while God is never in much of a hurry, He is never late. God will tell me when the timing of something is right. As His child, my job is not to try and speed up His clock, but to busy myself with His other works until He tells me when, and if, the timing is finally right.

Even a seemingly godly thing done for a reason that is not God-focused will displease the Lord and often produce negative results.

Sometimes, in our need for an immediate result, we fail to wait on God. If He doesn't respond on our very narrow timetable, we convince ourselves that He will remain silent forever, or worse, that His silence equals His approval.

How many of us are guilty of applying the culture of instant gratification to our relationship with God? Advertisers know they have an average of three seconds to grab a customer's attention. We live in a world of sound-bites and limited attention spans. The lives of many of God's children have detoured into the ditches and pits along the road because they simply did not have the patience to wait for God's perfect timing. When we fail to do so, we either miss out on His best, or we create a situation that will ultimately prove disastrous to our present and our future.

Debilitating Motives Seek Worldly Returns

If we are doing something for the expectation of worldly returns, it's a guarantee that we are not God-focused. That is not to say that worldly returns will not come. We get paid for the jobs that we do. Hopefully, our family loves and appreciates us for the time we pour into them. However, here we speak only of the reasons and motives for our choices. As followers of Christ, we are called to a spirit of sacrificial service. The First Epistle of John speaks of this truth:

> Don't love the world's ways. Don't love the world's goods. Love of the world squeezes out love for the Father. Practically everything that goes on in the world—wanting your own way, wanting everything for yourself, wanting to appear important—has nothing to do with the Father. It just isolates you from him. The world and all its wanting, wanting, wanting is on the way out—but whoever does what God wants is set for eternity. (1 John 2:15-17)[140]

Our Father is generous and loving. God desires to pour out a flood of His favor into our lives. He wants to see us fulfill our purpose and to bless us greatly in the process. However, if our hearts are focused on worldly returns, then we prevent the favor of God from entering into our lives.

Earning a good wage for the work that you do is a very good thing. However, if you are at a job only for the money, your spirit and energy will eventually shrivel, and you cannot reap the godly rewards that come from being planted in a field of God's selection. Serving your family is a godly thing, but if you do so in hopes of winning their love and affections, you will be sorely disappointed.

This is not an invitation to allow others to mistreat or abuse us. That is a recipe for misery and certainly not a reflection of godly love or victorious living. Though, there will be times when your spouse doesn't notice the kitchen is clean. There will be times when your kids will not appreciate that you have driven six hours for a softball game.

Hopefully, those around you will respect who you are, what you do, and that you are there with them. However, we must be ever mindful of the constant truth that we can never get from other people what we can only get from God. We will meet with much disappointment if we try. Our service, even to others, is a service to God. When we keep that perspective, our lives get more productive and less frustrating.

Debilitating Motives Mask the Truth

One of the most seductive aspects of debilitating motives is also one of the most dangerous and easily corruptible by the enemy. Debilitating motives often mask the truth behind the motive. Our anger and desire to get even may seem justified against someone who violated our trust or wronged us in some way. God gives us talents, so He must want us to have the praise of millions. If we are struggling financially, God will understand if we do not tithe. If we lack time in our schedule, God will understand if we never volunteer in our church or community. God gave us feelings, so it's okay if we lack the ability to control them or prevent them from ruling our life. The lies go on and on.

We have a human capacity to justify most any desire of our heart, no matter how wrong or ungodly. This ability to justify has been manipulated by the enemy to dissolve marriages, bankrupt companies, undermine churches, and sabotage the lives of so many of God's children.

Debilitating motives have another dangerous side effect. No matter how worldly justified the action may be, if our motives are debilitating rather than godly, they will always and inevitably backfire. God will make sure they backfire because He desires for us to have a heart like His.

This doesn't mean a perfect life. We all know that King David's life and choices were certainly not perfect. He sometimes wandered far from his Father's path. Still, he possessed a heart that consistently and inevitably refocused on God and His will. David had a heart *like* God because he had a heart *for* God. His heart was God-centered and God-focused. That didn't mean that he never made poor choices, mistakes, or fell short of the glory of God. David certainly did all of those things, at varying times.

Like David, we have all fallen short of God's glory many times. However, David learned from each mistake and never failed to turn to His beloved Father for redemption and a fresh start.

As long as we inhabit these fragile garments of flesh and blood, our hearts and our motives will get distracted. Our emotions will sometimes get the better of us. Other times, the enemy will temporarily win and change our focus onto something other than God. We can combat this by continually searching our motives and asking ourselves certain questions about our desires. Make your own list of questions with which to weigh your secret motivations. In the meantime, here is a good place to start:

- Is this consistent with God's Word?

- What is the Holy Spirit saying?

- Am I honoring my Father?

- Am I using God to justify a debilitating motive?

- Am I seeking something in the world that only God can provide?

- Am I usurping God's role as Lord of my life?

- Am I doing this in a spirit of turmoil/anxiety or in a spirit of peace/unison with God's will?

Until God calls us home, we will continue to live amongst the world, and have very real and earthly needs. We have bills to pay, kids to feed, taxes to file, deadlines to meet, dishes to do, dogs to walk, and meetings to attend. Jesus did not escape His earthly needs. He knew hunger. He grew tired and sleepy. He got angry. He felt pain and loneliness. He laughed. He cried. He celebrated and mourned. No doubt there were days that the hot desert sun sapped His physical energy. He was fully human and had many of the same needs and emotions we experience.

However, there is a very real difference between being *in* this world and being *of* this world. The difference between these two powerful positions is the direction of our focus. If we are in the world, yet focused on God, we become a formidable tool for God in His Kingdom. If we are focused on worldly things, no matter how grand or practical they may be, we will likely miss much of the extraordinary plans God has prepared for us. First John 2:15 says, *"Do not love the world or the things in the world. If anyone loves the world, the love of the Father is not in him."*[141]

We may stumble and fall, but if like David, we have a passionate love of our Father and a commitment to focus and refocus on Him, we can also have a heart like God.

PRAYER

Dear Lord, I seek only to serve You, know You, love You, and grow closer to You in an eternal relationship. Father, please search my heart and bring to my mind any debilitating or destructive motives that may be lurking. Please help me cast them out so that my heart may turn ever more to You and be transformed into a heart like Yours. Thank You for all that You do in my life. Amen.

CHAPTER FOURTEEN

EVEN THOUGH THE RIGHTEOUS MAY FALL

"...though the righteous fall seven times, they rise again..."
Proverbs 24:16 (NIV)

I recently read a story involving a twenty-some-thing job-seeker, and the CEO of a local job bank. The young job-seeker sent a friend-request to the CEO on a major professional networking website. They did not know each other and had never worked together. The job-seeker was attempting to build connections in hopes of landing a new job. This, as many people know, is a major no-no on certain social media sites. The CEO, who had nearly a thousand contacts, could have declined the invite or simply ignored the request. Instead, the CEO opted to email a lengthy, and many say hateful, critique of the twenty-something's lack of networking skills, and de-manded that the job-seeker never make contact again.

The young job-seeker responded by posting the email on several other social media sites, where it went viral. The CEO lost her job. Her reputation, built on helping people find work, was in a shambles. The networking contacts that she was trying so hard to build and protect were made useless within a matter of days.

The Word became flesh and made his dwelling among us. We have seen his glory, the glory of the one and only Son, who came from the Father, full of grace and truth. (John 1:14, NIV)

We all make thousands of decisions every day. Some of them are faulty and some are wise. However, precious few do we get to take back. *Do I have cereal or eggs for breakfast? Do I return this phone call or that one? Do I have one more drink? Do I return the flirtation of that cute stranger at the hotel bar?* The stories come in every shape and size. Some of them are mild and some will break your heart. Most begin cushioned inside the insidious normality of everyday life.

Sweeping across the cities of Europe, the plains of Africa, the deserts of the Middle East, and the small towns of the United States, there are many things that link us together as fellow travelers in God's remarkable creation of humankind. One of these threads that twine through every person who has ever lived, save for Christ Jesus. It is our propensity to use our free-will to make some really foolish, and sometimes stupid, decisions.

There may be more tactful ways to say it, but none as accurate. Even the wisest, most faithful, and most prudent among us still occasionally make really bad decisions. Some of them are small and easily recoverable. Some of them are painful and staggeringly life altering. Your intelligence, accomplishments, and seemingly put together life will not spare you from the occasional curse of bad judgment. If it has not touched your life, don't worry your time is coming. No one gets out of this life unscathed!

When we accept Christ as Savior, and invite the Holy Spirit to dwell inside us, our hope is that eventually, we will be filled with more of God and less of ourselves.

Scripture says that the Holy Spirit acts as our advocate, teacher, helper, and counselor. I don't know about you, but for most of the stupidest things I have ever done, there has been a voice in the back of my head that advised me against the bad decision. I ignored that wise counsel. God was guiding me in one direction, and I chose to ignore Him and go my own way. I may have had the *faith*, but not the *trust*, and certainly not the *obedience*.

The only person who can prevent you from reaching your God anointed destiny is you. The only person who can keep you from your Promised Land is you. The enemy can throw stones. He can whisper into your ear. He may try to lure and tempt you. However, the only person who can stand in the way of the mighty future that God wants for you…is *you*.

Sometimes, our mistakes carry with them consequences of staggering magnitude that will cost much in time, money, and willpower to make right. If you make a lousy investment, you may lose money. If you allow that one night's flirtation to go too far, you will end up spending far more time repairing your fractured marriage than the time you spent enjoying the encounter. If you get behind the wheel of a car after too many drinks, at minimum, reality will likely introduce you to the hospitality of the county jail, right before you wave goodbye to large chunks of money and your driver's license. King David learned firsthand the cost of terrible mistakes.

Trust in the LORD with all your heart and lean not on your own understanding; in all your ways submit to him, and he will make your paths straight. (Proverbs 3:5-6, NIV)

Arguably, there is no one in the entire Bible that was as blessed with God's anointing, and as guilty of bad decisions as David. Yet, in the entirety of His Word, God only referred to one person as a *"man after my own heart"*[142] *(Acts 13:22).* It was David. God handpicked the boy to succeed Saul as King of Israel. As David grew older, he carried with him the knowledge that he was God's chosen King.

Eventually, King Saul died, and David was crowned. King David united of the tribes, brought Israel and Judea together into one kingdom, defeated their enemies, and brought peace and prosperity throughout the land. He also brought the Ark of the Covenant to Jerusalem, and planned the first Temple. By any stretch of the imagination, he was a great King. He was the king of God's own selection. Ultimately, God would cut a Covenant with David.

*Our worst mistake is not
the end of our walk with God.*

Though, he was a great man in his public role, he made some horrible decisions in his personal life. He lusted after the wife of another man. Bathsheba was the wife of Uriah, a soldier in King David's army. Eventually, David committed adultery with Bathsheba and they conceived a child. David first schemed to manipulate Uriah into thinking that he was the father of Bathsheba's baby. When that failed, he sent him to the front lines to be killed. One of David's sons, Amnon, raped his own sister, Tamar. Amnon was later killed by his brother, Absolom. In rebellion, Absolom would later die trying to kill, David, his father.

David's decisions cost him dearly and he buried Amnon, Absolom, and the son he conceived with Bathsheba. God convicted the king through His Prophet Nathan: *"This is what the LORD, the God of Israel, says: 'I anointed you king over Israel, and I delivered you from the hand of Saul. I gave your master's house to you, and your master's wives into your arms. I gave you all Israel and Judah. And if all this had been too little, I would have given you even more. Why did you despise the word of the LORD by doing what is evil in his eyes?'"*[143] (2 Samuel 12:7-9)

Yet, this wasn't the end of David's story. He went on to marry Bathsheba, who he loved. She gave birth to another son, Solomon, who the Lord loved. King Solomon would succeed his father and become known, throughout eternity, for his wisdom and stewardship. King David would rule the united kingdom of Israel and Judea, until he was a very old man.

God would later praise David to King Solomon, saying: *"As for you, if you walk before me faithfully with integrity of heart and uprightness, as David your father did, and do all I command and observe my decrees and laws, I will establish your royal throne over Israel forever, as I promised David your father when I said, 'You shall never fail to have a successor on the throne of Israel"*[144] *(1 Kings 9:4-5).*

David's story did not end at his affair. It did not end at the murder of Uriah. It did not even end with the deaths of his sons. David's story did not end as a cautionary tale. How can it be that a man who had sinned so gravely, would later have God say of him that he had followed the Lord *"faithfully with integrity"*?[145] God knew David's heart. After all, it was a heart like God's own. David's heart not only turned towards God, but also towards His divine plan. The Amplified Bible translates Acts 13:22 this way:

> *"He bore witness and said, I have found David son of Jesse a man after My own heart, who will do all My will and carry out My program fully."*[146]

We can't fix bad decisions. Once an action is taken - good or bad - it can't be erased. We don't get to go back and change the past, or erase what has been done. We only get to decide what to do next. In Psalm 51, we hear the pain that David is pouring out to God. In his heartfelt repentance, we have guidance for reconciling ourselves to God after our own transgressions. We also see just how we can acquire a heart like that of our God. We do so by developing a heart that consistently turns toward God.

David Poured Out His Pain to God with Absolute and Raw Honesty

No matter how much pain a bad decision has caused those around us, it has also hurt us deeply as well. Our pain gets lost in the aftermath and the rubble. Those we have hurt have little time for our pain, and others have little concern. Still, the wounds we have inflicted on our own heart must be acknowledged and healed, or they will develop into deeper wounds. These wounds will ultimately transform into the bondage of unworthiness, shame, and self-defeat that will only lead us further away from God.

The pain we carry may have been inflicted recently or long ago. Its source could be external, or it could have been our own destructive natures. Regardless, hanging on to pain, even self-inflicted pain, does nothing to redeem us, or atone for our mistakes. However, it does numb the heart. If carried long enough, it will also harden our hearts. The Apostle Paul warned us about the dangers of a hardened heart in Ephesians 4:18: *"They are darkened in their understanding, alienated from the life of God because of the ignorance that is in them, due to their hardness of heart."*[147]

By its very nature, a hardened heart is alienated from God, blind to His glories, and separated from His miraculous healing. Only God can make us whole, but to receive that great healing requires a heart open to His healing love.

David Acknowledged His Transgression and the Severity of His Sin to God

How often have we heard others acknowledge what they did was wrong, but attempt to mitigate its severity, or offer justification and excuses? At one time or another, we have all offered excuses and justifications to ourselves or others. While it may be a common experience, there is no mistaking the pit that lies at the end of this path.

If we do not understand the severity of our actions, and acknowledge that understanding with the power of words, we have no hope of reconciling ourselves to God, receiving His forgiveness, redemption, and a fresh start. Without God's grace, we have no hope of reconciling ourselves to those whom we have hurt. Equally as important, we have no hope of being healed.

It is an overused cliché that *'hurting people, hurt people.'* It is overused because it is true. Most bad decisions come out of a separation from God. Hurt, fear, and shame often lie at the center of that separation. Before we can promise, with any conviction, to walk the path that God alone can make straight, our hearts must be healed. Before that healing can take place, our sin must be pulled out like a splinter. Only then can it be sat in the bright sunlight of God's mercy so that it has no power over our hearts or futures.

David Acknowledged That His Actions Were Undeserving of Forgiveness, but Could Only Be Reconciled By the Grace of God

If justice is receiving what we deserve, then mercy can be said to mean *not* receiving what we rightly deserve. Grace then might be described as *receiving* what we *do not* deserve. Not a single one of us are deserving of God's grace. Like His love, His grace is something that He freely bestows upon us as a gift. The grace of God cannot be earned. It is an extension of His love for us as His children, and from His grace flow every good and godly thing.

Through our Lord Jesus Chris we have "obtained access by faith into this grace in which we stand"[148] *(Romans 5:2)*. Grace is more than a perfunctory religious word tossed around in church. It is a condition of life as a redeemed child of God and a transformative force that bestows upon us the power to live out the new life we have been given.

If you are still living and breathing, then you are a member of the vast club of humanity that can honestly attest to being alive only by the grace of God. We depend on God's grace every single day. The Apostle Paul discussed the difference between justice and the grace of God when he penned Romans 6:23:

Romans 6:23 with key Greek transliterated words:
For the wages (*Opsōnia*) of sin (*Hamartia*) is death (*Thanatos*); but the gift (*Charisma*) of God is eternal (*Aiónios*) life (*Zoe*) through Jesus Christ our Lord.[149]

According to theologian William Barclay the word *Opsōnia* is a military term also used to mean the salary of a solider. "That is to say, if we had got the pay we earned, it would have been death," Barclay said in his book, *'New Testament Words'*. "Now *charisma* also is a military word. When an emperor came to the throne, or when he was celebrating his birthday, he gave his troops a *donativum* or *charisma*, which was a free grant of money, a free gift. They had not earned it as they had their *opsōnia*; they got it unearned out of the goodness of the emperor's heart."[150]

Thanatos is defined as "that separation…of the soul and the body by which the life on earth is ended."[151] The Greek word *aiónios* means "eternal, for ever, everlasting, world (began)."[152] *Zoe* is a word that means "the absolute fulness of life, both essential and ethical."[153]

God's gift of grace saves us from the death we have rightly earned, and delivers us into eternal and everlasting life. There is a reason that we never pray for God's justice, He just might decide to answer our prayers. At one time or another, we have all disobeyed God. We are all guilty of having made bad decisions. We are all deserving of God's justice. Despite this, God remains our loving Father. Like a loving human father, God may convict us of our wrong. He may impose the consequences of our behavior so that we learn valuable lessons. However, He will never stop loving us. It is out of the love only the Father can bestow, that He meets us with grace instead of justice. Like all gifts, we must receive God's gift of grace with a humble and appreciative spirit and a rejoicing heart.

David Asked For Mercy

God knows what is in our hearts. He walks before us and knows every step our feet will take. He knows the desires of our heart. He knows the needs of our present and our future. He knows all of this without a word ever leaving our lips. He knows our needs, even if we cannot form the words to express them. However, like any parent, God wants His children to come to Him and share our hearts openly. He wants us to ask. He doesn't want us to merely assume that because He knows our needs He will provide.

To receive our Father's forgiveness, all we need is to ask. If we pour out our true and repentant sorrow to God, He will not only forgive us, but He will also purify us of all unrighteousness, and grant us a fresh start. Though, first we must come to Him with everything. There is nothing that we can keep hidden or unspoken to God. We must come as we are, in all our messiness, and give it all to Him.

We serve a big God. We are children of the same God who created Heaven and Earth. Nothing is too big for us to bring to our *Abba*. He forgave David, who committed adultery and murder. He forgave Moses, who killed an Egyptian guard. He forgave Jacob, who deceived. God's love for us is so enormous that His only beloved Son came to die for us, even while we were still sinners *(Romans 5:8)*. The entire New Testament testifies to God's boundless love and remarkable mercy. We simply do not have the ability to out-sin our Father's ability to love and forgive, if only we come to Him, pour out our sorrow, and ask for His mercy.

God wants His children to come home. In whatever state we are in, with whatever burdens we carry, with whatever sin and wrongdoing that is in our past or our present, He wants us to come home to Him. Our Father can make a masterpiece out of a broken heart, if only we give Him all the pieces. Sweep up the shattered fragments of your life, your heart, your choices, and the rubble that you have left in your path. Bring every bit of it to the One who has the power to heal, redeem, and wash you clean.

We know that in all things *"God causes everything to work together for the good of those who love God and are called according to his purpose"*[154] *(Romans 8:28)*. However, for a variety of very individual reasons, there are some people who do not feel as though His words speak to their heart. It is possible for even the most faithful child of God to come to a place so bleak and painful that they can no longer hear their Father speaking into their life.

Sometimes, when we dwell in misery and pain, we simply do not hear when God speaks. Some people feel all alone in their sorrow, shame, and misery. Others come to feel that they have dug themselves into a pit so deep there is no way out, and not even God can hear their screams.

These are lies from the pit of hell. God is listening. He is speaking. Only He can heal your hurts and permanently lift you out of that pit. Call out to Him. Be willing to hear His voice, and receive His mercy. Isaiah 41:10 says, *"'Do not fear, for I am with you; Do not anxiously look about you, for I am your God. I will strengthen you, surely I will help you, Surely I will uphold you with My righteous right hand.'"*[155]

He wants us to talk to Him and willingly share our hearts with Him like a child coming home. If we want God's mercy and His grace we need to open our mouth and ask. If we want to be lifted out of the pit of our own making, then we need to call out to God and be willing to take His hand. If our desire is truly to be healed, forgiven, and made righteous again before God, then we must open our mouth and say, *'Have mercy on me, O Lord.'*

David Offered No Excuses

We often make the mistake of offering God excuses and justifications instead of our heartfelt honesty and repentance. An excuse or even a list of semi-valid reasons only serves to distance us from the severity of our actions. It reflects a heart that does not fully accept the seriousness of the transgression. How can God ultimately forgive us for something that we don't truly believe is entirely in need of forgiving? It also signifies that we are still trying to justify ourselves when only Christ Jesus can justify us.

God is not interested in our reasons, excuses, or justifications. He is only interested in our sincere and heartfelt acknowledgment of our actions, and our desire to repent. God already knows the content of our heart, but He still wants us to bring it to Him. It is our heart, not our well put together defense, that He is interested in hearing.

In 1 John 2:1, the Apostle John expresses his hope that believers should live without sin. However, if we do sin *"we have an advocate with the Father—Jesus Christ, the Righteous One."*[156]

In its original Greek, the word advocate is *paraklétos*. According to Strong's Exhaustive Concordance it means *"an intercessor,* consoler: - advocate, comforter."[157] In secular Greek, this word is often used to represent a legal advisor or advocate in court. In modern terms, this person could be thought of as a defense attorney. Jesus is our advocate! He is our defense attorney! Alleluia! Though, we have made many mistakes, and should rightly receive judgment and conviction, Christ pleads our case to the Father.

We serve a forgiving Lord, but we must follow David's example. Fall down before our Father, pour out our heart, repent of our sins, and ask for His forgiveness.

There is no better defense than the one provided by the beloved Son of God! By His blood, we are washed clean. He lived the life we could not live, and died the death we should have surely suffered. He did it all so that we could be made righteous in the eyes of our Father. Our Salvation requires our honest acknowledgment that we are unworthy to receive it.

Go to your *Abba.* Pour out your pain and repentance. Offer up no excuse or justification. Ask for His grace, mercy, and divine healing. Rest in the certainty of this truth: *"If we confess our sins, he is faithful and just and will forgive us our sins and purify us from all unrighteousness."*[158] (1 John 1:9)

David Expressed a Sincere Desire to Reform

If we have no true and heartfelt desire to change our behavior, then our words to God are empty shells. Only when our heartfelt sorrow is coupled with our sincere desire to change, will God pour out His grace into our lives. Like any parent, God's desire for His children is that we learn and grow into better and more faithful people.

For God to forgive us, we must be ready to receive forgiveness and believe we are worthy of redemption.

He desires that we grow from spiritual infancy into godly adults *(1 Corinthians 3)*. After the Israelites had wandered in the wilderness for forty years, God brought the second generation through the waters to Gilgal just in time to celebrate the Passover. This was the first time that they had celebrated the Passover in an area of the Promised Land. God had brought them full circle, back to the place where their parents had refused to venture. Their Father gave His Chosen People a second chance to get it right.

We all need second, third, and even fourth chances. God will continue to bring His children full circle until we learn the lessons He is trying to teach. We must be willing and ready to learn, and absorb His teaching. We must trade our ways for His ways. Only then, can we move forward on our anointed path and out of the wilderness.

David Had a Sincere Desire to Turn His Troubles into His Testimony

God lets nothing go to waste, not our victories, not our pain, not even our worst decisions. God uses everything for our good *(Romans 8:28)*. He is constantly at work in us and around us. He is continually preparing us for the next phase of our anointing.

When He breathed life into the universe and spoke mankind into existence, He gave us free-will. God walks before us, and He knows that sometimes we will use that free-will to make mistakes, defy Him, and rebel out of our lack of *faith, trust,* and *obedience.* Like any parent, if we are determined in our rebellion there will be times when He will get out of our way and let us learn the hard way. Our Father will still be there to help us pick up the pieces, if we ask, but He won't stop us from making the mistake.

As Christians, one of our directives from Christ Jesus is to go forth and spread the Good News of God to the world. Sometimes, out of the greatest negativity, and the greatest mistakes, comes our greatest testimony. Sometimes, it is our greatest failings and God's great love that brings forth our greatest opportunity to shower upon others the love and the grace that He first poured into us.

The nation of Israel doubted God many times before He finally spoke the condemnation found in Numbers 14. Proverbs 24:16 tells us that *"though the righteous fall seven times, they rise again."*[159] We have something the Israelites in the wilderness did not possess. We have God's saving grace poured out through the blood of our Savior, Christ Jesus. Praise God! It is the greatest gift God has ever bestowed upon mankind.

God's grace is a powerful blessing. The worst mistake that we ever make is not necessarily the end of our story. No one – not a single one of us – is defined by the stupidest thing that we have ever done. There is no uniqueness, no scandalous reality that differentiates our version of *stupid*, from that of the mass of humanity that has gone before us. As we stand at the crossroads of bad decisions, our futures are defined less by what has happened, and more by what we decide to do next. We will not escape the consequences of our decisions, good or bad. The first generation of Israelites to come out of Egypt paid for their lack of faith and trust in God by forsaking their right to the Promised Land. That is a mighty steep price to pay. Though, God also cares what is in our hearts. For those who love Him, who pursue Him, who believe Him, and who trust Him, the grace we can and will receive from Him is boundless and powerful.

So after your misstep, what is your next step? Are you going to crawl into a corner and hide from the light of day? Are you going to lie and hope no one asks too many questions? Are you going to cast yourself in the role of victim and ask the rest of the world for pity? Or are you responsible enough to accept the consequences? Are you honorable enough to attempt to put right what you made wrong? Are you wise enough to learn from the experience? Do you have enough strength to steadfastly refuse to allow your future to be shaped by your past? Are you going to pick yourself up, rely on yourself, and allow your heart to harden? Or are you going to fall down before God, pour out your heart to your Father, and cry out, *"Have mercy on me, O God, according to your unfailing love; according to your great compassion blot out my transgressions. Wash away all my iniquity and cleanse me from my sin"*[160] *(Psalm 51:1-2).*

PRAYER

Let us pray the words of King David found in…
Psalm 51:1-13

CHAPTER FIFTEEN

BREAKING THE CYCLE OF CIRCLES

The wind blows toward the south and
shifts toward the north. Round and round it
blows. It blows in a full circle.
Ecclesiastes 1:6 (GW)

*H*ave you ever felt stuck, in the same place, doing the same thing, and feeling the same way? No matter how far you walk, how hard you push, or how much you try, you just keep coming back to the same place. It may be different scenery, but you sure feel like you've gone around in circles, often in places you would prefer to have escaped long ago. Consider for a moment that this is not a figment of your imagination, and that you are, indeed, wandering in circles.

God not only tests us, but He brings us back around to the place of our testing until we pass. He will often bring us back around until we pass with honors. He will not allow us to break the cycle of certain seasons until we have fully learned, understood, and digested the lesson He is teaching. With each lesson we gain a tool that will help us in the next portion of our walk with Him. Sometimes, He will even bring us full circle to show us how far we have come in our journey.

Salvation may be instant, but a converted heart takes time to grow. When we accept Christ as our Savior and set our lives to follow after God, our eternal life has been secured. However, our emotions sometimes take time to catch up. Our mind may understand that we have become a beloved child of God, chosen, adopted, redeemed, anointed, and blessed. However, an intellectual *faith* and a converted heart are two very different things.

Blessed is the one who perseveres under trial because, having stood the test, that person will receive the crown of life that the Lord has promised to those who love him. (James 1:12, NIV)

Logically, we know that God has not brought us this far just to leave us now. We know in our minds that He is a faithful God. Yet, we grow so frightened when we are unsure of what to expect that we doubt God and turn back to our old ways that are comfortable and familiar. We return to the bondage from which God has already freed us. At least it is an existence that we know.

If we can look at the path of our life from the air, we would likely see that it forms more of a spiral towards a destination than a straight line. If you live long enough, you will come full circle. The scenery may be different, but the circumstances will be déjà vu. The cycles of our lives that keep repeating are not simply coincidence. Just as in His Word, that, which is repeated is important.

This resurrection life you received from God is not a timid, grave-tending life. It's adventurously expectant, greeting God with a childlike "What's next, Papa?" God's Spirit touches our spirits and confirms who we really are. We know who he is, and we know who we are: Father and children. And we know we are going to get what's coming to us—an unbelievable inheritance! We go through exactly what Christ goes through. If we go through the hard times with him, then we're certainly going to go through the good times with him! (Romans 8:15-17, MSG)

What has been your circle? Perhaps your circle is defeat, addiction, self-destruction, unworthiness, abandonment, sexual sin, abuse, or fear. How many times have you been pulled back into your old bondage? How many times have you cried out to God from the pit of your own creation?

We all stumble. We all fall. We all come full circle in one aspect or another. Inevitably, we have all cried out to our Father to save us from a pit. Some pits we may have dug ourselves. Some have been dug by other people who pushed us into them. Some pits may have been there all along, hidden by debris until we accidentally tumbled into their darkness. Regardless of how we arrived at the bottom of our pit, only God can permanently lift us out.

His love for us is as boundless as it is stubborn. If our heart is sincere He will lift us back onto solid ground. He wants His children to be close to Him. He wants us to stand firm on solid ground and walk proudly into our Promised Land. The path to get there may be short or it may take a lifetime. It mostly depends on us.

God's Word says that it is through testing that we are made, *"mature and complete, not lacking anything"*[161] *(James 1:4)*. God tested Abraham when He commanded him to sacrifice Isaac, the son given to him by God *(Genesis 22)*. God tested Joshua and the Israelites at Gigal when He commanded them to circumcise the sons of Israel before entering the Promised Land *(Joshua 5)*. God even tested Jesus by sending Him into the wilderness to be tempted by Satan before Jesus set out in ministry *(Matthew 4)*.

Abraham is the father of God's Chosen People. Joshua is the mighty warrior who conquered the Promised Land. Jesus is Lord and Savior. You cannot find three more important men in all of history or three more important God anointed purposes. God tested each of them in different ways and He did so just before sending them on a mighty segment of their walk with Him.

Jesus is the Son of God. Abraham and Joshua were chosen by God. Of course, our Lord could anoint and bless them, but how could anoint lives as broken as ours?

Even in our brokenness, we are His beloved children. First Peter 2:9 says that we are, *"a chosen people, a royal priesthood, a holy nation, God's special possession."*[162] Romans 8:17 says that we are, *"heirs of God and co-heirs with Christ."*[163] As His children, we also have a special anointing. Even before He created the earth, God knew that He would one day create you to fulfill a great and mighty purpose.

God will allow us to be tested and tempted in order to teach us. He does this not to find fault, but to perfect us and make us complete in Him. Through this refining, He is producing the abundant *faith, trust,* and *obedience* that is necessary to walk our anointed path. There are many reasons why God will bring us full circle. We will examine several of them in the coming pages. Whatever the reason or the method of refinement, God's goal is to bring us closer to Him. When our spirit touches the Spirit of God, and we rest confidently in our position as His beloved and fearfully made child, our *faith, trust,* and *obedience* is free to pour out of us. It produces a real and tangible earthly inheritance that cannot be matched this side of Heaven.

To Give Us a Second Chance

God brought the Israelites full circle to Gilgal. Though, this was the second generation out of Egypt, they certainly would have heard the stories their parents told. Some may even have been old enough to remember their escape from the Egyptian army, and that glorious moment when Moses raised his hand over the Red Sea and the Lord parted the waters before them so they could cross on dry ground.

We know that the Israelites had spent forty years in the wilderness because of their repeated refusal to trust and obey the Lord *(Numbers 14)*. Now God had brought the children of this first generation to the banks of the flooded Jordan River, where He held back the raging water so they could also cross on dry ground. There was no misunderstanding that God had brought them full circle. He was giving them a second chance to pass the test. In this case, the lesson to be learned, and the test being given, was one of trust and obedience.

Blessed is the one who perseveres under trial because, having stood the test, that person will receive the crown of life that the Lord has promised to those who love him. (James 1:12, NIV)

God instructed their leader, Joshua, to renew the Covenant of Circumcision. Rather than responding with doubt, this generation responded to God with radical *faith, trust,* and *obedience.* They circumcised all of the males of the nation. It had taken forty years in the desert before their mind caught up to the freedom of their soul. How long will it take our minds to catch up to the radical freedom in Christ that we are offered as a *charisma,* a free and unearned gift?

How long have you wandered in the wilderness, for no other reason than you simply cannot fathom the enormous favor that He is offering you in the land of His promise? How long will it take to cast aside the worry it will all go horribly wrong, and simply decide to trust that your Father has the situation handled? How long will it take for you to not only believe *in* Him, but also to *believe Him*?

God has performed monumental signs right in front of us. He has allowed us to bear witness to His magnificent glory. We can look back on our lives and see His real and active presence. Yet, when He brings us to the edge of His magnificent promise, a land flowing with milk and honey that is offered just to us, our minds cannot comprehend the enormity of the blessing.

Instead, our imaginations begin to dream up all that could possibly go wrong. We long for the familiarity of our tiny cell because the vastness of His promise is simply too frightening to comprehend. Instead of believing in God and His better plans that lead to abundance and victory, we long for the mediocrity of the desert.

Recently, I picked up a bake-at-home pizza from a local store. The nice young man behind the counter said they were running a special. I could add a whole container of cookie dough for only a dollar. Did I want the special? That's a silly question. It's a pound of fresh-made chocolate chip cookie dough for a dollar! Of course I want it! As he was ringing up my order, he told me that a surprising number of people actually turn down this deal. Who could turn down such a special offering?

How many of us give a similar response to God when He's offering us a special blessing prepared especially for us? The word '*no*' is so readily on our lips that it's often the very first word out of our mouth, even when we are being offered something wonderful. Our mind instantly looks for the catch, the downside, or the negative possibilities. Whether it is a pound of fresh-made cookie dough, or the land of God's promise, our first response is to say *'no'*.

It takes time for our mind to catch up to the enormous freedom and favor of God. Until then, we will be missing out on God's specially made joys and limitless blessings.

To Roll Away Our Reproach

God has great and mighty gifts that He wants to bestow upon his children, but He first needs us to be in a posture to receive the blessing. Have you ever been excited to give your child a brand new toy, but you wanted to first make sure they could receive the gift with a humble spirit?

In the Book of Joshua we see that God had very specific gifts in store for His Chosen People. He wanted to take away their shame. He wanted to help them claim the land of His promise, to bless them, and allow them to prosper in the land of abundance. However, He needed them to be in the right frame of mind to receive that gift. He needed them to appreciate the utter enormity of His offering and respond with *faith, trust,* and *obedience* so that they could maintain these precious gifts.

The first generation out of Egypt simply could not, or would not, receive His blessings. So God led them back through the wilderness until their children had come full circle. God gave the Israelites a do-over. Again, He asked for their *faith, trust,* and *obedience.* This time they obeyed without hesitation. Thus, God was able to bless them with a most special gift. He rolled away the reproach of Egypt from their lives *(Joshua 5:9)*.

He removed from them the shame and stigma of their captivity. He healed their hearts and lifted them from the pit of lingering negativity, helplessness, unworthiness, and humiliation associated with the bondage from which He had already set them free. Their minds had finally caught up to their souls. Their faith had gone from a mere hope in things unseen, to an absolute certainty in the only true and living God. When they were finally healed, they were ready to enter Canaan and take up the next phase of their walk with God.

It doesn't matter the pit from which God rescued us. It doesn't matter what individual sin, bondage, or shame from which He has freed us. Even though we may have stepped out of our shackles and breathed the fresh air of God's freedom, we still have lingering negativity clinging to us like bits of dryer lint and static cling. No one else may notice, but they will surely notice as we continue to stare at it, pick at it, and brush it off as though we have a nervous twitch. No matter how otherwise flawless we appear our mind is still focused on little bits of stuff still clinging to us.

No matter how far we have come in our minds, we are still the alcoholic who lost their home, the divorcee who couldn't keep their family together, the sexually promiscuous teen who slept with half the town, or the abuse victim who couldn't protect themselves. We still dwell in the past and use it as an anchor to hold us down. We use it because it is familiar. God wants to roll away every single bit of lingering negativity, stigma, and shame left over from your past. He wants to help your mind catch up to the radical freedom and abundant victory that is found only in Him.

To Show Us How Far We Have Come

In the course of our busy lives, we can often forget how far our journey of faith has come. So God will sometimes bring us full circle not to heal or refine us, but to show us just how far we have traveled in our walk with Him.

There was a godly woman who was a member of her local ministry. To know her now, you would never believe she had survived a past of childhood abuse, poverty, rebellion, sexual sin, and addiction. She dwelled in its defeat because it was all she knew. God lifted her from the pits of her own making and freed her from the captivity of her past. He brought her around in so many circles I am sure her path looked like a spiral ride at an amusement park. God just kept parting her waters and bringing her back to her Gilgal, until it finally clicked, and her mind caught up to her soul. With that, God rolled away every reproach of her past. He brought her into her Promised Land and ever since, He has poured onto her a flood of His favor. She wasn't just surviving anymore. She was thriving.

One day, she was approached about heading a new ministry outreach program that was starting in the very same neighborhood where her brokenness began. She thought that perhaps God was trying to teach her something new. She was nervous and in her anxiety she doubted that she was capable of carrying out this particular anointing. However, her faith and trust in her Father, who had brought her so far, was strong. Thus, she obeyed.

As she began this new phase of her walk with God, she didn't know what to expect. She prayed for the strength not to be pulled back into the life of bondage from which she was already freed.

We long for the familiarity of our tiny cell because the vastness of His promise is simply too frightening to comprehend

---

As she began her work with the new program, one day became two and before she knew it three months had passed. She had visited the dilapidated old apartment where she grew up. She had visited the places where she used to do drugs, and seen many of the old friends and neighbors that she used to get into trouble with as an adolescent. Finally, one day the revelation struck her like a lightning bolt from the sky. There was no danger of being pulled back into that old life. The experiences remained, but they helped build the woman she was today.

God had long since healed the brokenness and rolled away the shame of her past. He had long ago brought her out of her Egypt. He had so well prepared her that she could return to that land, not as a fugitive, but as an anointed child of God, and stare into the face of Pharaoh unafraid. God had not brought her back to test her, but to show her just how far she had come.

To Be a Testimony

D. T. Niles described Christianity as *"one beggar telling another beggar where he found the bread."* I can think of no better description, can you? One of the most important directives we have in our walk with God is to share our testimony with those we meet along the way. Jesus directed His disciples to spread the Good News of God throughout the world. As New Testament believers, we are also disciples of Christ Jesus. We share the same responsibility to let others know where we have found our daily bread. Acts 22:15 says: *"For you are to be his witness, telling everyone what you have seen and heard."*[164]

What does it mean to be a witness and to give testimony? Merriam-Webster Dictionary gives this definition:

> **Witness**: "a person who is present at an event (such as a wedding) and can say that it happened"[165]

> **Testimony**: "proof or evidence that something exists or is true"[166]

Faith may not be defined under a microscope, but for the men and women who are secure in their place as children of God, who know who He is, and who we are in Him, God is very much seen and known. He is not a distant presence. He is real, and alive, and active in our lives. When we listen and watch with an expectant heart, we can see and hear Him almost every single day. We are a witness to His active intervention in our lives and those around us. Our testimony is evidence of His presence.

Hopefully, you have spent some time looking back along the paths, curves, and spirals of your life, and have seen how far you have come. You have made note of all the times that God's presence was real, active, and tangible. You have recorded all the times when He lifted you from a pit, built your memory stones, or spoke into your life. Whether your walk with Him has been long or short, you have them. You have borne witness to God's work in the world. You have been present at the event. You can say that it happened. Your words are proof of the existence of God. Acts 1:8 says that, *"you will receive power when the Holy Spirit comes on you; and you will be my witnesses in Jerusalem, and in all Judea and Samaria, and to the ends of the earth."*[167]

Our lives can often be our greatest testimony to the glory and grace we have found in our God.

In her work with the new intercity ministry that godly woman had found another opportunity to serve the Lord. She shared her testimony of His real, tangible, and active presence. Her life was a testimony of God's redemptive power. She knew the bondage that existed in her neighborhood. God had freed her from that very same bondage. He had guided her path out of Egypt, healed her wounds, fed her, tested and refined her, and removed the shame of her past. Then, when she least expected it, He led her back into her Egypt so that others could see the light of God.

Not everyone is called to evangelize, but everyone can simply share their story with others. Sometimes, that is all God is asking us to do. Sometimes, the entire reason that He has brought us full circle is to share our story of His real, tangible, and active presence in our lives.

Our words are not the only way in which we can offer testimony to the glory of God revealed. Scripture makes clear that it's often our actions that provide our most powerful testimony to the world. Matthew 5:14-16 say: *"You are the light of the world. A city set on a hill cannot be hidden. Nor do people light a lamp and put it under a basket, but on a stand, and it gives light to all in the house. In the same way, let your light shine before others, so that they may see your good works and give glory to your Father who is in heaven."*[168]

Step out from under that basket. Put the light of God that shines through you, on a stand for the entire world to see. As you go about your day, be mindful that you are a walking, talking testimony. His seal is emblazoned on your head with anointing oil. You are a representative to everyone you encounter (family and stranger alike) to the power, grace, love, abundance, and redemption that can only be found at the foot of the Cross. There are folks who may never pick up a Bible, but they will come to know God through your words and actions.

If you choose to be mean, angry, and spiteful, then that is how others may come to see your Father. You are His ambassador to the world. Your words and actions directly help form the world's impressions of your God. How do you want to represent the One True Living God?

It's a big responsibility, but your Father will be right there with you. His Spirit is already inside you, providing guidance and counsel. Allow God's light to shine through your fragile earthen vessel. Allow Him to guide your words, actions, thoughts, and decisions so you can live in glorious alignment with His heart and His will. Make this a part of your daily prayer life.

God did not create you to sit under a basket and hide from the world. He created you to shine brightly with His light. Our Father is constant and unchanging. His light does not alter based on your circumstances.

It is illegal to practice Christianity in North Korea. It's a death penalty crime to preach the Gospel or even possess a Bible. Often Christians are placed in forced labor camps. Many die from hunger, disease, or heavy burden. Others are executed. However, their captors have learned that they must separate Christians from non-Christians, because the light that shines through these Christian martyrs, even as they bear the burdens of heavy labor and death, often cause even more conversions within the camps.

Think about it for a moment. The way in which these children of God live their lives, offers such testimony to the presence of God that others come to know Him through them. Even in the midst of such great suffering, their lives provide a light to the world. No matter what their captors may try, these brave men and women are a city set upon a hill that simply cannot be hidden.

In a constantly changing world, ours is a God that has been constant and unchanging since before the creation of time. He was the same yesterday, as He is today, and will be tomorrow. So is His light. The light of God that shines through the fragile earthen vessels of our lives is also powerful and unchanging. It does not diminish or alter depending on our mood or circumstance.

The world will come to know our Father, in part, through the living testimony of our lives. So, what is stopping you from being a light on a stand for the entire world to see the presence of God?

Whether you are ready to share all or part of your story with others, there is nothing stopping you from allowing God's light to shine through your life so that others, *"may see your good works and give glory to your Father who is in heaven"*[169] *(v. 16)*. As God's children, shouldn't that be one of our greatest daily goals?

What glory would be provided to the Kingdom of God if every single day, each and every one of us set a goal to find just one person or situation in the course of our day to bless! It doesn't have to be big or grand. Blessing someone could take the form of holding open a door, paying for a stranger's coffee, checking in on an elderly neighbor, or kind words to a passing stranger. We can all find small ways in the course of our day to allow our lives to be a testimony of God's boundless love.

More people have come to know the Most High God, receive His redemptive love, and live in true relationship with Him through the power of love, than by any other source. Words do not convert the human heart. Condemnation never saved a human soul. Only the grace of God!

Unless you are living in relationship with God, it is unlikely that you will feel the conviction of your sins. Even the Scripture that He breathed into life is mere words on the page to someone whose heart is not filled with the love of God. How many people who fill the pews on Sunday morning are reading His Word out of religious obligation, rather than a passion to know the heart of God revealed?

If our *faith*, *trust*, and *obedience* to the Lord are based on anything other than our passionate love of our Father, then it will be in constant danger of crumbling when life gets hard. But if we love God, we will follow Him anywhere, even through the darkest valley or the most barren desert. It is our love that produces the *faith*, *trust*, and *obedience* that leads straight to our Promised Land. It is our love for our Father than invites His presence into our lives. It is our love for our God that gives us the strength to trust Him and obey Him, even when the road ahead is uncertain. Every good and godly thing in all Creation begins with His love.

Sometimes, it takes a while before we are ready to fully trust God to be exactly who He says that He is, and to do what He says that He will do. Sometimes, it takes even longer for us to believe Him when He says we are his cherished children. But like any loving parent, our Father, wants us to succeed, to thrive, to flourish, and to reach our

Promised Land. He is the God of second chances, and third chances, and forth chances. If our hearts are sincere, He will lift us out of the murky and mired pits, bring us full circle, and roll away our reproach. He will prepare us, fully and completely, to claim the land of milk and honey and defend the ground on which we will stand. Alleluia!

PRAYER

Dear Father, Thank You for every second, third, fourth, and fifth chance that You have given me. Thank You for loving me so much that You have never given up on me, even in the moments when I have doubted You. Thank You for believing in me even in the moments when I have given up on myself. Thank You for wanting even more for my life than I could possibly dream of wanting for myself. Thank You for rolling away the reproach of my past, forgiving me of my sins, and leading me towards the land of Your promise. Please allow me to be a testimony to Your glories. Let Your light shine through my life so that all that cross my path will come to know You. Amen.

CHAPTER SIXTEEN
WHEN THE ENEMY COMES

And the great dragon was thrown down, that ancient serpent, who is called the devil and Satan, the deceiver of the whole world —he was thrown down to the earth, and his angels were thrown down with him.
Revelation 12:9 (ESV)

To walk with God means to understand that we are, at all times, in a battle of spiritual warfare. As we walk the path God has anointed, we must navigate between the ditches that could leave us broken and in desperate need of repair. We must be wary of deadly snakes that slither across our path, and boulders that roll down from the mountains to block our route or crush our spirit. If allowed, the enemy will sap our strength, prey on our emotions, and ultimately corrupt our walk with God.

We must also remember an important aspect of this struggle. Satan's fight is not with people, it's with God. He uses people as weapons in the war he is waging with God. What an effective tool! The Lord is our Father. We are the apple of His eye *(Psalm 17:8 and Deuteronomy 32:10)*. Every parent knows that there is no pain as great as seeing your child hurt or led astray. So a fallen angel, who cannot attack God directly, is left only to launch attacks against the one target that will hurt the Father most…His Children.

When you go to war against your enemies and see horses and chariots and an army greater than yours, do not be afraid of them, because the LORD your God, who brought you up out of Egypt, will be with you. (Deuteronomy 20:1, NIV)

Our battle against Satan is no different from a battle against any formidable enemy. As soldiers on a battlefield, we must be well armed and possess good armor. We must also have accurate knowledge of our enemy, their plans, and their tactics.

The Lord walks before us. He equips us with everything we might need to fulfill His anointed plan *(Deuteronomy 31:8)*. When the Israelites entered the land of Canaan, they were more of a large camp than a future settled kingdom. As they were preparing to fight the formidable army of the Canaanites, God gave to them the rules of warfare found in

Deuteronomy 20. The very first verse of this chapter tells the Israelites not to be afraid when they see the horses and chariots of their enemy.

Horses and chariots were the tanks of the ancient Near East, and the Canaanites had them in abundance. How could you not be afraid if you have only a sword and you are staring down the gun turrets of an entire Abram's tank division? However, the Israelites had something mightier than any chariot or any tank. They had the anointing of God to fight a divine battle. The favor of God poured out upon them and united with their faith to form a shield. His Word shot forth from them as a fearsome sword. His Holy Spirit formed their rear guard.

God has equipped and armed us with every tool needed for spiritual warfare.

As the Israelites stood on the edge of their Promised Land, they stood in the knowledge that they were heirs to the Covenants God made with Noah, Abraham, and with Moses. We too, are heirs to those sacred Covenants. We are also descendants of Abraham. Just as the Lord poured out His favor upon them as a shield and gave them His Word as their sword, so too, does He equip us for divine battle.

Hebrews 4:12 tells us that, *"the word of God is alive and active. Sharper than any double-edged sword, it penetrates even to dividing soul and spirit, joints and marrow; it judges the thoughts and attitudes of the heart."*[170]

If our battle is divine then, like Joshua entering Canaan, we have been anointed by God. His Word is our sword. Certainly, no battle can be more divine than that waged against the forces of darkness.

If you have not already encountered the enemy in your walk with God, just wait because he will arrive eventually. He has arrived in the path of every child of God who has ever lived and breathed from the moment of his fall from Heaven. No child of God has ever left this earth without at least one encounter with the enemy. It's an encounter that not even Jesus escaped.

We know from Ephesians 6, that God has armed us for this battle. He has equipped us with the full armor of God *(v. 11)*, the belt of truth *(v. 14)*, the breastplate of righteousness *(v. 14)*, the shield of faith that extinguishes *"all the flaming arrows of the evil one"*[171] *(v. 16)*, the helmet of Salvation, and the *"sword of the Spirit, which is the word of God"*[172] *(v. 17)*. We stand armed and ready, and dressed in the full armor of God so that *"when the day of evil comes, [we] may be able to stand [our] ground"*[173] *(v. 13)*.

God has not only well equipped us, but He has also provided us insight into the ways and tactics of our enemy. In Matthew 4, the newly baptized Jesus is led into the wilderness to be tempted by Satan. The enemy does his best to lure the Son of God into forsaking His Father and joining the enemy. Matthew 4 is remarkable in many ways, not least of which is within this chapter, God has given us powerful insight into how Satan operates, and ultimately how he can be defeated.

Satan Came When Jesus was Close to Victory

Matthew 3 tells us that Jesus was baptized by John in the River Jordan. As He arose from those waters, the Heavens opened, and the Spirit of God came down like a dove. Jesus heard the voice of God say, *"This is my Son, whom I love; with him I am well pleased"* [174] *(v. 17).* As Christians, we long to please God. We long to hear Him say the words, *'You are my child, whom I love. In you I am well pleased.'*

As soon as Jesus was baptized, he went up out of the water. At that moment heaven was opened, and he saw the Spirit of God descending like a dove and alighting on him. And a voice from heaven said, "This is my Son, whom I love; with him I am well pleased." (Matthew 3:16-17, NIV)

After His time in the wilderness, God's plan for Jesus was to begin His ministry. He would head to Galilee, then to Nazareth, and to Capernaum beside the Sea of Galilee. While walking beside this large lake, He would encounter two future disciples, brothers Simon Peter and Andrew.

This moment in human history would ultimately lead to the Salvation of the world. Standing there in the wilderness, Jesus stood on the precipice of unimaginable victory. It was the victory that God had sent Him to fulfill. It was the victory of Salvation over damnation and life over death. The ministry to which Jesus was about to embark would ultimately be the deliverance of humanity. It would be a staggering defeat for the enemy and his plans.

For Satan's evil plans to work, he needed to stop Jesus before His ministry began. The enemy carefully chose this moment in the wilderness to come to the Son of God. Jesus was physically weakened, and He had yet to embark on His Father's anointed ministry.

Behold, I have given you authority to tread on serpents and scorpions, and over all the power of the enemy, and nothing shall hurt you. (Luke 10:19, ESV)

Fasting for forty days and nights, Jesus' fully human body would have been weak and hungry. Being alone in the wilderness, he was also isolated from human contact. Satan knew this might be the only chance he had to fulfill his evil plot. This is one of the enemy's common tactics. In fact, it's a tactic that he employs so often, we can be nearly certain that if he enters our path with a vengeance, we are on the precipice of a great victory in Christ.

Satan did not come to Jesus spewing venom and hatred. Certainly, he can and does do that and more, but often he is far more subtle. The voice in which Satan speaks often sounds like our own voice as it whispers the negative thoughts of our deepest worldly fears and insecurities. Worldly fear, anxiety, and insecurity are not God-given emotions. They do not dwell in the Spirit of God. They are not part of God's Kingdom. However, they are nourished and cultivated by the enemy. The value of these emotions to Satan's plan is enormous. They provide an oversized door into our otherwise well-fortified spiritual defenses.

How many times have negative thoughts, rooted in worldly fear and insecurity, run through your mind? Thoughts like: *I'm not good enough. I'm not worthy. I've failed before. Why would they want me? I'm overweight. I'm ugly. Why should I even try?* How have these thoughts interrupted your God anointed destiny?

How many times have these thoughts entered your mind when you stood at the edge of a great opportunity? Perhaps, a promotion has come open and you are trying to decide whether to apply. Maybe, you have just begun a potentially wonderful relationship. You may have an idea to start a new business. Just like he did to Jesus, Satan often comes when we're at the precipice of some of our greatest victories in God's divine plan.

The enemy is the ultimate opportunist. He comes when it's in his best interest to attack. He is not going to put forth the effort unless there is something in it for him. There are times when we are doing such a good job of sabotaging ourselves that Satan need only cheer us on from a distance.

Then there are times when we pose a threat to his plan. That certainly was the case with Jesus in the wilderness. Regardless of the reason he comes or how many millennia he has spent honing his tactics, the enemy has no more power over us than we allow. God gives us the authority to rebuke Satan, just as Jesus did.

Satan Tempted Jesus with What His Fully Human and Weakened Body Craved Most

Satan comes when we are weakest. He evaluates our desires and our vulnerabilities. He feeds on our fears and our insecurities. When he has studied us long enough to have learned the chinks in our armor, he comes.

Satan decided that his best hope was to come after Jesus when He was weakest. His fully human body was hungry and tired. That's when Satan came. He challenged Jesus, *"If you are the Son of God, tell these stones to become loaves of bread"*[175] *(Matthew 4:3).*

Have you ever tried fasting for just a day or two? How about a restrictive diet or fasting before blood work? Our bodies almost scream for the food that is being denied. That loaf of freshly made bread never looked as good as when you know that you can't have it. Jesus wasn't fasting for a day or two. He was fasting for forty days and nights!

Fasting has been an important part of Jewish life since the Exodus. It would have been a significant part of Jesus' life as well. God proclaimed the tenth day of the seventh month *(Yom Kippur)* as a day of fasting for the Israelites. Moses fasted for forty days and nights before recording the Ten Commandments on Mount Horeb. The Prophet Elijah traveled for forty days without food. Individual fasting served many purposes. An Israelite could fast as an act of submission, an expression of grief or remorse, or part of spiritual preparation. However, at its heart, each purpose was a closer connection to God.

In this wilderness of spiritual preparation, the enemy came to tempt and manipulate. Place yourself in Jesus' sandals for a moment. How delicious that bread must have sounded out there in the desert. Jesus certainly could have turned every stone in the desert into fresh bread. However, it would have come at a steep price. That which tastes delicious for a few fleeting moments would have also meant surrendering the battle to Satan. How often do we face similar temptations? Something sounds so wonderful that we are tempted to surrender ground to the enemy in exchange for a few brief moments of pleasure.

What is it that you want most? Some people crave food or shopping to drown their emotions. Others crave drugs or alcohol. Others crave attention, respect, affirmation, compliments, success, acknowledgment, or perfection. This list goes on. What do you hunger and crave the most in your life? Even if we don't consciously understand what individual cravings drive our behavior, we can be certain that the enemy will figure it out eventually.

Our cravings do not have to be bad to be manipulated by the enemy. A desire to be successful is not negative if it does not impact your hunger for God. However, it's a potential chink in our armor that could be attacked by the enemy. This is why it's important for us to understand the emotional motives driving our behavior. It is also important to identify what we crave physically, emotionally, spiritually, and why we desire them.

To be one step ahead of the enemy and prepared for when he comes requires us to understand our potential vulnerabilities. If we desire to live victoriously, then we must be aware of all that the enemy can manipulate and use to subvert our walk with God.

We also see another tactic at play in Matthew 4:3. Satan challenged Jesus to prove He was the Son of God. For many of us, we might have been tempted to display our God-given power to the enemy. We may have wanted him to have no uncertainty that we had the ability to crush him under our heel. Perhaps then, he would leave us in peace. However, Jesus knew without a shadow of a doubt that He was the beloved Son of God. He had nothing to prove, and certainly nothing to prove to the enemy. Jesus had absolute God-given power and authority over the enemy and all his evil forces. He also had confidence in who God is and who He is in God.

As the adopted sons and daughters of God, the co-heirs of Christ, we have this same power and authority over the enemy. We can have the same steadfast confidence in our position as the beloved child of God that Jesus displayed.

Like Jesus, all we must say is, *"get out of here, Satan"*[176] *(Matthew 4:10)* and he will be gone. Luke 10:19 tells us that God has *"given [us] authority over all the power of the enemy, and [we] can walk among snakes and scorpions and crush them. Nothing will injure [us]."*[177]

You have power over the enemy. He cannot hurt you. Let that sink in for a moment. Embrace it. Own this Biblical truth. This authority is your right as a beloved child of God. Satan certainly does not want you to know that he is powerless. However, the enemy is indeed powerless before you, just as he was powerless against Jesus in the wilderness. You simply have to claim that power.

In Christ, we have become the son or daughter of God. Nothing can hurt us. We are forever under the protection and dominion of the Most High God. Satan can tempt, manipulate, even threaten and frighten, but he cannot directly harm us. Our Father simply will not allow it!

Satan Manipulated the Word of God

Satan's power is limited. He can only function under very specific circumstances. Because of this, he often relies on manipulation as a strategy. We see this clearly in Matthew 4:5-6, just as we see it in Genesis 3, in the Garden of Eden. When Satan's first, more direct approach failed to work, he decided on another scheme. This time he twisted the Word of God.

When Jesus rebuked Satan's direct challenge, Satan took Him to Jerusalem to stand on the highest point of the Temple. There, Satan referenced a passage from Psalm 91 when we said, *"If you are the Son of God, jump off! For the Scriptures say, 'He will order his angels to protect you. And they will hold you up with their hands so you won't even hurt your foot on a stone'"*[178] *(Matthew 4:6)*.

Satan's love of half-truths and sly deception is evident in this passage. Psalm 91 does say that the Lord will order His angels to protect Him so that He will not even injure His foot on a stone. However, as with everything, context is important in Scripture. Here is the entire passage from Psalm 91 in context:

If you make the LORD your refuge, if you make the Most High your shelter, no evil will conquer you; no plague will come near your home. For he will order his angels to protect you wherever you go. They will hold you up with their hands so you won't even hurt your foot on a stone. You will trample upon lions and cobras; you will crush fierce lions and serpents under your feet! (v. 9-13)[179]

"*If you make the LORD your refuge, if you make the Most High your shelter*"[180] *(v.9).* That is a pretty significant portion to leave out, don't you think? Satan took the parts of God's Word that suited his purpose, twisted them to fit his desires, and then attempted to use those verses to manipulate the Son of God. This is a tactic the enemy still uses today because it can be effective. After all, who can argue with God's own divinely inspired Word? When Scripture is taken out of context and used for evil, it is important that we challenge it! Jesus sure did! In Matthew 4:7, Jesus cites Deuteronomy 6:16 saying, "*The Scriptures also say, 'You must not test the LORD your God.'*"[181]

If only Adam and Eve would have had such *faith, trust,* and *obedience* to their Father, perhaps things would have worked out very differently in the Garden. I don't think either of them woke up on that now notorious morning and said, '*I want to succumb to the enemy, defy God, and forfeit our right to Eden.*' Few of us ever wake up with that intention in our heart, and yet, sometimes that is what we do.

Satan began his manipulation of Eve with a simple question, "*Did God really say you must not eat the fruit from any of the trees in the garden?*"[182] *(Genesis 3:1).* When we begin to parse the Word of God like an attorney in a court of law, we are dangerously close to the pit of legalism.

In Eve's case, Satan did not try to overtly separate her from the Lord. He didn't try to say that God was unkind for denying her the knowledge of good and evil. He made the case that she was mistaken about what God really wanted and intended for her life in the Garden.

Satan used the same tactic with Jesus as he did with Eve. After all, God loves His children. Satan challenged that if God truly loved Jesus, He would send angels to prevent His fall. He challenged Eve that because God loved her, He really didn't want to deny her the delicious looking fruit or the knowledge of good and evil.

This is a dangerous, and as we have seen, sometimes successful strategy of the enemy. It works because it preys on the secret desires of our heart. Surely, our loving Father would want us to have *every* desire of our heart, right? Wrong! Some of the things we want are very bad for us. Some things we want will separate us from our eternal Father, from our Kingdom destiny, and eventually from our Promised Land. Like every good Father, God longs to say *yes* to His children. However, our good and perfect Father will never say *yes* to us when the most loving and responsible thing to do is to say *no*.

Satan may have won his battle in the Garden, but he most assuredly lost in the wilderness. The enemy failed miserably in his effort to lure Jesus away from His anointed path because Jesus knew the Word of God. There is a very real reason God instructed His children to affix His Word to our heart and soul *(Deuteronomy 11:18)*, to write them on the tablet of our heart *(Proverbs 7:3)*, and keep them always on our lips *(Joshua 1:8)*. If we have feasted on and absorbed His Word, Satan is powerless to use our Father's Word against us.

Satan does not always need to manipulate God's Word for an unholy purpose. Far too frequently we do his job for him. Combine the convenient justification of God's Word manipulated out of context with a secret desire of our heart and it becomes a powerful force that can override our better judgment and even the conviction of the Holy Spirit.

Tell Satan at the top of your lungs:
'Get out of here, Satan!
I worship the Lord and serve only Him!'
Then watch him run back to hell.
The enemy is no match for the child of God!

When we have ventured, or have been lured, so far away from God that we can easily ignore the Holy Spirit's conviction, we have indeed entered a very dangerous place. Satan's own words in Matthew 4:5-6 inadvertently reveal just how dangerous of a territory this can be.

Satan challenged Jesus to jump off the tallest peak of the Temple in hopes that God would divinely save Him. When we seek to manipulate the Word of God to justify our own desires, we are the ones jumping off a very high peak.

In his confrontation with Jesus, we see another aspect of Satan's manipulative side. The Apostle Paul wrote about it in his second letter to the Corinthians: *"No wonder, for even Satan disguises himself as an angel of light"*[183] *(2 Cor. 11:14).*

Eventually, the enemy will come into the life of every Christian. He will cloak himself in whatever attire might accomplish his evil intent. Sometimes, he is dark and menacing. Sometimes, he disguises himself in the light of an angel. Other times he spouts fearsome threats. He will even recite verses of God's divinely inspired Word. Satan will use whatever works.

As we prepare to do battle with the enemy we cannot forget that Satan himself was once an angel in God's Heavenly Kingdom. He had once shined with the light of God, until his own pride, envy, and rebellion got him cast out of Heaven. Satan is good at pretending to be what he is not. Regardless of his experience or skill at this manipulation, like all of Satan's strategies this one is also easy to rebuke. There isn't a single tactic that Satan can form against us that we do not have the authority and ability to rebuke if we stand firm as a child of God.

Like Jesus, we have the power to rebuke the enemy and send him running back to the pits of hell. We have the Sword of His Word. If we want to unmask Satan, then we must keep the Word of God in our heart and on our lips, wield them like a double-edged sword, and seek the Lord as our refuge. As children of the Most High God, we can and will reveal the enemy as a powerless imposter, unable to stand against anyone in God's Kingdom.

Satan Tried to Tempt Jesus into Trading the Worthy for the Easy

In Satan's final attempt at luring Jesus from God's path, he took Him to a mountaintop and showed Him all of the kingdoms of the world, promising to give it all to Him if only He would worship Satan. He tried to tempt Jesus into trading what was worthy for what was easy.

It might be easy to dismiss this idea. Of course, Jesus was never going to give way to the temptation of Satan! However, just for a moment consider the fate that awaited Jesus at the end of His earthly ministry.

*God is faithful, and he will not
let you be tempted beyond your ability...
(1 Corinthians 10:13, ESV)*

The nations of the entire world already belonged to the true Kingdom of His Father. They were already His by right as the beloved Son of God. However, He was going to pay a high price. Jesus was going to suffer unimaginable torture, torment, and humiliation. He was going to purchase the Salvation of the entire world with His blood. He was going to die the death we should have died so that we could live a life we could never earn.

With those horrific scenes fresh in our mind, let's turn back to the offer that Satan made to Jesus. He offered the kingdoms of the entire world in return for bowing down before the fallen angel. If you knew that horrific pain, humiliation, and ultimately death awaited you, and you had an offer to escape it all and receive great riches instead, which future would you pick?

We surrender much of our earthly inheritance as God's beloved children when we elect to take the easy way to our desire, instead of the right way to our Father's will.

Before you say that this is simply not in the realm of possibility, consider how many people make such trades every day. How many people have you personally seen take the easy way to their desires, instead of the right way to the will of God? The circumstances and choices may be different, but the ultimate perilous trade is the same. They decide no one will get hurt if they cheat on the science test. They defend the simple flirtation as meaningless. They justify the good results and ignore the evil means of a plan. How many such trades have you witnessed? Perhaps, you have even made a few. In doing so, you may not have bowed down and worshiped Satan. However, you surely allowed him a strong foothold into your life. You've also certainly (though unintentionally) done his bidding.

Every single time we trade what is worthy and godly for what is easy and wrong, we are most certainly doing the enemy's job for him. We already know if our actions are wrong or inconsistent with God's plans for our life. The Holy Spirit tells us loud and clear. Still, the lure of the easy, the new, and the worldly can cause even otherwise faithful and devout Christians to fall into a muddy and mired pit. To find examples of Satan's success in this area of temptation we need only look around at popular culture, turn on a television, or pick up a magazine.

We can take another lesson from this last gripping encounter between Jesus and Satan described by the Apostle Matthew. We can see just how simply and effectively Jesus defeated the enemy.

In response to Satan's offer of all the kingdoms of the entire world in exchange for Jesus bowing down in worship to the evil one, Jesus responded this way: *"Get out of here, Satan...For the Scriptures say, 'You must worship the* LORD *your God and serve only him.'"* [184] *(Matthew 4:10)*

Satan certainly does not want the world to know this poorly kept secret. We are the children of the Most High God. We have been given authority to rebuke the enemy and send him running back to hell. When Jesus ordered Satan to leave, he left. He had no choice. Afterwards, the angels of Heaven came and tended to Jesus.

So the next time you feel physical temptation, the pull to select the easy over the worthy, the sapping of your strength, the negative influence of your mood, the manipulation of God's Word, depressing and shaming thoughts that seep into your head, or any of Satan's much used strategies, repeat the words of Jesus. Say them loud and clear and with the full confidence that you are the child of the Most High God with the authority to crush the enemy under your heel. Tell Satan at the top of your lungs, *'Get out of here, Satan! I worship the Lord and serve only Him!'* Then watch him run back to hell. The angel of darkness is no match for the child of God!

God Leads Us to Be Tested

Matthew 4 reveals another important thing. It tells us that God not only allowed Satan to tempt Jesus, but He guided Jesus to the location of the temptation. Why would God do such a thing? Isn't our battle difficult enough without directing us into the lion's den?

Faith untested is simply an idea. It is a lovely notion that holds no strength, weight, or power. Like a sword tempered in fire, our faith grows when tempered by the fires of testing, trial, and temptation.

No matter what Satan whispers into our ear, he has no power to cause us injury.

It is often in the midst of our own personal darkness that we can most clearly see the light of God. In those moments our intellectual faith is transformed into a converted heart. We go from *hoping* that we are who God says that we are, to knowing with unyielding certainty. We go from thinking that God is *likely* who He says that He is, to having real and tangible proof.

The secular world often asks how Christians can believe in something we cannot see. I disagree with the very premise of the question. I have seen God show up in my life, time and time again. I can point to real and tangible moments in which I have reached victory only through the divine hand of a merciful and loving God. When our faith has been tempered by fire, it is no longer a hope. It is no longer a wonderful intellectual notion. A faith that has been tried and tested doesn't just have feet. It has arms, and legs, and a head that can shout *'Alleluia.'*

Our testing is the gift by which God tempers our faith with fire, and forges us a shield and armor. His Word becomes our sword. We can know with certainty that God is with us, even in the darkness, and in the quiet moments when we can no longer hear His voice. We know it because He has never failed to be there before. This is a certainty that every child of God can have. We stand on Holy Ground beside the commander of His army. His Spirit guides and strengthens us.

God Teaches Us to Wield the Sword

To have possession of a mighty sword is one thing, to know how to wield it so that we may be a powerful force for God's Kingdom against the enemy, is quite another. It is not enough that we read Scripture and attend worship. We must absorb the Word of God as spiritual food so that when the enemy comes, when the doubters appear, and the critics arise, His Word will be always on our lips and we may speak it in unison with the Holy Spirit.

The author of the Epistle to the Hebrews provides a strong conviction of believers who, by their lack of action, have chosen not to grow their spiritual maturity. *"There is much more we would like to say about this, but it is difficult to explain, especially since you are spiritually dull and don't seem to listen. You have been believers so long now that you ought to be teaching others. Instead, you need someone to teach you again the basic things about God's word. You are like babies who need milk and cannot eat solid food"*[185] *(Hebrews 5:11-12).*

These are strong words, and they reflect an important decision that every believer will face. It is a decision that will define our relationship with God and help determine whether we will claim our Promised Land.

I dare say that there are many believers who love God and sit in the front rows of church, but rarely spend time feasting on His Word the other six days. Far from being able to rebuke the enemy, if he came disguised in the light of an angel they would not even recognize him. They may sit on the front row of church, but they absorb God's Word only when it is spoon fed on Sunday morning. They have opted for a diet of milk instead of solid food, and chosen to remain spiritual infants.

The letter to the Hebrews was originally addressed to the New Covenant community that had steadily grown since the Resurrection of Christ. It had been formed of people who had repented and accepted Jesus Christ as their personal savior. They had the yoke of law removed and had been given, *"the perfect law that sets you free"*[186] *(James 1:25).* Still, they struggled.

They were torn between the ways of the world and the ways of God. Some were being tempted to return to their old ways and beliefs. They were uncertain of God and who they were in relationship to Him. They may have believed *in* Him, but they did not *believe Him.*

Satan loves nothing more than an uncertain Christian. Uncertainty breeds doubt, fear, insecurity, and anxiety. It can be easily manipulated and twisted. If we are fearful, insecure, uncertain, and anxious, then we are silent in the face of great challenge. If we do not rest firmly upon our Lord, upon who He is, and who we are in Him, then we are left to be pushed, and pulled, and battered by the enemy.

God Matures Us into Mighty Warriors

His Word tells us clearly that we must give up the milk of our spiritual infancy, and feast at the grown-ups table. We must meditate and absorb His Word as though it is spiritual food. It is the only food that will sustain us eternally. We must be in the habit of using the Word of God, as the Holy Spirit directs us, in our daily lives.

We must also have the discernment to speak in a manner that allows others to hear our message. It is not the job of others to try to interpret what we really mean. It is our responsibility to speak in a way they can clearly receive.

We cannot forget that how we communicate something is just as important as the substance of our communication. Both of these elements have equal importance. Do our words come across as angry, judgmental, arrogant, terse, uncaring, hypocritical, or otherwise unloving and unworthy of the monumental love and grace found in God? We can recite the entire Bible cover to cover, but if we do so in a manner that is unloving, we have failed to serve our God.

As Joshua entered the Promised Land, God instructed him to have the Word always on his lips. That is exactly how Jesus triumphed over Satan in the wilderness. He knew God's Word. It was a part of Him. When Satan came, it was His Word that was instinctively on the lips of Jesus.

Satan will come eventually into the life of every believer who walks with God. Our victory lies greatly in our preparation. Spend some time with God and take stock of your areas of potential vulnerability that can be exploited by the enemy. Ask God to bring to mind all of your worldly fears, conflicts, insecurities, uncertainties, doubts, and anxieties. Bring them to your Father, and see what He has to say.

The greatest thing we can leave for generations to come is a legacy of faith in a big and loving God.

Let's see how God's Word rebukes Satan's appeal to some very common fears and insecurities.

Satan Says: You are not good enough. You are unworthy. You are a terrible sinner.

God Says: You are My Temple. My Spirit lives in you. I loved you so much that even while you were still sinning, I sent My Son to save you and give you eternal life, if only you believe. *(1 Cor. 3:16, John 3:16-17, and Rom. 5:8)*

Satan Says: You have failed many times before. You're too weak to accomplish anything.

God Says: I will help you up when you fall and lift you up when you are bowed down. All you need is My grace. My power works best in weakness. *(Ps. 145:14, 2 Cor. 12:9)*

Satan Says: If God loved you He would end your troubles.

God Says: I test you so you will be strong, of good character, able to endure, and filled with hope. Through it all, I pour out my love into your heart. *(Romans 5:3-5)*

Satan Says: Everyone hates you.

God Says: If you were still of the world the people would love you because you would still be one of them. Instead, you are with Me, so they hate you, but only because they hated Me first. *(John 15:18-19)*

Satan Says: You are flawed and ugly.

God Says: Your body is a beautiful temple built for the My Spirit whom I have given you. I have bought you for a high price. You are My masterpiece and your appearance glorifies Me. *(1 Corinthians 6:19-20 and Ephesians 2:10)*

Do not stop with this list. Make your own list of how God answers your individual fears and insecurity.

Our goal is to dwell closely with God and reach the land of His promise. Though, it's not simply enough that we claim the land. We are going to have to defend the land from every attempt by the enemy to reclaim it. The enemy may come subtly or he may come with force, but rest assured that he will come. He will try his best to throw us off our land, undo the mighty work that God has done in our lives, and separate us from our Father. However, even his best plans are doomed to failure unless he can convince us to cooperate with him.

Why would we ever cooperate with Satan? That seems a ludicrous thought! Until you stop to consider how often we cooperate with him in our own defeat every day. How many times a week do you absorb the negative voices of others? How many times a day do you repeat them in the form of bad reports, gossip, or faithless words? How many times a day do you allow your mind to drift towards the worst possible outcome of a situation? How often do you assume that something is impossible in your life? How many times have you looked at a magazine and wished your body looked like those on the cover?

Every single time we allow the negativity, the standards of the world, the faithless words of others, or the self-defeat of our own nature to interfere in our walk with God, we are unintentionally cooperating with the enemy and forsaking our rightful inheritance as God's beloved child.

After the Book of Joshua details the conquest of the Promised Land, we are given the Book of Judges. It is filled with examples of how the Chosen People of God relinquished their right to their Promised Land for a season or a generation. They did so by forgetting their history with God. In the routine of everyday life, they let their guard down. What one generation fought so hard to achieve, subsequent generations lost. They did so simply because they forgot the past and failed to pay attention to the present. We cannot afford to be so lax in our lives that we forsake the inheritance we have fought so hard to claim.

Neither can we simply assume that future generations will hang on to the victories that we have won. To defend the ground upon which we stand and ensure that future generations also claim their inheritance in God's promise, we must pass down a heritage of *faith*, *trust*, and *obedience* to a big and loving God. We must tell the stories of our memory stones. We must proudly show our battle scars. We must teach future generations to wield the sword and shield which God has given to us. We must live our lives as a living testimony to God's faithfulness so when future generations ask, we can tell them what God has done. We must leave a legacy of believing what God says and does, not simply believing in His existence.

We must walk with God.

PRAYER

Dear Lord, Thank You for shielding me and arming me with every tool needed to fight the evil one. Thank You for guiding me and training me in all that I need to stand against the slings and arrows of the world. My faith in You is my shield. Salvation is my helmet. Your Word is my sword. I know that Heaven is Your throne and the Earth is Your footstool. Everything is under your authority. I stand firm in the knowledge of who You are and who I am in You. I am Your beloved child. I claim my inheritance. You have given me the power to crush the enemy and all his forces and this, I do in Your name. Amen.

CHAPTER SEVENTEEN
PARALYSIS OF FEAR

*"Be strong and courageous. Do not fear or be
in dread of them, for it is the Lord your God who
goes with you. He will not leave you or forsake you."*
Deuteronomy 31:6 (ESV)

ear is a complex emotion. It can be good and godly. It can also be a tool for the enemy to twist our path from that which God has anointed. The difference between the two types of fear can be found in context.

Fear can sometimes be the way that God warns us of impending danger. Every woman has experienced being alone in an isolated area and feeling that sudden urge of fear, even before seeing a stranger lurking. That is the kind of fear that can help to keep us safe.

I love nature documentaries with gorgeous panoramas and the stunning beauty of God's creation. Inevitably, there is a scene with antelopes, zebras, or wildebeest happily grazing and drinking. The audience may know that lurking nearby are hungry lions, but the herd is gleefully oblivious. Then, suddenly, the massive herd bolts in unison away from the area they were previously enjoying. They did not see the lions. They may not even have smelt the lions. Their gift of fear had somehow alerted them to danger and they responded without a second thought.

"Who gives intuition to the heart and instinct to the mind? Who is wise enough to count all the clouds? Who can tilt the water jars of heaven when the parched ground is dry and the soil has hardened into clods?" (Job 38:36-38, NLT)

(God speaking to Job)

Humans also have the same gift of fear and the ability to perceive it supernaturally. The word *supernatural* is defined as, "of or relating to an order of existence beyond the visible observable universe."[187] Can you think of a better description of God's periodic communication style? It exists beyond the world's definition of the visible and the observable. It cannot be quantified in a lab. Though, we as His children hear the communication clearly.

Isaiah 6:9 tells us that because of the people's unbelief, God instructed Isaiah to inform them they would "'be ever hearing, but never understanding; be ever seeing, but never perceiving.'"[188]

God can and does communicate to us in many different ways. He can send other people, orchestrate events, or even send us an angel and a burning bush. Many times, He communicates to us supernaturally, through our gifts of perception. Sometimes, it takes the form of our gift of fear and our ability to sense danger. Sometimes, it may be that voice in the back of our mind that says, *'pause at the next stoplight'*, only to narrowly avoid an accident. Sometimes, it is an odd feeling that tells us to stay away from a certain person or situation.

These are not simply good and godly. These are God's communication to us, and evidence of our real and tangible relationship to Him. Though, not all fear can be so defined. Fear mixed with anxiety, doubt, and uncertainty has no place in the Holy Spirit. This worldly fear does not come from God and as surely as you read these words, this kind of fear will be used by the enemy.

To reach our highest anointing,
our faith must be constantly renewed.

Have you ever been shark diving, or watched a documentary of the adventure? To attract the sharks, boat crews will use chopped up fish and fish blood to *chum the waters*. Sharks possess a keen sense of smell. It does not take them long to follow their nose to the source of a new meal. This is what our fears do for the enemy. Our fears attract the enemy to the source of a new meal.

We are all imperfect creatures. We all stand on feet of clay. We all have fears of some kind. Even our most seemingly illogical fears usually have some basis in reality. We often have tangible evidence to support them. We can point to a specific event or set of circumstances and say *'see this is why (fill in the blank)'*.

I have never been the most coordinated person in the world. As a young child, I fell so often that my family considered fitting me for a football helmet. As an adult, I have a fear of heights. I need only look at the faded childhood scars to count my evidence. Perhaps, you have had a failed business and you are afraid of starting another one for fear it may also fail. Perhaps, you have been divorced and are afraid of beginning a new relationship because it might also end. Perhaps, like Job, you have known both great joy and great loss, and now you are afraid of happiness for fear it might lead to loss and pain.

Our fears are valid to us. Over time, we can find further evidence to reinforce them. Oftentimes, we can be so afraid and convinced that an outcome is set in stone that we inadvertently cause the very thing we fear.

Worldly fear comes from a variety of places, but the root of each one eventually winds back to the same sources:

- ➢ Not fully absorbing who God is, what He says, what He does, and who we are in God.

- ➢ Not trusting ourselves in God.

- ➢ Not trusting God to do what He says He will do.

- ➢ Not accepting God's direction.

Every fear comes down to a limited trust in God, and a lack of fully internalizing the His Word. Think about that for a moment and apply it to your fears.

Whether your fear is heights, divorce, failure, or any one of a million secret fears that we all harbor, they grow in a mind, and flourish in a spirit that is unfilled by the spiritual food of our Father and hesitant to trust Him.

The roots of worldly fears are
lack of faith and trust in God.

We have talked a lot about trusting God and feasting on His Word, but trusting is not as easy as it sounds. We live in a fallen world that does not value the things that God indicates are valuable. Our society tells us that the Bible is merely a collection of stories and allegories handed down from one generation and culture to another. Not everyone has had the privilege of witnessing a burning bush and receiving specific instructions.

I dare say a lot folks – even a lot of good church going Christian folks – hedge their bets just a little. They may go to church and even serve God, but they don't have time to spend with Him the rest of the week. They may come to Him when something big is happening in their lives, but they don't talk to Him every day. Or they may have a great inner dialogue with God, but they would be embarrassed to speak words in prayer aloud with friends and family.

Still others, may mention to friends that their family goes to church, but they don't dare invite them or mention Scripture to them for fear of being labeled as *'one of those Christians'*. Do any of these sound familiar?

Our hesitancy keeps us one step removed from God. We feel safer standing on our own two feet instead of sitting out on the furthest limb with God. However, no matter how firmly we stand, we are mortal and stand on feet of clay *(Daniel 2:31-33)*.

Fear eventually leads to physical, emotional, and spiritual paralysis. We are so afraid to do anything that we do nothing. When the enemy comes - and he will come - our lips are silent and unable to utter any rebuke. Our feet are melded to the earth. We can offer no defense when he smells our specific fears and whispers them back to us in familiar voices. When God tells us to charge forth to a mighty destination on our anointed path, our feet remain so frozen by our fears that they will not budge.

What does God say about our fears?

> *Isaiah 41:13: For I am the LORD your God who takes hold of your right hand and says to you, Do not fear; I will help you.*[189]

> *2 Timothy 1:7: For the Spirit God gave us does not make us timid, but gives us power, love and self-discipline.*[190]

> *Psalm 27:1: The LORD is my light and my salvation—whom shall I fear? The LORD is the stronghold of my life—of whom shall I be afraid?*[191]

If God is adamant that there is nothing on earth that we should fear, He is equally adamant that there is only one source in all of existence to which we should direct our fear and reverence. Him! Fear of the Lord is a godly fear. Proverbs 1:7 tells us that, *"fear of the LORD is the beginning of knowledge, but fools despise wisdom and instruction."*[192]

Do not let your hearts be troubled and
do not be afraid. (John 14:27, NIV)

There are few words in the English language that properly convey the often misinterpreted phrase, *fear of the Lord*. Far from meaning that we should hide ourselves from a wrathful God, the word *fear* in this context, implies a form of celebratory awe, a reverential submission, a sacred adoration, and an obedient respect to our Heavenly Father. To *fear the Lord* is to revere Him. It means to fear the consequences of sin. It means to know God and to trust Him. When we live in celebratory awe, reverential submission, and obedient respect to the Most High God, we grow closer to Him and firmer in our relationship to Him.

Think of God's relationship with us as the relationship of a loving father to his child. A father's love cannot be earned or lost. It is the natural outpouring of his role as a good Father. His natural instinct is to love and shower upon his child all the blessings that he can give. His job is to teach his child, nurture them, impose the consequences of bad decisions, and grow them up into mighty men and women of faith. If He has done his job well, His children will have great love for Him, respect, reverence for him, and an unwillingness to cause him disappointment. This is also our relationship with our eternal Father.

Faith is not something that is instilled once and then forgotten. Like a car, it must be regularly refilled. We must renew our faith, or over the course of many miles we will run dry. No matter how many times that God has showed us His love, grace, loyalty, devotion, and favor, our imperfect natures can cause us to forget.

Even before God led His People out of bondage in Egypt, He performed awe-inspiring signs in their presence. Before and after He parted the Red Sea and drowned their enemies in the crashing waves, He had led their way and sustained them. God had been faithful. He showed up, in ways both big and small, along every step of their journey. They were alive only because the hand of God was laid upon them as a protective shield, yet when times looked dire, they doubted God more than once. Even as they stood on the edge of a great promise, they doubted Him again.

Moses had sent men to do reconnaissance on this new land and its people. When the men came back they said:

> *"We can't attack those people; they are stronger than we are...The land we explored devours those living in it. All the people we saw there are of great size. We saw the Nephilim there (the descendants of Anak come from the Nephilim). We seemed like grasshoppers in our own eyes, and we looked the same to them." (Numbers 13:31-33)*[193]

As the word spread amongst the people they began to rebel and said:

> *"If only we had died in Egypt! Or in this wilderness! Why is the LORD bringing us to this land only to let us fall by the sword? Our wives and children will be taken as plunder. Wouldn't it be better for us to go back to Egypt?" (Numbers 14:2-3)*[194].

Only twelve people in the entire nation had seen these massive armies. The remainder had never even ventured into the land. Yet, upon hearing the dire words of a few people, the entire nation was convinced that the Promised Land was a doomed venture that would leave them, and their families, dead by the swords of their enemies. They had forgotten how God bent Pharaoh to His will. They had forgotten the manna from heaven, the pillar of cloud and fire, and the parting of the Red Sea.

They heard a dire prediction and leaned upon the power of their fears, anxieties, uncertainties, and imagined horrors. They convinced themselves that their worst nightmares were true, and they acted upon that false belief. After 400 years in Egypt, they had finally come to the edge of the Promised Land, and their imagined fear was so strong that they were willing to return to slavery rather than take a few more steps forward into abundant victory.

Sounds familiar to me, how about you? Haven't we all stood were the Israelite's stood at that moment? How many times has God sustained us? How many times can we say that we have been victorious only because God showed up? How many times can we say that we, or those we love, are alive only because God laid His hand upon us as a protective shield? How often has He led us by pillars of cloud and fire? How has He supernaturally provided for us and removed the obstacles in our path? Yet, when times look dire, we grow fearful, anxious, uncertain, and consumed by imagined horrors.

Worldly fear fills us with anxiety, doubt, and false belief. It will attract the enemy and lead to physical and spiritual paralysis.

In Biblical language, things that are repeated have great emphasis. As Joshua led the second generation of Israelites to claim the land of promise, God said to him, *"Have I not commanded you? Be strong and courageous. Do not be afraid; do not be discouraged, for the LORD your God will be with you wherever you go"*[195] *(Joshua 1:9).* Now, Joshua was a mighty warrior. He was God's chosen and anointed leader of the Israelites. He was the general, hand-selected by God, to claim the Promise Land occupied by the very formidable Canaanites. Yet, God was repeating His instructions to Joshua not to be afraid? Yes!

God walks before us. He sees every step along our journey before our feet have touched the ground. He knew that even a mighty warrior, blessed with God's favor, can and will grow fearful when faced with a dire situation or an imposing obstacle. God was reminding Joshua of a truth that the warrior already knew, that God had been with him before, He would be with him now, and in the future. It is a reminder that Our Father gives to us every day and longs for us to hear and absorb as eternal truth.

Repeat the words from Joshua as a personal declaration: *The Lord my God is with me wherever I go!*

Let that rest for a moment. Absorb it. Digest the enormity of that statement. God is with you wherever you go. He walks before you. He shall be with you *"even unto the end of the world"*[196] *(Matthew 28:20).*

"The Lord your God will be
with you wherever you go."
(Joshua 1:9, NIV)

We must renew our faith, lest our human fears grow, until we are paralyzed and unable to move. We renew our faith in many different ways.

➤ Attend a church regularly that fills you with godly energy and vigor.

➤ Join a small group Bible study with other men and women of faith.

➤ Find a way to serve others in His name. Whether it is a missionary trip, helping neighbors, caring for shelter animals, or serving food in a soup kitchen, find a way to put feet to your faith.

➤ Talk to God throughout the day. Our prayer life need not always be formal. Talk to Him as though to an earthly father or a friend. Chat with Him.

➤ Read Scripture daily. Meditate on His Word. Speak it both aloud and in your mind. Allow your mind, heart, and spirit to absorb the miracle of it all.

➤ Keep a faith journal. It does not have to be long or fancy. Jot down your feelings, verses that inspire you, ways in which God is moving you. Most importantly, keep note of the times that God has shown up in your life both big and small. Whether it is finding $20 in your old coat pocket when you were short of money or curing a disease, write it down and read it often.

➤ Take your faith outside of the church doors and into the mission field that is your daily life. Live it. Speak it. Find ways to make your life a testimony.

➤ Get into the habit of bringing everything before your Father. Bring all of your worries, hopes, desires, fears, questions, concerns, and struggles to Him. Trust that He can and will handle things. Ask Him for His will and guidance in each situation. Then go where He is leading you.

Spiritual paralysis can also indicate that another issue is at work – a battle between what we want and what the Holy Spirit is telling us. There are times when we want something badly, but God is strongly moving us in another direction. If our relationship with Our Father is deep and personal, we will find it difficult to ignore Him. Still, the pull of our own personal desire is strong.

What we are wanting doesn't have to be bad. It may just be something that is not God's plan for our lives. It could be a job that we really want, a person that we would like to marry, or a city where we would like to move. If we have a plan that is directly contrary to God's plan we can feel a type of paralysis. The pull of our personal desire is countered by the pull of God's divine plan. In these moments, it is our obedience that is tested.

What regular appointment do you have with God in order to refresh and refill your faith and your spirit?

We know that God's plan will prevail. We know that His plans are greater and better than ours. Our *faith* leads to our *trust*, which sees evidence in our *obedience*.

To fully embrace God's plan in preference to our plan is not a sacrifice. Quite the contrary, to embrace God's will over our own is to accept a bigger and better future than anything we could ever accomplish on our own. It is to leave the wilderness that is so familiar, for the Promised Land of milk and honey. It is to run to our *Abba*. Given the choice, I'll take the Promised Land. How about you?

PRAYER

Dear Lord, fill me with a renewed faith in You. Allow me to feast upon Your Word and put feet to my faith. Prune away my worldly fear and fill me with reverence for You. In the face of the enemy and in the face of my own worldly desires, let my *faith* and *trust* produce a perfect *obedience* to Your will. I know that yours is a plan greater than anything I could create. Replace my paralysis of fear and indecision with a passion to run hard after You. Amen.

CHAPTER EIGHTEEN

WHEN OUR VESSEL RUNS DRY

And without faith it is impossible to please him,
for whoever would draw near to God must believe that he
exists and that he rewards those who seek him.
Hebrews 11:6 (ESV)

We know that Joshua was a great man of *faith, trust*, and *obedience*. He steadfastly believed God in the face of every obstacle on the Israelite's Promised Land journey. Throughout his story, there has been little indication that Joshua ever doubted that he and his fellow Israelites were God's Chosen People. When Moses' spies returned from Canaan it was Joshua and Caleb, who stood against their bad report. When others wanted to run, they wanted to charge ahead and claim the land. When the people began to rebel, it was Joshua who urged them to stand with the Lord.

"If the LORD delights in us, he will bring us into this land and give it to us, a land that flows with milk and honey. Only do not rebel against the LORD. And do not fear the people of the land, for they are bread for us. Their protection is removed from them, and the LORD is with us; do not fear them." (Numbers 14:8-9)[197]

Joshua was a man who passionately believed God and His Word. He was a man who believed that God was on their side and would bring the walls of their enemies crumbling down. As we journey with him we see that, so far, he has been right. So, what happens when someone who is accustomed to running hard after God, runs full force into a wall that doesn't come crumbling down? What happens when our earthen vessels run dry? To answer this question we are going to skip ahead and join the Israelites in the seventh chapter of the Book of Joshua.

Even the most passionate followers of God will occasionally feel empty, alone, and doubtful.

Here, we find Joshua and the Israelites already across the Jordan River and into Canaan. With the help of the commander of God's army, the Israelite army has taken Jericho and burnt it to the ground. We will come back to this pivotal point in their journey. For now, what we need to know is that they had been greatly victorious at Jericho. God had allowed them to take the silver, gold, and articles of bronze and iron for the treasury of the Lord's House. However, they were prohibited from taking any valuables for personal property.

Fresh off such a mighty win, Joshua sent men to spy on the city of Ai, near Beth Aven. The men came back and reported, *"Not all the army will have to go up against Ai. Send two or three thousand men to take it and do not weary the whole army, for only a few people live there"*[198] (Joshua 7:3).

Even if we don't know exactly what is coming, we still cringe at these words. By now, we know that testing God is never a good idea. In taking such an utterly nonchalant attitude towards claiming the Promised Land, they were most definitely testing the Lord. It should come as no surprise when we learn that the men of Ai chased the three thousand Israelites from the city gates, killing thirty-six of them. Joshua 7:5 tells us that the hearts of the Israelite army *"melted in fear and became like water."*[199]

Up until now, Joshua has been pretty unflappable in the face of every obstacle. We all know someone who reminds us a little of Joshua. We all have that certain someone who always seems to have everything put together. They never seem to be in a hurry or frazzled. They have the perfect words for any situation. Their house is spotless. Their kids are always perfect. They volunteer for everything and still find time to make a four course meal for their family. They sit on the front row at church. They seem to have a perfect relationship with God, a perfectly blessed life, and a perfect faith. No matter what comes up in their life, they believe God and His Word.

We usually don't like these people very much. Well, at minimum, we usually have a slight love-hate relationship with their life as seen from the outside. We all know that no one has a perfect life, no matter how things may appear on the surface. Just as there is no perfect life, there is also no perfect faith. Everyone will have moments of doubt, loneliness, and despair.

Look back at the stories of most of the great men and women of Holy Scripture. From Abraham and David to Peter and Paul, each of them experienced a moment of despair in which they felt alone. Christ Jesus was the only perfect human being ever to walk the face of the earth and yet, even He cried out on the Cross, *""Eli, Eli, lema sabachthani?" which means "My God, my God, why have you abandoned me?""*[200] *(Matthew 27:46).*

Joshua will have such a moment in the aftermath of this first great loss in the Promised Land. Joshua tore his clothes and fell face down onto the ground in front of the Ark of the Lord. Knowing what we do about Joshua's faith and trust, his words to God may seem a bit out of character:

> *"Alas, Sovereign LORD, why did you ever bring this people across the Jordan to deliver us into the hands of the Amorites to destroy us? If only we had been content to stay on the other side of the Jordan! Pardon your servant, Lord. What can I say, now that Israel has been routed by its enemies? The Canaanites and the other people of the country will hear about this and they will surround us and wipe out our name from the earth. What then will you do for your own great name?" (Joshua 7:7-9)*[201]

"If only we had been content to stay on the other side of the Jordan!"[202]*(v. 7).* This sounds a bit like the words spoken by the Israelite community upon hearing the bad report of the spies Moses had sent into Canaan.

The Bible does not seek to sugarcoat the lives of God's best. Don't you just love that about His Word? God lays everything out there for us to read, to know, and to absorb. He knows that at some point along our journey, we will need to know that we are not alone in our season, or our feelings. Sometimes, our feelings are of being alone, unheard, forsaken, doubtful, angry, or just simply empty. Sometimes, no matter what we do, our earthen vessel just seems dry, and God seems to be so very far away. In the aftermath of the defeat at Ai, Joshua's faith appears to have run desperately dry.

However, things turned out differently for Joshua than they had for the first generation of Israelites. God answered him, and said, *"Stand up! What are you doing down on your face?"*[203] *(Joshua 7:10).*

The Lord told Joshua that a member of the Israelite community had violated His instructions, stolen prohibited items from Jericho for their personal possession, and lied about taking them. He commanded Joshua and the people of Israel to consecrate themselves, and then remove the wrongdoer from their community. Achan, from the tribe of Judah, admitted to the wrongdoing and for his crime he would pay with his life.

Afterwards, the Lord said to Joshua, *"Do not be afraid; do not be discouraged. Take the whole army with you, and go up and attack Ai. For I have delivered into your hands the king of Ai, his people, his city and his land"*[204] *(Josh. 8:1).* God kept His promise. He delivered the city of Ai, its king, and all of its people and possessions into the hands of Joshua and his army. Not a single survivor was left by the end of the day. This is a very different outcome than the one experienced by the first generation of Israelites when their faith had run dry.

So, what did Joshua do differently?

Joshua Quickly Turned to God

One generation was barred from the Promised Land. Their children grew up to conquer the land with God's help. If I were to put my finger on one single element that separated these two generations and the results they achieved, it would be the speed in which each generation turned to God in both good times and bad. This is pivotal not just for claiming the land, but also for keeping it.

Both generations ultimately turned to God when disaster struck. However, the Israelites under Moses took a lot longer to come to the Lord and were quick to forget His faithfulness. The second generation did not make this same mistake. This is a pivotal difference between these two reactions and results.

From the beginning of the campaign to claim the land, we have seen Joshua experience moments of fear and nervousness. However, he was quick to turn towards God for strength and resolve. He may have felt alone and forsaken after this first great defeat in the Promised Land, but he still had faith enough to turn to God in his grief, fear, and pain.

We will all have times of doubt, struggle, and defeat. Like Joshua, we will all fight impossible odds. What distinguished Joshua is his immediate willingness to lay all of this down before God. He didn't spend a lot of time complaining and blaming. He swept up every bit of doubt, struggle, and defeat, and brought it all to his Father. We will see a similar quality in Israel's second monarch, David.

*In our times of emptiness, loneliness, and
doubt we remain on our Kingdom path
by bringing all of our emotions to God.*

What makes these men remarkable is not perfection or even great accomplishments. Though, certainly both men would accomplish mighty deeds in their lifetime, they were both far from perfect. They both made mistakes. However, they were clear about who God is and who they were in relationship to Him. They understood that no one, but God could hold the title of perfection. They also understood that every victory they experienced was won by the hand of God acting through them. What kept their mistakes from becoming barriers that forever blocked their path to God's promise was their willingness to turn to Him in their shame, grief, doubt, fear, and defeat.

We learn a powerful lesson from the testimony of these two mighty men of God. Our Father doesn't ask us to be perfect. He would never set up such an impossible goal for His children. He wants us to understand that all perfection, all success, and all victory come from Him. Each of these may flow through us as empty earthen vessels, but they originate with God. He is the source of our strength, our faith, our hope, and our victory.

Though, we may face setbacks and defeats, they will remain only temporary if we keep our focus on God and His divine plans. When our faith rests in Him, rather than in ourselves, He will lift us up though we may fall *(Psalm 37:24)*, give us hope though we may despair *(Jer. 29:11)*, offer strength though we may fear *(Deut. 3:22)*, and fights for us though we may be unable even to move *(Exod. 14:14)*. His righteousness goes before us and His glory forms our rear guard *(Isaiah 58:8)*. Can we ask for anything more? God alone brings victory. Consider just two of these verses.

> **Exodus 14:14:** "The LORD will fight for you; you need only to be still."[205]

> **Deuteronomy 3:22:** "Do not be afraid of them; the LORD your God himself will fight for you."[206]

The transliterated Hebrew word for fight in both of these verses is *lacham*. It means "fig. to *consume*; by impl. to *battle*…devour…fight…overcome, prevail, (make) war."[207] The Lord will not simply fight for us, He will devour whatever obstacle or enemy stands between us and the destiny He has planned for us.

We need never be reluctant, ashamed, or fearful to come to our Father, even in the face of a great mistake. These are most especially the times in which we need our Heavenly Father most.

In the midst of our joy and our grief, and every single moment in between, we need our God. We most especially need Him when we have stumbled. We need Him when we have ended up in a darkened pit. We need Him when we do not think we have the strength to carry on. We need Him when we have made such a mess of things that we have no idea how on earth we can ever clean it up. We need Him when we are heartbroken, defeated, fearful, fallen, shattered, angry, and ashamed. In our weakness, His power is strong *(2 Corinthians 12:9)*. He can, and will, lift us up, renew our strength, purify us, and give us hope once more. He will do all of this and more, but only if we have the faith to turn to Him. The longer we try to go it alone and do it alone, the longer we deny ourselves the love, grace, faithfulness, and power that only God can bring.

Joshua Allowed God to Refill His Faith

Unlike our trust, which requires active and intentional participation on our part, our faith is a free gift bestowed upon us by our Father. We receive this gift of faith so that we may know God and live in true relationship with Him. Still, our faith is not a never-ending well. It is not bestowed once and then left alone to collect dust on a shelf. Nor is it intended to remain stagnant and forever stunted. With God's help, we are meant to grow our gift of faith into a powerful force in God's Kingdom.

In 1 Kings 17:8-16, the Prophet Elijah arrives in the village of Zarephath. There, he sees a widow gathering sticks. He asks her for a cup of water and some bread. The widow replies that she has only a handful of flour and some cooking oil, but not a single piece of bread. She has so little food that she fears for her life and that of her son.

Elijah told her, *"Don't be afraid! Go ahead and do just what you've said, but make a little bread for me first. Then use what's left to prepare a meal for yourself and your son. For this is what the LORD, the God of Israel, says: There will always be flour and olive oil left in your containers until the time when the LORD sends rain and the crops grow again!"*[208] *(v. 13-14).*

She did as Elijah asked and there was food every day for the prophet, the widow, and her family. In keeping with the Lord's promise, her flour remained plentiful and her oil did not run dry.

Each time he said, "My grace is all you need. My power works best in weakness." So now I am glad to boast about my weaknesses, so that the power of Christ can work through me. (2 Corinthians 12:9, NLT)

We see a similar scene in 2 Kings 4 with Elijah's successor, the Prophet Elisha. When a widow had fallen into such debt and poverty that she might lose her sons as slaves to the debt collector, Elisha asked what she has in her home. The widow replies that she has a little oil.

He tells her to gather as many containers together as she can find from friends and neighbors. Then, she is to go inside, shut the door, and pour her oil into each of the containers.

She filled every container to its brim, yet never ran out of oil. Only when there were no more jars to fill did the oil stop flowing. The profits from those oil jars allowed her to buy the freedom of her sons, pay all of their debts, and supply them an income for survival.

The oil referred to in both of these chapters is olive oil. It was highly valued and used in daily life for everything from cooking and medicinal cures, to holy anointing. This oil remains so closely associated with the divine that it's still in use today in Christian churches as anointing oil.

We are a bit like these jars. As we pour out our oil onto others, God constantly refills our jars. In our most perfect walk with God, we are empty vessels constantly being poured into by God and constantly pouring out love and blessing onto others. Like the widow, our oil only stops flowing when we no longer have a place to pour it.

———

Heal me, O LORD, and I will be healed; Save me and I will be saved... (Jeremiah 17:14, NASB)

———

Though, there are times when our earthen vessels are so cracked and broken that no matter how rapidly they are refilled, they seem to no longer hold a single drop of oil. Our containers are dry and we find ourselves in a pile of clay shards and dust. There are moments, and even seasons, when we lack the strength to move forward. The weight of our circumstance and emotions feel like a lead anchor around our neck.

Perhaps, like Joshua, you have suffered a staggering defeat and are overwhelmed at its potential repercussions. Maybe your spouse has asked for a divorce. Maybe your child has been in an accident. Maybe you are caring for a loved one with a terminal diagnosis. Maybe you lost everything to a bad financial deal. The list of possibilities is both endless and highly personal. The one thing each of them has in common is the overwhelming sense of hopelessness and despair that will shroud not only your present circumstance, but also your view of the future.

We are resilient and strong. We can walk through fire and face down mighty armies, if we have the hope of God securing our future. However, when that hope is crushed under the weight of despair and fear, our legs buckle and our fragile vessels break and crumble.

We cannot repair the cracks in our vessels any more than we can refill our own jars, or discover the purpose of our lives by reading self-help books and looking deeper inside ourselves. We didn't create ourselves. We didn't knit together our DNA. We didn't breathe life into our mortal bodies. We are created beings. The source of our purpose, our healing, and our renewing is always our God. The same God who created us, knitted us together, and breathed life into us. The sooner we look to God in every situation, the happier and more successful our lives will become, the closer our relationship with Him will be, and the closer to our Promised Land we will venture.

One of God's specialties is healing the broken. His power is made perfect in our weakness. God doesn't just stop pouring into us because our hearts and souls are too broken to hold His blessings. He continues to pour into us even as He restores us and mends our broken places. Psalm 147:2-3 reminds us of the mercy and healing of God: *"The LORD builds up Jerusalem; He gathers the outcasts of Israel. He heals the brokenhearted And binds up their wounds."*[209]

Our *Abba* heals our broken hearts. Though we are outcasts, He gathers us up and invites us into His city to make our home. When God is the source of our strength, though our legs may buckle, He will carry us through. When He is the source of our healing, though we may bleed, He will bind up our wounds and make us whole again.

He brought me up out of the pit of destruction,
out of the miry clay, And He set my feet
upon a rock making my footsteps firm.
(Psalm 40:2, NASB)

God is constantly pouring into us. Just like the widow with many oil jars, the flow only ceases when we no longer pour our blessing onto others. This is part of our role in His Kingdom and as His children. We remain whole and filled with God's glory when we remain focused on Him instead of the troubles that inevitably pass through our lives.

Joshua knew this well, and in His despair, He turned to God. He knew that God alone can make straight what was once crooked, and heal what was once broken. Our hearts may be shrouded and even temporarily angry at God for allowing such pain to enter our lives. However, as children of the Most High God, we must also remember that our Father is the source of all goodness, all healing, all life, and all victory. He alone can turn death to life again. He alone can turn our greatest defeat into our greatest victory. Our *Abba* can do it! He will do it! He certainly did it for Joshua.

This mighty warrior and great military leader turned to his God. He fell down on his face before the Ark and poured out everything to the Father who has the power to redeem every defeat and mistake we could ever make.

What we do with our emotions
plays a large role in determining whether
we claim and keep our Promised Land.

For a mighty healing to take place, we must do as Joshua did, and go to the Lord. We must be near Him. We must also develop a practice of remaining with Him and focusing on Him throughout our day. Only then can we ensure that when darkness and despair comes we will not have far to travel to the meet our Father.

We do this by spending time with Him in prayer, feasting upon His Word, worshiping Him, and experiencing fellowship with His other children. We do it by talking with Him daily, listening expectantly for Him, trusting Him, loving Him, obeying Him, believing Him, and serving in ways that will please Him.

Joshua Did Not Blame God

We gain nothing when we play the victim with God. After all, He is the one who gave us the gift of free-will. We have the choice as to whether to believe Him, follow Him, and obey Him. True, our lives will be a whole lot more difficult, empty, and unfulfilling when we choose to ignore His path, but we still have the choice. Blaming God for the bad results of choices we have made is a lot like taking your parent's car without asking and then blaming them when you dent the fender. It will also produce about the same results.

How many people do you know who spend a day, a season, or even a lifetime angry with God? They will gladly recount all the ways they believe God has let them down. They claim to care very little for God. Their heart is hardened by their lack of trust and understanding. Their stories are filled with all the ways that God has short-changed their lives. We know from our own memory stones that this could not be further from the truth. Their stories do not reflect the Most High God.

Our Father is the essence of generosity and love. If we ever stop and truly listen to the stories of those who blame God and drill down to the core of their message, we often hear the truth. For much of what they are angry with God about, the originating source of the issue is often their own actions and choices. They are blaming their Father because they wrecked the family car and He will not buy them a new one.

323

There are times when we may experience anger at our Father. It may not be wise. It certainly will not get us anywhere productive. However, it is common and I believe, like all parents, our Father knows our heart. However, He will still be quick to correct it. If we make the bigger mistake of blaming our Father, He will surely set us straight. Though, if we let Him, He will also bring us comfort and healing. However, the longer we spend caught up in our own anger and resentment, the longer that healing will take, and the longer our journey to His promise will be sidetracked.

Sometimes, the pits we end up in are those we have dug ourselves. The ground may have been soft, the enemy may have handed us the shovel, but we dug the thing ourselves. We could be wise, take responsibility for our choices, and ask God to rescue us from the mess of our own making. Instead, we often stomp our feet, cross our arms, and blame God for our predicament. Blaming God for our mistakes and choices may feel good in the short-term because it soothes our egos and temporarily keeps us from feeling the burden of our responsibility. Though, it does nothing to get us out of the miry clay and set our feet on firm rock.

Joshua understood this and he poured out everything before the Ark of the Lord. He grieved. He expressed fear of what the future held. He had many regrets. He even whined a bit. Though, He never blamed God for his decisions or those of his fellow Israelites.

Like every good father, God wants us to learn the important lessons He is trying to teach. He has gifted us with free-will. If, by this gift, we decide to take up residence in the muddy pit, then in the pit He will leave us. However, He will never abandon us. He will never be far from us. The moment we cry out to our Father for help, He will lift us out and set our feet on solid ground. It doesn't matter what mess we've made. God will help us put it right, if only we ask Him. Our *Abba* will purify us and give us a fresh start, but first we must have the courage to acknowledge that we've made the mess and need His help.

Joshua Waited for God

God only speaks to accomplish something, whether by breathing life into the universe or imparting information and instruction. He does not speak just to hear His own voice. There will be times when God is silent because He wants us to wait on His timing. While He is never in a hurry, He is also never late. Throughout His Word we see that God has always shown up in the lives of His Chosen People. Joshua knew this and even in his despair he had the faith and trust to be patient, though certainly not silent.

Just because God isn't talking does not mean that we should remain silent. Our Father wants us to cry out to Him and tell Him everything that is weighing on our heart.

He already knows the content of our heart. He understands our feelings even before we have made sense of them ourselves. However, God also knows that acknowledging and speaking them to Him is a vital part of our healing process. Thus, He wants us to bring to Him all of our fear, grief, mess, despair, and brokenness.

Even when God is silent, He is still listening and He is still present. Much trouble has been caused in the life of God's children because they decided not to wait on God. We know how failing to wait on God's timing resulted in the Israelite's first king being the selfish and cruel Saul instead of David, the man after God's own heart.

Waiting on God's instructions is as vital to our victory as obeying them when they come.

The Israelites had not been defeated at Ai because they faced a more imposing force. They were not even defeated simply because of the horribly nonchalant attitude they took towards conquering the land of God's promise. Joshua and his army were defeated because some amongst them had violated God's commands, taken prohibited items from Jericho, and then lied about their disobedience. If Joshua had attacked Ai again before receiving instruction from God, not only would they have been defeated again, but it may have been much worse.

Being in a hurry to right our wrongs is not a bad thing in itself. However, when we go about it in a manner that is inconsistent with God's wishes or when we have failed to learn His wishes altogether, we run the very real risk of making things much worse. We are on very dangerous ground, indeed, when we try to simply guess the will of the Most High God. We are doomed for disaster if we dare try to treat our mere guesses as His instructions.

Joshua Immediately Obeyed God

One of the key elements that distinguished the second generation out of Egypt from their parents was their willingness to immediately obey God, and to rectify and repent any wrongdoing. When Joshua cried out to God, his Father heard his cries and He said to Joshua:

> *"Get up! Why have you fallen on your face? Israel has sinned; they have transgressed my covenant that I commanded them; they have taken some of the devoted things; they have stolen and lied and put them among their own belongings. Therefore the people of Israel cannot stand before their enemies. They turn their backs before their enemies, because they have become devoted for destruction. I will be with you no more, unless you destroy the devoted things from among you. Get up! Consecrate the people..."* [210] *(Joshua 7:10-13)*

Indulge me. Allow me to try to say this in a way we might recognize as coming from the mouth of an earthly father: *'Get up. Stop crying. You disobeyed me. You did something wrong and you're going to fix it, but I'll help you. I am not abandoning you. Now, go get ready.'* If you are a parent, you have likely said something very similar to your own children at one time. The words may be stern. They certainly leave little room for doubt over your displeasure at the disobedience. However they also relay the love of a parent who is teaching their child to walk in the way that is right. God does the same with His children.

He Knew Partial Obedience Equals Rebellion

We have two choices in life. We can do things God's way or we can do things our way. There is no middle ground. We cannot obey God only up to a point and then expect His favor. To walk with God is to surrender our lives and our plans to our Father, the Most High God.

Joshua knew that God had not led them so far only to abandon them in Canaan. God's chosen leader possessed the kind of *faith* and *trust* that produces the fruit of complete *obedience*. Joshua surely had a special anointing, but so do we. We are also His Chosen People and His Royal Priesthood *(1 Peter 2:9)*. We fool ourselves and greatly undermine our highest destiny if we falsely believe that God's best and brightest somehow had greater *faith, trust,* and *obedience* than anything we could muster. They were still as fully human as you and me.

We know that our Father will not ask of us anything that we cannot bear. We must also understand that He will never ask of us anything that is impossible. Every single thing that He will ask of us is completely doable. It may be difficult. It may challenge us in ways we never thought possible. However, it can be done and with His help, it will be done, if only we hold to the *faith* and *trust* that produces complete *obedience*.

If we believe that our Heavenly Father wants the best for us, that His plans are greater than ours, and He has never failed to show up before, then why would we want to do things any other way but God's way?

Joshua Did Not Grieve Alone

Joshua 7:6 says that upon the Israelites defeat at Ai, *"Joshua tore his clothes and fell to the earth on his face before the ark of the LORD until the evening, he and the elders of Israel. And they put dust on their heads."*[211]

Tearing clothing, wearing sackcloth, growing or cutting hair, and the sprinkling of dust or ash on the head were common symbols of mourning, deep repentance, and humility in ancient Israel. David tore his clothing, wept, and fasted upon learning of the death of King Saul. In today's Christian churches we see another use of ash as a symbol of humility and repentance. Each year, the season of Lent begins with Ash Wednesday and the marking of ashes on the foreheads of believers who gather in repentance.

In his mourning, Joshua was not alone. He was with the elders of Israel. No matter what level of grief or regret that we may experience in certain seasons of our life, we are not meant to weather them without the fellowship of others who share our path. God created people as the body of His church so that we may come together as a solid, stable, and cohesive family in Christ. As brothers and sisters, we are a family united by God to serve and walk with Him.

God is with us every moment. We are certainly not alone in our mourning. Our Father never abandons us. Still, we need other people who will fall down before God with us and share our grief. We need fellow travelers on this most glorious journey with God who will sprinkle dust on their heads and share our pain.

Who will be there on the ground with you before God? Who will cry with you? Who will pray at your side? These are important questions to consider and important faith-filled relationships to cultivate.

PRAYER

Dear Lord, Thank You for loving me and walking with me. Thank You for never leaving me alone in my times of fear, defeat, doubt, and emptiness. Let Your will be done in my life. I turn to You in my darkness and I know that You will fill me up with renewed faith. I know that Your path leads to victory beyond my understanding. I know that You walk before me and prepare a path just for me. It is a path filled with Your glories. Please renew my faith and pour into me as Your beloved earthen vessel. Amen.

CHAPTER NINETEEN
JERICHO SIZED VICTORY

But thanks be to God, who gives us the
victory through our Lord Jesus Christ.
1 Corinthians 15:57 (ESV)

Most of us pray for our lives to be tranquil, quiet, and drama free. We get pretty upset when life comes out of nowhere and disturbs our peaceful times. Many of us question God. We ask or even demand, *'God, why would You bring this into my life?'* We long to quickly get back to our comfortable normality.

Our messy moments come in every shape and size. Their only consistent element is their seeming appearance from out of nowhere. Sometimes, these moments really do appear out of nowhere, but more often, we are simply just good at putting on blinders in the morning and keeping those rose-tinted glasses perched on the tip of our nose.

Sometimes, messy moments come with the phone call from the doctor saying you, or a loved one, has a serious illness. Sometimes, the moments come with the discovery of a betrayal, a child failing school, termination of a job, the failure of a business, a divorce, or a bankruptcy.

Moses answered the people, "Do not be afraid.
Stand firm and you will see the deliverance the
LORD will bring you today. The Egyptians
you see today you will never see again."
(Exodus 14:13, NIV)

In these moments we pray for God's rescue. We pray for Him to return our lives to peace and quiet. Even though He loves us greatly, it is a prayer that He will rarely answer. He wants us to have peace. However, He wants us to have the peace that comes from working in unison with Him towards His purpose for our life, and for His Kingdom. Maintaining the quiet status quo and achieving God's greatest victories rarely go hand in hand. In these moments we have only two choices:

(A) We run and hide; or

(B) We march forward and take the walls of Jericho.

Here is one aspect of our walk with God that few people will mention because most do not want to hear. God did not create us for the easy times. He did not breathe life into us for the times of peace and tranquility. These are our rest periods when we can regroup and regain our strength for the battles ahead. He created us for the messy periods, the turbulent times, and the crisis moments. Why?

Because these are the moments when all of the chess pieces are in midair and nothing is set in stone. These are the moments when we, as earthen vessels, have the greatest opportunity to effect change. We have the chance not just to change the ending of the game, but to change the game itself. It is in these moments that we can create something mighty. These moments allow us to change the face of our lives and the lives of those that come after us. In the midst of such moments people are freed, lives are saved, and wonders are created. During one such moment God's nation was born.

Twice the Israelites stood within reach of the Promised Land. Twice they stood on the edge of the land of milk and honey, which God had promised to their forefathers. Twice they faced a mighty foe. Twice they faced the choice that we all face in the midst of difficult and messy seasons of our lives. They could run and hide, or they could march straight ahead and claim God's enormous promise. The first and second generations chose radically different options and received radically different outcomes.

As we come to the close of our journey together within these pages, we will join each of these great generations on the edge of Canaan. We will explore the choices they made and the results they received. Through their lives, God has given us guidance to the claiming of our own Promised Land, and to the choices that we will be asked to make.

Option (A): The Choice to Run

We join Moses and the Israelites in the Book of Numbers. It has only been two years since they came out of slavery in Egypt. Their minds would still be fresh with the witness they bore to the mighty hand of a faithful God. God had sent Moses to lead His people out of slavery in Egypt. He had set plagues upon Pharaoh to force the ruler to His will. He had led them by a pillar of cloud by day and a pillar of fire by night. He had parted the Red Sea so they could cross on dry ground. He had drowned their enemies in the waters of that Sea. He had fed them with food from the sky and made the bitter water sweet to drink. He had brought water from a rock to quench their thirst and continued to sustain them in the wilderness.

Finally, the Lord commanded Moses, *"Send some men to explore the land of Canaan, which I am giving to the Israelites. From each ancestral tribe send one of its leaders"*[212] *(Numbers 13:2)*. Moses obeyed. He dispatched a leader from each of the twelve Tribes, out of the Desert of Paran and into the land of Canaan to conduct surveillance. Moses instructed the men to gather practical information that would be needed in formulating a strategy: *"See what the land is like and whether the people who live there are strong or weak, few or many. What kind of land do they live in? Is it good or bad? What kind of towns do they live in? Are they unwalled or fortified? How is the soil? Is it fertile or poor? Are there trees in it or not? Do your best to bring back some of the fruit of the land."*[213] *(Numbers 13:18-20)*

The spies explored the land and found that it did indeed flow with milk and honey. The ground was fertile and they brought back grapes, pomegranates, and figs. They also brought back a bad report that the people who lived there were powerful giants and their cities were heavily fortified.

This was no deterrent for Caleb and Joshua, who were among the twelve spies. The two men strongly believed God and stood against their ten comrades. Caleb and Joshua believed that if God was fighting on their side, no enemy could ever stand against them.

However, their fellow spies were fearful and that fear activated their imagination. They were certain their enemy was more powerful. They said, *"We can't attack those people; they are stronger than we are"*[214] *(Num. 13:31).* We have seen how they spread the bad report amongst the nation saying the *"land we explored devours those living in it"*[215] *(v. 32).*

Have you ever met someone whose fear and anxiety continued to grow before your eyes? The more they gave voice to their fears, the more their imaginations run wild.

We've discussed the various types of fear that we experience as part of our human nature. The fear we see these ten spies displaying is not the fear God has given us. The fear they show is bred from a lack of faith and trust in God. Their memories of God's faithfulness have been short. They judged the size of their God by their circumstances. This is a recipe for disaster every single time.

Our Father created the entire universe, every planet discovered and yet to be discovered. He placed every single star in the sky. He created every animal, every plant, and every person by His hand. What circumstance in our lives, could ever be bigger than the God who did all of this? Only Caleb and Joshua held firm to this truth. They judged the size of their circumstances by the size of their God.

These ten spies made another grave error. They continued to give voice to their fear and anxiety with faithless words that articulated their lack of trust. Our words and our thoughts have power. What we concentrate on flourishes and grows. What we ignore shrivels and dies. Have you ever sat and stewed over a small problem? Have you spent hours talking about it to friends under the guise of trying to make a decision? Have you been the friend who has spent hours listening to such a fearful person?

How quickly has that relatively small and solvable problem grown into the full focus of their life and the enormous boulder in their path? All from faithless words and a lack of trust, fermented in a faithless imagination. We spend enough of our Christian lives fighting off attacks from the enemy, why do we want to aid him with our own attacks from within?

As the chapter continues, we see exactly how powerful words of fear can become. Soon the report of the spies spread through the entire Israelite community. The fears, anxieties, faithless words, and self-destructive imaginations of ten men grew to become the grumblings of a nation. They eventually drowned out the voices of Caleb and Joshua. Our fearful natures often find even inaccurate bad news easier to accept than good news.

Later, we will see the mighty reward that great faith and focus on the good news of God will bring. For now, we see just how dangerous this inclination to assume the worst can be in our walk with God and our journey to our Promised Land:

> *That night all the members of the community raised their voices and wept aloud. All the Israelites grumbled against Moses and Aaron, and the whole assembly said to them, "If only we had died in Egypt! Or in this wilderness! Why is the LORD bringing us to this land only to let us fall by the sword? Our wives and children will be taken as plunder. Wouldn't it be better for us to go back to Egypt?" And they said to each other, "We should choose a leader and go back to Egypt.*[216] *(Numbers 14:1-4)*

Out of a community of more than 600,000, only twelve men had explored the land and seen the enemy firsthand. Each of those twelve has seen the exact same fertile fields and fortified cities. Ten of them saw the obstacles and assumed the worst. Two of them saw the same hurdles and knew that the Most High God keeps His promises.

The community's fears so fermented in their imagination that they had already assumed all was lost before they even saw the enemy for themselves. They would rather have returned to slavery in Egypt than face the horrible future they had dreamed up out of a few faithless words and the embers of uncertainty.

How many of us have done this? How many of us have looked at an obstacle in our path, forgotten how faithful

God has always been, imagined the worst possible scenario in our minds, and then acted as if it had already become truth? We see our spouse talking to an attractive stranger and suddenly this is evidence of our worst fear of adultery and divorce. Our company is suffering financial losses, and suddenly we see this as evidence of our worst fears of bankruptcy and foreclosure. Even when the evidence before our eyes is objectively serious, such as a grim medical diagnosis, we read the statistics and forget the faithfulness of the God from whom all healing comes.

How many of us can recognize ourselves in this first generation of Israelites out of Egypt? How many of us have seen God show up in our lives in big and mighty ways, but when an obstacle triggers our fears we buckle, weep aloud, assume the worst, and believe all is already lost. How many times have we opted to return to mediocrity, or even bondage, rather than charge a fearsome foe?

If we are not alert, we are all at risk of falling into this particular pit. It is a pit dug by specific actions and choices. We dig this pit when…

- ➤ We fail to discipline our minds and our emotions.

- ➤ We judge the mightiness of our God by the perception of our circumstances.

- ➤ We listen to our fears and the voice of the enemy, instead of listening for the voice of God and the divine counsel of the Holy Spirit.

- ➤ We give voice to faithless fears.

> ➤ We give the enemy a doorway into our mind.

> ➤ We fail to remember God's love and faithfulness.

> ➤ We select our ways over God's will and divine plan.

> ➤ We view our circumstances through the filter of fear instead of the mirror of His Word.

> ➤ We act upon a truth invented by our perception of our circumstances, rather than the truth of His Word.

> ➤ We fail to have *faith*, *trust*, and *obedience* to our eternal Father.

As Chapter 14 continues, we see Moses pleading with God to forgive the Israelites. God did forgive them, but He added something that should give us all great pause before considering Option A. God prohibited every living adult, with the exception of Joshua and Caleb, from ever stepping foot in the Promised Land. They lost their inheritance as descendants of Abraham. They lost their right to God's promise all because they allowed their fear to produce the bad fruit of unbelief and rebellion.

This first generation of Israelites out of Egypt stood on the edge of the Promised Land. They had every promise of a faithful and loving God stretched out before them, and yet they allowed their fear and unbelief to deprive them of victory. They lived out the remainder of their days without ever stepping foot in the land they had been waiting for their entire lives. They remained forever in the wilderness.

Even in the darkest night, amidst the bleakest silence, or facing the gravest foe, God will not abandon you. He certainly did not abandon this first generation of Israelites. The Israelites abandoned God. They allowed their fear to overwhelm their faith and in so doing, they also deprived themselves of God's best. Even in the midst of rampant rebellion, God still rewarded great *faith*, great *trust*, and great *obedience*. The faithless words of fear had not phased Caleb or Joshua. They were still willing to claim the Promised Land. As it turns out, they were the only ones among their peers who would ever live to see it.

Even after the people's rebellion, God did not abandon the Israelites. He continued to sustain them in the wilderness until one generation had passed and another had risen. It is comforting to know that God is still faithful even in the face of our mistakes. Our Father never abandons His children. He always keeps His promises. He will prepare and provide for every journey He asks us to undertake. He could have left those who rebelled to starve in the desert, but they were His Chosen People and He was their God.

It may be comforting, but it's not a life that I want, do you? Would you be content to live your life forever out of reach of your Promised Land because you lacked the courage to believe Him? Do you want to be merely sustained in the wilderness or do you want to live every ounce of God's promise for your life? Do you want the abundance and victory only God can provide? Do you want to make it to your Promised Land? Do you want to shout out and watch the walls of your Jericho crumble to the ground?

Option (B): The Choice to Claim the Land

As we examine our second option, we come to the first chapter of the Book of Joshua. The Israelites have remained in the desert until everyone who was of military age at the time of the Exodus from Egypt has died, except for Joshua and Caleb. We now meet the second generation that God raised up in place of their rebellious parents.

This generation was either born in the wilderness or were children during the Exodus. Moses, the only leader most of them had ever known, had died. God has now selected a new leader, Joshua. His anointing is to claim the land God promised Abraham's descendants. Standing in their way is a flooded river, fortified cities, heavily armed militaries, mighty giants, and their own fears.

Things are not much different from the last time that God brought His Chosen People to this location. Some could argue that the situation is even a little more daunting. After all, when the previous generation arrived, they didn't have to cross the flooded Jordan River. One thing was drastically different this time around. The people were different. They had perfected their *faith, trust,* and *obedience* to God. They believed their Father.

When asked to renew the Covenant of Circumcision, this generation obeyed. When asked to cross the flooded Jordan River, whose waters were held back by God, they obeyed. When asked to erect memory stones, they obeyed. They trusted God. They believed Him. They went where He lead them.

Do you remember how this second generation responded to Joshua's anointing as the successor to Moses? They vowed to follow Joshua faithfully because God was with him as their new leader. They vowed that whoever rebelled against Joshua should be put to death. The community asked only that God remain with him and that Joshua be strong and courageous *(Joshua 1:16-18).*

Those who think they can do it on their own end up obsessed with measuring their own moral muscle but never get around to exercising it in real life. Those who trust God's action in them find that God's Spirit is in them—living and breathing God! Obsession with self in these matters is a dead end; attention to God leads us out into the open, into a spacious, free life. Focusing on the self is the opposite of focusing on God.
(Romans 8:5-6, MSG)

Their lives attest to the incredible strength and victory that is released when a trusting and believing child of God acts in alignment with God's will and His better plan. When we invite God to fulfill His plans through our purely human lives, the impossible becomes possible. We serve the God who created Heaven and Earth. Every time we cooperate with His better plan He gives us a chance to come closer to the divine, and better know His incredible heart.

Thomas Paine wrote, *"What we obtain too cheaply, we esteem too lightly."* God didn't simply hand the Israelites the keys to their kingdom. He certainly could have. God can do anything He desires. But in the Promised Land, He wanted His Chosen People to cherish and maintain the promise He was giving them. He needed them to work, and strive, and even sacrifice to obtain their Promised Land so that they would esteem it greatly. He helped them. He sent the commander of His army to fight beside them.

God does the same for us today. He knows that nothing is more deeply cherished than that which we have to work hard to achieve. Just like the Israelites, if we want to live in our Promised Land, then we will have to take up the fight. We have to claim the land. Though, if we have the *faith* and *trust* that produces the *obedience*, then God will supply us some pretty mighty assistance.

Our Father is generous with His blessings and favor. He does not withhold or restrain the gifting of His best to be ungenerous. He wants to ensure that we respect our Promised Land as the mighty gift that it is, and cherish it accordingly. He wants us to work, to strive, and even to sacrifice for it. God wants to ensure that it is not obtained too cheaply, so that we will not esteem it lightly.

As Joshua neared Jericho, he saw a man standing before him with a drawn sword. Joshua asked the man, *"Are you for us or for our enemies?"*[217] (Joshua 5:13). The man replied, *"Neither...but as commander of the army of the LORD I have now come"*[218] (v. 14). He did not come to choose a side. He had come to simply take over.

God does everything by His divine plan. By the gift of free-will, we have the choice to follow Him or to disobey Him. However, the one thing that we can never do is ignore Him. God will make His voice heard. He will make His instructions known.

The first town that the army came to was Jericho. It was surrounded by a walled fortress with barred gates. No one was allowed in or out. The people of Jericho were expecting them. Can you think of a more difficult obstacle in your path than a fortified city that knew you were coming? As they approached the city, God gave Joshua instructions that were as unusual as they were specific.

God's words are recorded in Joshua 6:2-5:

> *"See, I have delivered Jericho into your hands, along with its king and its fighting men. March around the city once with all the armed men. Do this for six days. Have seven priests carry trumpets of rams' horns in front of the ark. On the seventh day, march around the city seven times, with the priests blowing the trumpets. When you hear them sound a long blast on the trumpets, have the whole army give a loud shout; then the wall of the city will collapse and the army will go up, everyone straight in."*[219]

Anyone who has watched a few war movies knows that a fortified city is either taken by overwhelming force or surrounded and starved out. One method would incur heavy losses and the other would most likely take many months. Joshua, who was a great military leader, would have known this all too well.

God's instructions must have sounded as strange to Joshua's ears as they do to ours. If I were in Joshua's place, I can think of a million questions to ask God. However, Joshua did not ask a single one. Instead, he listened and he obeyed.

God's instructions are not always going to be logical by the world's standards. God's plans are divine. He does not have to provide a reason or explain His thinking. Our Father is generous and sometimes He will shed light on a reason, but most often no reasons will come.

Our obedience follows our trust. Our trust follows our faith. These are the moments when we must put feet to our faith. We have a choice to make. We either stick with God or we run and hide. We either believe these things or not:

God is exactly who He says He is.

God can do exactly what He says He can do.

God will do exactly what He says He will do.

We are exactly who He says that we are.

We can do exactly what He says that we can do.

Has God ever asked you to do something so seemingly ludicrous to the outside world that you might be exposed to untold criticism or ridicule? Has He ever asked you to walk around a fortified city with an Ark, priests, and soldiers for seven days while blowing a horn in order that the walls might actually crumble? What did you do?

Many of us may have feared the scorn of our peers. We may have been too embarrassed to obey God's instructions. If Joshua and his army had similar feelings they sure did not show them. They responded the same way they had ever since God anointed Joshua successor to Moses. They did exactly what God had commanded. They marched around the city for six days and the priests blew rams horns. On the seventh day, Joshua gave the order.

> *Joshua 6:16-17: The seventh time around, when the priests sounded the trumpet blast, Joshua commanded the army, "Shout! For the LORD has given you the city! The city and all that is in it are to be devoted to the LORD."*[220]

> *Joshua 6:20: When the trumpets sounded, the army shouted, and at the sound of the trumpet, when the men gave a loud shout, the wall collapsed; so everyone charged straight in, and they took the city.*[221]

How magnificent of a passage: *"Shout! For the LORD has given you the city!"*[222] God does not leave us unprepared for the mission He asks us to undertake. He walks before us just as surely as He walked before Joshua into the land of Canaan. He has given us the city. All that is required of us is the *faith, trust,* and *obedience* to shout to the walls.

When we are following where God is leading, our victory is already assured. Sometimes, it will take seven days. Sometimes, it will take seven years. Sometimes, it may not resemble the victory for which we have prayed. But if we, *"have faith as small as a mustard seed, [we] can say to this mountain, 'Move from here to there,' and it will move"*[223] (*Matthew 17:20)*, or shout to the wall and watch it crumble.

Joshua and his men can teach us a great many things! Here are just a few:

➤ Faithful obedience to God, especially in the face of great difficulty or risk, brings victory. Often it brings Jericho sized victory!

➤ The power, plan, and mind of God are simply beyond our human understanding. To spend time questioning and second-guessing God, only delays and diminishes the victory that He has planned.

➤ When we have fallen so head-over-heels in love with God that we are willing to follow Him anywhere without hesitation, we get the privilege to watch Him do truly incredible things.

➤ God keeps His promises. On this His Word is clear. Deuteronomy 7:9 says this: *"He is the faithful God who keeps his covenant for a thousand generations and lavishes his unfailing love on those who love him and obey his commands."*[224]

➤ If we have *faith* and *trust* enough to *obey* God when He commands us to shout at the wall, He will bring it crumbling to our feet.

➤ It does not matter how many times we may fall. We must get back up, wipe the dust from our clothes, and continue on our journey of walking with God.

➤ Walking with God requires actions. Ours is not a dead ideology or a passive faith. James 2:26 says, *"As the body without the spirit is dead, so faith without deeds is dead."*[225] It is not enough to say, 'I believe in

God,' but sit by doing nothing. Our victories are delivered by God, but He still requires us to work for them. Our Jericho victories are going to require great *faith, trust, obedience,* and great work.

➤ Sometimes, God will ask us to do things that may not be very comfortable, or even logical by worldly standards. However, God's ways are not the world's ways. Our job is to obey, not to second guess.

➤ Claiming our Promised Land is not a onetime fight. It is a journey and a continuing effort to develop a heart like God and stand firm on the foundation of His truth.

➤ There will be times when God will ask us to cross a flooded river. He will ask us to step into a new landscape for which we have no previous experience. We will have to take a leap of blind faith and trust, and believe that our God will hold back the water.

➤ In our walk with God, there will be times when no gray area exists. We either, claim His promise and walk so far out on the limb that if God is not active and present we will surely perish, or we can live forever in the mediocrity of the wilderness.

If God is standing with you who can stand against you? Only you! Only you can stand in the way of your Promised Land. Only you can reject God's favor. Only you can refuse the anointing that God has planned for your life. Only you can block the journey to your greatest destiny and your highest victory. Satan cannot do that, he does not have the power. Your past cannot do that, Jesus has redeemed every part of you. Your friends and family certainly cannot do that because no man can stand in the way of the Lord.

As we face the difficult and messy moments that will inevitably come along in our walk, let us pray to have the faith of Joshua and shout at the wall so we may watch it crumble. Let us get out of our own way. Most importantly, let us get out of God's way. Let us have a faith strong enough to trust that God always keeps His promises. Let us have a trust mighty enough that we believe without question that God will deliver us victory over the enemies we will face in life. Let us have obedience resolute enough to follow the instructions of God even when He says to march ahead confidently and face a fearsome enemy.

———————

Are you willing to go out on a limb with God?
Are you willing to trust Him without hesitation and embrace the big and bold life He is calling you towards?

———————

I do not want to live my life only to perish in the wilderness. How about you? Do you want to simply get by, or do you want to reach the land that your Father has prepared just for you? Do you want to experience the victory and abundance that can only come from the hand of God? Will you journey there with me? Let's pick up that sword and shield and march into that land together!

Can you picture it with the gift of your imagination? Can you feel the warmth of His light on your face? Can you smell the sweet liberty in the air and see the abundance all around? Can you feel the freedom that comes when all the weight and shackles of your past have been laid down? Can you hear His voice saying, *'welcome My beloved child'*? My heart swells at the thought! How about you?

What do you want? What do you truly want in this incredible journey that you are taking with your Father? Do you want to know the existence that can only come from a close personal relationship with God? Do you want to live out the God anointed purpose for your life and reach your highest destiny in His Kingdom? More than anything, do you want to live God's best plan for your life, to walk so closely with Him that nothing can separate you, and to never ever stop loving and believing Him? I pray all this, and so much more, over you my sweet friend.

We know that our Salvation is only just the beginning of our journey. It's a journey that will last not just a lifetime, but an eternity. So, from now until eternity, let's approach this amazing gift of life with a fresh faith, a bold trust, and a radical obedience. Let's agree that our lives are no longer normal, business as usual. Let's surrender everything to the God who knit us together and loves us with a boundless passion. Let's stop struggling in the wilderness to simply get by and start claiming the abundance, victory, and purpose that God has already spoken over our lives.

Take down that dusty crown and claim your rightful place as a beloved child of the King of Kings, the Most

High God, the Creator of Heaven and Earth. Surrender the anxiety and worry over what the future holds and rest firmly in the knowledge that you have asked your Father, and if it's His will, then it will be yours *(1 John 5:14-15)*. Even if it's not God's will, believe with a heart that knows God's love and faithfulness, that what He has in store is even better than you could ever conceive.

I have dearly loved this journey we have taken together with God in these pages. It has been a wild and beautiful adventure. My heart is overflowing with gratitude for God's amazing grace and faithful love, and for your incredible companionship along this road. But our journey with our God cannot be contained within the covers of a book. There is a more beautiful and wild adventure awaiting us along our walk with Him.

By our gift of free-will, we can obey God or we can disobey Him, but we can never ignore Him.

Come with me. Let's join hands as we have the *faith*, *trust*, and *obedience* to dip our toes into the rushing waters of the Jordan River and watch with wide-eyed wonderment at the miracles our Father will perform. Those giants and mighty armies are no match for our God!

We may be grasshoppers in our own eyes, but to our Father, we are His beloved adopted, chosen, redeemed, forgiven, and blessed children. We are His masterpiece! We stand on the solid rock of His trust. The helmet of Salvation is on our head. The shield of faith is in one hand. The sword of His Word is in our other hand. The commander of His army stands before us. The Holy Spirit is behind us forming our rear guard. The same God who created the universe has already prepared our way! Our hearts are filled with a boundless faith, trust, obedience, love, and expectancy in the One who set us free. Let's leave the sands of this desert together and claim God's sovereign promise! Come on! Let's walk with God to the other side of that muddy riverbank!

PRAYER

Dear Lord, Thank You for Your mighty hand that fights my battles, prepares my way, and declares victory over me and my family. Please let my *faith* and *trust* in You produce an unquestioning *obedience* to Your will. Speak the words and I shall march in the direction of Your will. I relinquish all that is mine so that I may follow hard after You and Your anointed path for my life. I love You so very much! I praise Your mighty name. I claim my place as Your precious child. Let my actions and words glorify You. Let me honor Your Son and His Sacrifice in all that I do. Let my life be a testimony to the amazing power, love, and grace that resides in a close walk with You. Amen.

Discussion Questions

Chapter 1: To Know Him Is To Trust Him

1. Have you ever been called to do something difficult for God? What was it?

2. Have you been called to show godly love to someone who wasn't very lovable? How much *faith, trust, obedience,* and love for God did it take to obey?

3. Looking back over the last year of your life can you recall the times when God has shown up in your life or those around you?

4. How often do you cooperate with God? How often do you go out on a limb with Him?

Chapter 2: My Sheep Shall Know My Voice

1. What is God whispering or shouting to you lately?

2. What has God asked that you said *yes* too lately?

3. Are you feeling the pull of the Holy Spirit, but haven't said *yes*? Why?

4. Do you have a daily appointment to spend time with God and His Word? If not try making one.

5. How does that time help shape the rest of your day?

6. Have you ever realized in retrospect that God was speaking into your life? What did you learn?

Chapter 3: Preparing the Way

1. What bondage still holds you captive?

2. Can you list your greatest memory stones?

3. Can you list the memory stones God has been building in your life over the last year?

4. What branches has God pruned in your life lately?

5. What branches still need to be pruned?

6. Have you been to Gilgal? Has God removed your covering? If not, have you asked Him?

7. What still inhibits your close relationship with God?

8. What is still holding you back in the wilderness?

Chapter 4: Refine Us Like Silver

1. How has God's refinement been evident in your life? In what ways are you stronger, better, or more prepared to claim your Promised Land?

2. Looking back over the last week, the last month, the last year, can you see God's testing and refining at work in your life? What method(s) has God been using to refine you?

3. What areas can you identify that are in need of greater refining so that they may be made stronger, more solid, and more whole? List them and then ask God to prepare you in these areas. Better yet, start to work on these areas yourself, with God's help.

Chapter 5: An Expectant Heart

1. What do you believe God for in your life?

2. Looking back over your life can you think of times when you have limited your expectation of God, brought before Him only selected aspects of your life, or asked of Him only mediocre outcomes?

3. Has God stopped the sun and moon in your life? Have you come to Him with an expectant heart? When has He shown up in mighty way(s)?

4. How does your relationship with God improve when you expect the best from Him? How does your relationship with other people change?

5. How does expecting His best change your situation?

Chapter 6: I'll Take the Brick, Thank You

1. What pebbles and bricks is God sending your way? What direction do you feel God leading you towards?

2. Whether you have chosen to follow those nudges or ignore them, what has been the outcome?

3. What would you do if you knew you could not fail?

4. How does your world change when you are quickly obedient to God?

5. How has your *brick wall moments* helped prepare you for your Promised Land?

Chapter 7: Junk in Your Trunk

1. Do you struggle with unrepentant guilt or shame? If so, list them or simply speak them to God. Ask for His mercy, His grace, His forgiveness, and His healing?

2. Do you struggle with false guilt? If so, list them here or simply speak them to God. Ask for His divine healing to mend all of the broken places that He finds and to bring your mind and heart into the same freedom that He has delivered your soul.

3. Looking back over your journey how has guilt, false guilt, and the shroud of shame affected your life and your choices?

4. What will you do differently now that God has forgiven you, lifted this shroud, and freed you from the bondage of false guilt and shame?

Chapter 8: Training For the Promised Land

1. In the last year what has God asked of you that required extreme *faith*, *trust*, and *obedience*?

2. What keeps you from going out on the furthest limb with God?

3. What mistakes has God allowed you to travel full circle to revisit? How have they helped train you for your anointed journey?

4. What areas do you remain shackled to by choice?

Chapter 9: Listening To Your Father

1. How often do you hear God speaking into your life?

2. Have you received what you believed at the time to be divine communication, but it made you uncomfortable and anxious? Can you better identify the source of that communication now?

3. How does envisioning God's Word coming alive in your mind change your relationship to Scripture?

4. Have you experienced a time when God asked something of you that did not fit in with your own plans? What did you do? How did you feel?

5. Have you experienced the peace that comes from acting in accordance with God's will?

Chapter 10: It Took a Goliath

1. What have been the obstacles and crisis moments in your life? How have you faced your giants? How has God helped bring you to victory?

2. What have you learned from those challenges? How have they prepared you to accomplish greater things in your journey with God?

3. How has God shown up in your crisis moments?

4. How can you better embrace these experiences?

5. How have you approached your crisis moments? What was in your heart and on your mind?

Chapter 11: Doing What God Is Blessing

1. In the course of the next week, write down all of the opportunities that you have found to be a blessing to others.

2. Make a list of all that you are grateful to God for pouring into your life. Each time you pray be sure to thank Him first for these gifts.

3. What are the desires of your heart?

4. What prayers are you praying that are big enough to excite the God who created Heaven and Earth?

5. When you step outside what the world says is *realistic*, what can you and God create together?

Chapter 12: The Illusion of Control

1. What are you struggling with at this moment that needs to be surrendered to the Lord of your life?

2. How do you feel about surrendering control to God?

3. Can you list the top five things in your life that you hold tightly in the palm of your hand? Can you find the extreme *faith, trust,* and *obedience* to list these out loud to God and surrender them to Him so He may fulfill His plans and His best in your life?

4. Have you faced a situation that required extreme *faith, trust,* and *obedience*? What memory stones did you take from your adventure with God?

Chapter 13: Motive Matters

1. Earlier you listed the desires of your heart. Spend time in prayer over these desires. Ask God to reveal the motives of your heart regarding them. What have you discovered?

2. Whether it is love, appreciation, material reward, or another reason, what do you continually seek from those around you?

3. What is your reaction or feeling when you fail to receive what you are seeking?

4. How do you master those feelings and discipline your mind?

5. How have hidden motives impacted your life?

Chapter 14: Even Though the Righteous May Fall

1. What sins and mistakes do you still need to pour out before the Lord?

2. What testimony has come from your mistakes?

3. What testimony and memory stones has God-given you by covering your sins and mistakes with His grace and forgiveness?

4. Is there someone, even yourself, you still need to reconcile with after a transgression?

5. Have you allowed God to heal the self-inflected wounds caused by those transgressions?

Chapter 15: Breaking the Cycle of Circles

1. What circles has God been leading you through? Is there a pattern in your life that just keeps repeating itself time and again? What keeps you entangled by the same patterns?

2. How can you better recognize these circles and cooperate with God to break the cycle?

3. What is one thing you can do today in order to help break your cycle?

4. How have these circles kept you in the wilderness?

5. List the times in which God has shown up in incredible ways. Would you be comfortable sharing any stories as a testimony to others, if God asks?

6. Is there a reproach that God still needs to roll away? Have you asked Him to bring you to Gilgal? Have you been willing to cross the Jordan?

Chapter 16: When the Enemy Comes

1. What does Satan whisper into your ear? What does God have to say about it? How can His Word be a guard against the enemy?

2. Has Satan ventured into your path? What have you learned? How have the encounters better prepared you for greater victory in your journey with God?

3. What are the negative effects of spending too much time concentrating on the enemy?

4. Satan loves to use disguises. What disguises has he used in your life?

5. How has the enemy attacked you, your family, or those around you? Have you recently experienced a spiritual attack? Why do you think he used the weapons that he has chosen?

6. God can use everyone and everything, even the enemy, to accomplish His better plan. Have you experienced what seemed, at first, to have been a setback, but God later turned into a victory?

Chapter 17: Paralysis of Fear

1. How have your fears kept you from achieving great things with God? How has it prevented you from reaching your Promised Land?

2. How has the enemy used and manipulated your fear? In what ways have you allowed it?

3. How has fear affected your life?

4. How does fear inhibit your relationship with God?

5. What have you felt paralyzed over?

6. Review your list of memory stones. Weigh your fears against God's continued love and faithfulness. What have you discovered?

7. Have you let go of your wilderness plans in preference for the fulfillment of God's plans?

Chapter 18: When Our Vessel Runs Dry

1. Describe your empty vessel moments. How have you approached them? What have you learned?

2. What is your greatest advice to others who may be facing a time of loneliness, doubt, or despair?

3. How do you prevent your moments of loss and despair from becoming a permanent obstacle to your walk with God?

4. What regular practices do you prioritize to refill your faith?

5. In what ways do you regularly pour out your blessings onto others? List how you have served Him in the last week or month. Have there been opportunities that you overlooked?

6. In your darkest times, who are your faith partners? Who will join you in falling down before the Lord?

Chapter 19: Jericho Sized Victory

1. What is your current Jericho?

2. In the past, what has been your reaction to the formidable obstacles in your path? What would you change if you could? How do those lessons affect your current choices?

3. Have you ever chosen Option A? What did you learn? Have you chosen Option B? What happened?

4. Are you ready to leave your wilderness behind? Are you ready to claim your Promised Land?

5. What does victory look like to you? God's idea of victory may look a little different. Would you recognize God's victory when you see it?

6. What victories have you been standing in the way of achieving? Why? How? What are concrete steps that you can take to get out of God's way?

7. What obstacle(s) stand in the way of claiming your Promised Land? What has God's love and faithfulness shown you about the obstacle(s)?

8. Jericho's fortifications were a massive obstacle for the Israelites. However, God used that obstacle to show His power to the Canaanite kingdoms and help the Israelites conquer the Promised Land. With God's help, how can you use your greatest obstacle to help achieve great victory?

9. What has God asked of you that would seem ludicrous by worldly standards? Did you obey? Why? Why not? What did you learn?

10. Can you see yourself in the first generation of Israelites out of Egypt? Has God led you to the edge of something great, but your fear got the better of you? What have you learned from the experience? How will you be better prepared the next time?

Write your questions, thoughts, and any insights that God brings to mind.

A FEW FINAL WORDS...

This has been an incredible journey! From the first moment that God planted the seeds of this book in my heart, until the moment when I penned its final words, He unfolded a message before me that I pray will be as beautifully transforming to your life as it has been for mine. This book has been not simply an adventure, but an all-consuming passion that I could not dare ignore.

Through this journey God has placed very specific requirements upon my life and upon the writing of this book. Some have been easy and obvious. Some have been difficult and highly personal. However, if we know anything about our role as children of God, we know that whether His instructions make sense to our fully human minds or not, our job is to obey. Whether His request is as simple as turning left at the next stoplight, or as bold as marching around a walled city carrying the Ark of God, we are to obey. Nothing beneficial will ever come from questioning or second-guessing our Father's ways or His plans.

Right now, you are reading one of the requirements He placed upon me as I wrote. These final pages began as very ordinary acknowledgments. I know that acknowledgments rarely come at the end of a book and they usually include at least the first names of those being thanked.

In my first draft of this manuscript the acknowledgments appeared at the very beginning, right between the copyright pages and the table of contents. It made sense to me, but God had other ideas. It wasn't until I thought this book was nearly complete that He gave me one final and very clear requirement:

Nothing shall come before His Name.

God was very clear that nothing was to come before Him. Not even well-intentioned recognitions of those who have supported me along this journey could be placed ahead of God and the message of this book that he had written in my heart. This book would not be complete until the recognition of others was placed is submission to the recognition of Him and the Scriptures that He breathed into existence.

Not to us, O LORD, not to us, but to your name goes all the glory for your unfailing love and faithfulness.
(Psalm 115:1, NLT)

Psalm 96:8 says, *"Give unto the LORD the glory due unto his name: bring an offering, and come into his courts."*[226] As New Testament believers we are not required to make the offerings described in the Law of Moses. However, God does require offerings of His children. To follow hard after God requires nothing less than the complete surrender of our lives to the will and plan of the Most High God. We must lay down everything at the foot of the Cross, if we are to ever pick up that crown and claim our rightful place and our rightful inheritance as His beloved children.

If we are to reap a godly reward and claim the victory and abundance that God has proclaimed over our lives, then we must keep Him first in all that we do. We cannot just praise His name on Sunday mornings and go about our lives as business as usual the other six days. Jesus came to transform the world and overthrow a legalistic status quo. Business as usual simply cannot coexist with a life lived in the presence and anointing of the Most High God.

But to all who did receive him, who believed in his name,
he gave the right to become children of God...
(John 1:12, ESV)

The Lord said to Abraham, *"I am God Almighty. Live in My presence and be blameless"*[227] *(Genesis 17:1)*. To live in the presence of God, there are a lot of folks who will have some restructuring to do in their lives. Even those of us who like to think that our lives are structured to prioritize God first above all things, still need to remember that this is not a onetime event. Every morning, we must make the decision to place God first and live in His presence. Nothing can come before God, not our relationships, our jobs, our desires, not even our family.

If we hope to live abundant, victorious, and godly lives, then we must let go of the ordinary and claim the miraculous. We must surrender our comfort zones and pick up our anointing. We must stop listening to what the world, the modern day religious Pharisees, and the enemy proclaims, and start remembering what God has spoken over us. We must stop living a passive faith, and start embracing the extraordinary lives He has called us to lead as disciples of Christ and children of the Most High God.

If we are going to do any of this successfully, then we must put Him first in all we do, live in His presence, and pray to have His hand over our lives.

You will make known to me the path of life; In Your presence is fullness of joy; In Your right hand there are pleasures forever. (Psalm 16:11, NASB)

The Apostle Paul praised the faith displayed by the impoverished churches of Macedonia, saying, *"they gave themselves first to the Lord and then by the will of God to us"*[228] (2 *Corinthians 8:5*). I can think of no better verse to exemplify the priorities we are required to maintain in our own lives. We give ourselves first to the Lord, and then by His will, we can give energy and attention to ourselves, our families, our friends, our jobs, and our community. But it is only through our relationship with our God that we can fulfill any of these roles successfully.

In this final requirement, God turned a few simple thank you's into a bold reminder of the extraordinary and anointed lives He calls us to lead. In my gratitude I am left breathless in the radiance of His generous love.

I lack the words to properly express my gratitude to God for the overwhelming faithfulness, boundless love, immeasurable grace, and unreasonable mercy that He has poured into my life. The infinite patience He has shown me, the memory stones He has built, the forgiveness, and undeserved favor to which He has graced me, leave me not simply without words, but often in such pure wide-eyed wonder that I forget to breathe. How grateful I am that our beloved Father knows our hearts and that His Spirit speaks the words that we sometimes simply cannot find!

"I came that they may have
life and have it abundantly."
(John 10:10, ESV)

Second only to my gratitude to God, is my unending thankfulness for the family and friends that He has so lovingly placed into my life. I am grateful for the unending support and lavish love each of you pour into my life. I need only look around me to see in bright and vivid colors the commandment of Jesus - to love one another as He first loved us - brought to life in real and tangible ways. I am blessed to be surrounded by true servants of God, whose love for the Father and His children is evident daily.

To my mother, who has read each installment of this book and listened excitedly to each new thought and chapter that God placed in my heart, thank you, not just from the bottom of my heart, but the tips of my toes. Thank you for never failing to be God's cheerleader in my life and celebrating each new anointing.

To the love of my life, thank you for your unending patience during the long hours and late nights God and I have spent together in the preparation and writing of this book. Thank you for your unshakable love, tender encouragement, and daily example of how one servant of God who is willing and ready to be His hands and feet, can impact the world and His Kingdom for the better.

To my beloved cousin and her incredible husband, thank you for the faithful love and blessings that you have brought into my life. Thank you for modeling to the world what it means to walk with God. Your lives and your marriage shine so brightly with the presence of God that you offer a living testimony to all who are blessed to know you. I love you more than words can say.

Most especially I want to thank *you* for joining me on this journey with God through the desert, across parted waters, and towards the land of Promise. It has been an incredible and beautiful adventure. I have so cherished our time together. My heart swells at the thought of what our Father has planned for us next as we walk with Him with fresh faith, bold trust, and incredible obedience.

I have done my best to fulfill the requirement that God placed on my heart in the writing of this book. I submit it humbly to your hands and trust that the Lord will do with it what He sees fit to do. As for me, I now come to my knees in thankfulness to our God and humble prayer on your behalf, my cherished friend. May you bask in the lavish love of the God who calls you His beloved child.

End Notes

CHAPTER ONE

[1] John 13:35 (NIV)

[2] Mark 14:36 (ESV)

[3] Romans 8:17 (NIV)

[4] "Pistis." No. 4102. Thayer and Smith. "Greek Lexicon entry for Pistis." "The KJV New Testament Greek Lexicon." Bible Study Tools.

[5] "Pisteuo." No. 4100. Thayer and Smith. "Greek Lexicon entry for Pisteuo." "The NAS New Testament Greek Lexicon." 1999. Bible Study Tools.

[6] Ephesians 2:8 (ESV)

[7] James 2:26 (ESV)

[8] Jeremiah 29:11 (ESV)

[9] "Trust." "Merriam-Webster". 2014. www.merriam-webster.com.

[10] Strong, James. "Hupakouó." No. 5219. "The Exhaustive Concordance of the Bible." 1890. Jennings & Graham.

[11] "Hupotasso." No. 5293. Thayer and Smith. "Greek Lexicon entry for Hupotasso." "The NAS New Testament Greek Lexicon." 1999. Bible Study Tools.

[12] "Hupo." No. 5259. Thayer and Smith. "Greek Lexicon entry for Hupo." "The NAS New Testament Greek Lexicon." Bible Study Tools.

[13] Strong, James. "Akouó." No. 191. "The Exhaustive Concordance of the Bible." 1890. Jennings & Graham.

[14] Strong, James. "Tassó." No. 5021. "The Exhaustive Concordance of the Bible." 1890. Jennings & Graham.

[15] Hebrews 11:8 (NIV)

CHAPTER TWO

[16] 2 Corinthians 11:2 (NIV)

[17] 2 Timothy 3:16-17 (NIV)

[18] Exodus 20:13 (NASB)

[19] John 14:26 (ESV)

[20] "Coincidence." "Merriam-Webster." 2014. www.merriam-webster.com.

[21] Job 12:10 (ESV)

CHAPTER THREE

[22] Exodus 25:10 (NASB)

[23] Exodus 25:17 (NASB)

[24] Exodus 25:22 (NASB)

[25] Romans 8:15 (NASB)

[26] MacLaren, Alexander. "Joshua 4". "MacLaren Expositions of Holy Scripture." 1826-1910.

[27] Joshua 4:6-7 (ESV)

[28] Joshua 4:9 (ESV)

[29] Joshua 5:9 (NIV)

[30] Numbers 13:32-33 (NLT)

[31] Joshua 5:1 (NIV)

[32] "Galal." No. 1556. Brown, Driver, Briggs and Gesenius. "Hebrew Lexicon entry for Galal". "The KJV Old Testament Hebrew Lexicon". Bible Study Tools.

[33] Hebrews 4:13 (NIV)

[34] Luke 12:3 (NIV)

CHAPTER FOUR

[35] Marcinko, Richard. "Leadership Secrets of the Rogue Warrior: A Commando's Guide to Success." 1996. Simon & Schuster.

[36] Ephesians 6:13-17 (NIV)

[37] Isaiah 48:10 (NIV)

[38] "Refine." "Merriam-Webster." 2014. www.merriam-webster.com.

[39] "Kakopatheia." No. 2552. Strong's Exhaustive Concordance. Biblehub. 2014.

[40] James 5:10 (KJV)

[41] 1 Corinthians 10:13 (NIV)

[42] White Alasdair. "From Comfort Zone to Performance Management." 2009. White & MacLean Publishing.

[43] 1 John 2:6 (NIV)

[44] Proverbs 21:2 (NIV)

[45] 1 Corinthians 10:13 (MSG)

[46] "Peirasmos." No. 3986. Thayer and Smith. "Greek Lexicon entry for Peirasmos." "The KJV New Testament Greek Lexicon." Bible Study Tools.

[47] Matthew 17:20 (NIV)

CHAPTER FIVE

[48] Joshua 10:12-14 (NIV)

[49] Joshua 10:13-14 (MSG)

[50] Romans 9:8 (NIV)

[51] Exodus 23:20 (NLT)

[52] 1 Corinthians 2:9 (NIV)

[53] Deuteronomy 31:8 (NIV)

[54] Exodus 19:5 (NLT)

[55] "Segullah." No. 5459. Brown, Driver, Briggs and Genesis. "Hebrew Lexicon entry for C@gullah." "The NAS Old Testament Hebrew Lexicon." Bible Study Tools.

[56] 1 Peter 2:9 (NIV)

[57] Jeremiah 1:5 (NIV)

[58] 1 Peter 5:6 (NLT)

[59] Ephesians 2:10 (NLT)

[60] Psalm 46:10 (KJV)

[61] Psalm 46:10 (HCSB)

[62] Mehrabian, Albert. "Silent Messages". 1971. Wadsworth.

CHAPTER SIX

[63] Numbers 14:20-24 (NIV)

[64] "Gilgal." No. 1537. NAS Exhaustive Concordance of the Bible with Hebrew-Aramaic and Greek Dictionaries Copyright © 1981, 1998 by The Lockman Foundation

CHAPTER SEVEN

[65] Ecclesiastes 12:14 (NIV)

[66] 1 John 1:9 (NIV)

[67] 1 John 5:14-15 (NIV)

[68] Joshua 5:9 (NIV)

[69] Psalm 44:15-16 (NIV)

[70] "Galgal." No. 1556. Brown, Driver, Briggs and Gesenius. "Hebrew Lexicon entry for Galal." "The NAS Old Testament Hebrew Lexicon." Bible Study Tools.

[71] Romans 10:10-11 (NIV)

CHAPTER EIGHT

[72] Exodus 3:8 (NIV)

[73] Numbers 14:3 (NLT)

[74] Joshua 5:13-15 (NIV)

[75] Joshua 1:16-18 (NIV)

[76] Joshua 1:18 (NIV)

[77] 2 Corinthians 4:7 (NIV)

[78] 1 Kings 19:12 (KJV)

CHAPTER NINE

[79] John 10:27-28 (NIV)

[80] Romans 8:14 (NIV)

[81] Luke 6:46 (ESV)

[82] Luke 6:46-47 (MSG)

[83] Luke 6:47-48 (NIV)

[84] Jude 1:19 (NIV)

[85] Instinct." "Oxford Dictionaries.com." 2014. oxforddictionaries.com.

[86] John 1:14 (ESV)

[87] Strong, James. "Sarx." No. 4561. "The Exhaustive Concordance of the Bible." 1890. Jennings & Graham.

[88] John 6:53 (NASB)

[89] "Phago." No. 5315. Thayer and Smith. "Greek Lexicon entry for Phago." "The KJV New Testament Greek Lexicon." Bible Study Tools.

[90] 1 Corinthians 15:58 (ESV)

[91] "Perisseuo." No. 4052. Thayer and Smith. "Greek Lexicon entry for Perisseuo." "The KJV New Testament Greek Lexicon." Bible Study Tools.

[92] Luke 18:17(NLT)

[93] Exodus 33:7 (NIV)

CHAPTER TEN

[94] 1 John 2:27 (ESV)

[95] "Chrisma." No. 5545. Thayer and Smith. "Greek Lexicon entry for Chrisma." "The KJV New Testament Greek Lexicon." Bible Study Tools.

[96] Strong, James. "Chrió." No. 5548. "The Exhaustive Concordance of the Bible." 1890. Jennings & Graham.

[97] "Consecrate." "Merriam-Webster". 2014. www.merriam-webster.com.

[98] 2 Corinthians 1:21-22 (NIV)

[99] 2 Corinthians 1:22 (NIV)

[100] Strong, James. "Christós." No. 5547. "The Exhaustive Concordance of the Bible." 1890. Jennings & Graham.

[101] Exodus 3:11(NIV)

[102] Exodus 4:13 (NIV)

[103] John 4:10 (NLT)

[104] John 4:26 (NLT)

[105] John 4:39 (HCSB)

[106] Acts 13:22 (NIV)

[107] Exodus 3:21 (NIV)

CHAPTER ELEVEN

[108] Strong, James. "Berakah." No. 1293. "The Exhaustive Concordance of the Bible." 1890. Jennings & Graham.

[109] Strong, James. "Barak." No. 1288. "The Exhaustive Concordance of the Bible." 1890. Jennings & Graham.

[110] Exodus 3:14 (NIV)

[111] Strong, James. "Emeth." No. 571. "The Exhaustive Concordance of the Bible." 1890. Jennings & Graham.

[112] Mark 14:36 (NLT)

[113] "Abba." No. 05. Thayer and Smith. "Greek Lexicon entry for Abba." "The NAS New Testament Greek Lexicon." 1999. Bible Study Tools.

[114] "Ab."No. 02. Brown, Driver, Briggs and Gesenius. "Hebrew Lexicon entry for 'ab (Aramaic)." "The NAS Old Testament Hebrew Lexicon." Bible Study Tools.

[115] Genesis 1:1-3 (NIV)

[116] Ephesians 2:10 (ESV)

[117] Romans 8:16 (NIV)

[118] Psalm 139:14 (NIV)

[119] Psalm 139:15-16 (NIV)

[120] "Golem." No. 1564. Brown, Driver, Briggs and Gesenius. "Hebrew Lexicon entry for Golem". "The NAS Old Testament Hebrew Lexicon." Bible Study Tools.

[121] "Galam." No. 1563. Brown, Driver, Briggs and Gesenius. "Hebrew Lexicon entry for Galam". "The NAS Old Testament Hebrew Lexicon". Bible Study Tools.

[122] "Addereth." No. 155. Brown, Driver, Briggs and Gesenius. "Hebrew Lexicon entry for 'addereth." "The NAS Old Testament Hebrew Lexicon." Bible Study Tools.

[123] 1 Thessalonians 5:16-18 (NIV)

[124] Psalm 18:1-2 (NIV)

[125] Psalm 18:6 (NIV)

[126] Foster, David. "Small Groups as Programs are Failures Because They Have the Wrong Purpose." www.davidfoster.tv. June 20, 2008

[127] Ibid.

[128] John 13:34-35 (NIV)

[129] 2 Samuel 7:5-7 (ESV)

CHAPTER TWELVE

[130] Exodus 32:9 (ESV)

[131] 1 Samuel 8:7-9 (NIV)

[132] "Happy." "Merriam-Webster.com." 2014. www.merriam-webster.com.

CHAPTER THIRTEEN

[133] Mark 10:21 (NIV)

[134] Genesis 4:6-7 (NIV)

[135] Proverbs 21:2 (NIV)

[136] Romans 12:1-2 (NIV)

[137] Romans 12:19 (NLT)

[138] Genesis 12:3 (NLT)

[139] Romans 8:1 (NLT)

[140] 1 John 2:15-17 (MSG)

[141] 1 John 2:15 (ESV)

CHAPTER FOURTEEN

[142] Acts 13:22 (NLT)

[143] 2 Samuel 12:7-9 (NIV)

[144] 1 Kings 9:4-5 (NIV)

[145] 1 Kings 9:4 (NIV)

[146] Acts 13:22 (AMP)

[147] Ephesians 4:18 (ESV)

[148] Romans 5:2 (ESV)

[149] Romans 6:23 (KJV)

[150] Barclay, William. Pg. 64. "New Testament Words." 1964. SCM Press Ltd.

[151] "Thanatos." No. 2288. Thayer and Smith. "Greek Lexicon entry for Thanatos." "The KJV New Testament Greek Lexicon." Bible Study Tools.

[152] Strong, James. "Aiónios." No. 166. "The Exhaustive Concordance of the Bible." 1890. Jennings & Graham.

[153] "Zoe." No. 2222. Thayer and Smith. "Greek Lexicon entry for Zoe." "The KJV New Testament Greek Lexicon." Bible Study Tools.

[154] Romans 8:28 (NLT)

[155] Isaiah 41:10 (NASB)

[156] 1 John 2:1 (NIV)

[157] Strong, James. Paraklétos. No. 3875. "The Exhaustive Concordance of the Bible." 1890. Jennings & Graham.

[158] 1 John 1:9 (NIV)

[159] Proverbs 24:16 (NIV)

[160] Psalm 51:1-2 (NIV)

CHAPTER FIFTEEN

[161] James 1:4 (NIV)

[162] 1 Peter 2:9 (NIV)

[163] Romans 8:17 (NIV)

[164] Acts 22:15 (NLT)

[165] "Witness." "Merriam-Webster." 2014. www.merriam-webster.com.

[166] "Testimony." "Merriam-Webster." 2014. www.merriam-webster.com.

[167] Acts 1:8 (NIV)

[168] Matthew 5:14-16 (ESV)

[169] Matthew 5:16 (ESV)

CHAPTER SIXTEEN

[170] Hebrews 4:12 (NIV)

[171] Ephesians 6:16 (NIV)

[172] Ephesians 6:17 (NIV)

[173] Ephesians 6:13 (NIV)

[174] Matthew 3:17 (NIV)

[175] Matthew 4:3 (NLT)

[176] Matthew 4:10 (NLT)

[177] Luke 10:19 (NLT)

[178] Matthew 4:6 (NLT)

[179] Psalm 91:9-13 (NLT)

[180] Psalm 91:9 (NLT)

181 Matthew 4:7(NLT)

182 Genesis 3:1 (NLT)

183 2 Corinthians 11:14 (NASB)

184 Matthew 4:10 (NLT)

185 Hebrews 5:11-12 (NLT)

186 James 1:25 (NLT)

CHAPTER SEVENTEEN

187 " Supernatural." "Merriam-Webster." 2014. www.merriam-webster.com.

188 Isaiah 6:9 (NIV)

189 Isaiah 41:13 (NIV)

190 2 Timothy 1:7 (NIV)

191 Psalm 27:1 (NIV)

192 Proverbs 1:7 (NIV)

193 Numbers 13:31-33 (NIV)

194 Numbers 14:2-3 (NIV)

195 Joshua 1:9 (NIV)

196 Matthew 28:20 (KJV)

CHAPTER EIGHTEEN

197 Numbers 14:8-9 (ESV)

198 Joshua 7:3 (NIV)

199 Joshua 7:5 (NIV)

200 Matthew 27:46 (NLT)

201 Joshua 7:7-9 (NIV)

202 Joshua 7:7 (NIV)

203 Joshua 7:10 (NIV)

204 Joshua 8:1 (NIV)

205 Exodus 14:14 (NIV)

206 Deuteronomy 3:22 (NIV)

207 Strong, James. "Lacham." No. 3898. "The Exhaustive Concordance of the Bible." 1890. Jennings & Graham.

208 1 Kings 17:13-14 (NLT)

209 Psalm 147:2-3 (NASB)

210 Joshua 7:10-13 (ESV)

211 Joshua 7:6 (ESV)

CHAPTER NINETEEN

212 Numbers 13:2 (NIV)

213 Numbers 13:18-20 (NIV)

214 Numbers 13:31 (NIV)

215 Numbers 13:32 (NIV)

216 Numbers 14:1-4 (NIV)

217 Joshua 5:13 (NIV)

218 Joshua 5:14 (NIV)

219 Joshua 6:2-5 (NIV)

220 Joshua 6:16-17 (NIV)

221 Joshua 6:20 (NIV)

222 Joshua 6:16 (NIV)

223 Matthew 17:20 (NIV)

224 Deuteronomy 7:9 (NLT)

225 James 2:26 (NIV)

226 Psalm 96:8 (KJV)

227 Genesis 17:1 (HCSB)

228 2 Corinthians 8:5 (ESV)

www.ingramcontent.com/pod-product-compliance
Lightning Source LLC
Chambersburg PA
CBHW051938090426
42741CB00008B/1185